The Garage Sale Decorator's Bible

HOW TO FIND TREASURES, FIX THEM & FURNISH YOUR HOME

WRITTEN AND ILLUSTRATED

BY

SHELLEY KINCAID

FELINE BOOKS

Illustrations:	Shelley Kincaid
Editor:	Martha King
Cover Photo:	Avanti
Cover:	John C. Otto Co.

ISBN 0-9655461-1-X

Printed in the United States of America

Publisher's Cataloging in Publication
(Prepared by Quality Books Inc.)

Kincaid, Shelley.
     The garage sale decorator's bible : how to find treasures, fix them & furnish your home / written and illustrated by Shelley Kincaid.
     p. cm.
     Includes index.
     ISBN 0-9655461-1-X

     1. Interior decoration--Handbooks, manuals, etc. 2. Garage sales. I. Title.

NK2115.K56 1997   747' .1
                         QBI97-40033

ACKNOWLEDGMENTS

There are many people I wish to thank for their contribution to the writing and publication of this book:

My sister, for encouraging me to write this book and for giving me many hours of counsel.

In the early stages of this project, many friends and family members offered valuable ideas, criticism, feedback, encouragement and support. My thanks to Debbie Brateman, special friends and garage sale~ing buddies.

I owe much to Martha King, who carefully read and re-read chapters at the shortest notice, giving generously of time that she did not have. Her suggestions were always helpful, informative and wise. I will always be grateful for her editing expertise and enthusiasm for this project.

Last and very important is my husband Steve who shares my enthusiasm for sale~ing and never complains when he has to unload a van filled with furnishings and carry the items either upstairs or downstairs or when I change my mind--upstairs or downstairs again! He has become very adept with a saw, hammer and nails and after five years of "seeing is believing," rarely shakes his head and tells me it can't be done!

TABLE OF CONTENTS

"HOW TO" INSTRUCTION INDEX

FOREWORD

Garage sale~ing just kind of happened to me by accident. In fact, I had never even heard about garage sale~ing until my dearest friend, Kate told me that the pieces I was admiring at her home were all bought at garage sales. I was shocked and surprised! I must admit, I thought to myself how could a person buy other people's old and used things? But her things were gorgeous. I admired them and wished I had them in my home, plus I couldn't go out and buy them anywhere.

I guess I was kind of a snob. I had always purchased name brands and shopped only the finest stores. I even insisted on having an interior designer present just to change out a candlestick or two!

I frequented stores and decorator showrooms every week just to see all of the beautiful things that were available and to plan my rooms--what I would put here and there and everywhere.

Interior decorating and accessorizing was my passion.

Throughout the years, I had acquired some beautiful designer pieces and lots of accessories that meant a lot to me. I worked hard and saved hard so I could have beautiful things. I had time payments and lots of interest charges just so I could furnish my home with elegant things.

You can't begin to imagine how my dreams were shattered when we lost everything in a long distance move. When I say lost everything--I mean everything!

My husband was transferred to another state and his company moved us. It was the easiest move I've ever done. The movers came in, removed everything from the cabinets, wrapped them in paper, packed and loaded. They did everything.

After our house full of treasures arrived at our destination, we had to store everything in the mover's warehouse until we could find a suitable place to live. It took us six weeks of checking out neighborhoods and looking at houses to find just the perfect place. It was a 3,000 square foot two-story house with five bedrooms and three bathrooms, a full basement and a great big back yard. This house would hold all of our treasures and display them beautifully.

I couldn't wait for the day when the moving van would come and unload all of the furniture, knick knacks and things that I had collected over the past 20 years. I had already picked out where everything would go.

Well, the movers finally came, and when they started unloading the van and bringing in the furniture, it became apparent that something was very wrong. Everything they took off the truck was damaged. Every box, every chair, every piece of furniture, every treasure, every little trinket that we owned was damaged. The sofa and chairs looked like they had been picked up by a fork lift truck that missed! The wooden pieces of furniture were wavy and veneers were buckling. Boxes of dishes, glasses, statues, lamps and flower pots were crushed and as you can well imagine . . . I was crushed too-- very crushed!

When I tell everyone this story the first thing they ask is, "Didn't you have insurance?" Yes, we had insurance--or so we thought! We certainly paid the extra price for full replacement value insurance, but, when the movers received the replacement estimates, they balked, and refused to pay on some technicality.

We argued with the insurance company for months, meanwhile living in our large home with no furniture, no appliances or dishes to eat on. I went to the discount store and bought the bare minimum until we could get the insurance company to pay for our damaged belongings.

Since the move was a corporate one and my husband's company was responsible for the move they wanted us to settle. With jobs the way they are I'm sure you know what we did. We settled.

The settlement wouldn't begin to pay for replacing the damaged furnishings and accessories, but I thought with the settlement I could pay to have some of the items restored to their original quality. What I didn't know is when an insurance company gives you a settlement on damaged items, they then own the items and they take them away. So there we sat in our big beautiful empty dream house with enough money to fully replace maybe one piece of furniture.

You rationalize that it's just stuff, and thank God for everyone's health and all the usual. You try to pick up and get on with your life.

One day, our new neighborhood was having a community flea market and we decided to go, just to meet the neighbors and show our support. It was a day that has forever changed our lives!

While strolling through the flea market meeting new neighbors and friends, I found some kitchen gadgets and lots of little items that would cost $2.00 or $3.00 brand new for only 5¢. I found a beautiful crystal lamp, the kind that I had been wanting to get for the bedroom for only $5.00. This was easily a $100 lamp! I found a French style double dresser that was much nicer than the one my daughter had in her room and it was only $20. I opened the left hand drawer and saw the name brand carved into it. It was a quality piece! There were candlesticks and picture frames and my husband's favorite kind of wine glasses that he got for only 25¢ each.

There were drapes and curtains and bed linens--not your typical flea market junk but items that were brand new and still in their original packaging for less than $1.00.

Our van looked like a gypsy caravan when we finally left. We couldn't believe our incredible good luck! Such bargains for such wonderful things!

We were hooked instantly! From that point on, every weekend we drove around the neighborhood looking for garage sale signs. The more we "sale~ed", the more I knew I could elegantly decorate the entire house with garage sale treasures and I was committed to doing just that. My challenge and goal were to furnish the entire house from top to bottom with garage sale bargains. Not only was it economical, it was fun too!

I already knew how to refinish furniture as I

had done a little of this before. I had always been handy at crafts and was always figuring out ways to build things or do things or decorate things. I always wanted to learn how to re-upholster and unbeknownst to me, so did my husband. We were learning new things about each other and learning how to do new and fun things together. We bought sofas and chairs and bought a "how to" book on upholstering. We soon learned new and better ways to upholster and ended up throwing the book away.

I would find pieces of furniture that I somewhat liked, but perhaps didn't like certain parts. The legs would be wrong or the handles wrong or some little something would be wrong with it. It soon became apparent that I could change the legs, hardware, handles or drawer fronts and turn a piece of furniture into exactly what I wanted with other bits and pieces of garage sale bargains.

The more we "sale~ed," the more fun it became and we couldn't believe the wonderful buys we found. Really unbelievable buys! Items that you would find at designer showrooms and in the latest decorator magazines for only a few dollars at garage sales.

Our big empty house is now bursting at the seams with items that we dearly love and treasure. Garage sale~ing has become a way of life for us and all of our friends too!

Fortunately, I was able to attain my goal of decorating and furnishing the entire house with garage sale bargains.

At last count we have 14 televisions, five VCRs, four deep freezers, three refrigerators, eight computers, two printers, closets full of wonderful linens, a fully equipped kitchen and everything else you can imagine!

Friends and relatives no longer come in for the holidays just to visit. They also come to go garage sale~ing with us. They usually fly into town, then rent a van to hold all of their garage sale bargains and drive back home. People who have never "sale~ed" in their lives can't wait to come here and LEARN how to "sale!"

Our dinner parties always turn out the same with each guest being kind and admiring this piece or that. Of course I say, "Thank you, that cost $2.00!" or "Thank you, that cost 25¢" or "Thank you, that cost $1.00!" Our guests think we've gone mad but the evening usually ends up with a complete tour and a promise to take them sale~ing with us that weekend!

Over the years, friends, relatives and neighbors have told me, "You should write a book." I didn't know how to write a book, but I'm having fun learning! What I hope to do is share some ideas with you, and help you have everything you want for pennies, make your dreams come true, and have a wonderful fun filled time doing it! You can throw your credit cards away, they don't take them at garage sales. You can say good-bye to monthly payments and debt and still have everything you've ever wanted.

Garage sale~ing is for everyone--women, men and children. Women may have to drag husbands along the first few times, but when a man finds that first "real bargain"--that perfect hard-to-find wrench or saw blade for 25¢, he'll start coming around. In my husband's case, it was the wine glasses. You never know what it will be--you never know what you're going to find!

"GARAGE SALE~ING IS LIKE A BOX OF CHOCOLATES--YOU NEVER KNOW WHAT YOU'RE GONNA GET!"

CHAPTER ONE

GARAGE SALE~ING WILL CHANGE YOUR LIFE

A NEW LIFESTYLE

PLAN AHEAD

HOW TO SALE

EARLY BIRDS

PRICES

DEALERS

ALWAYS ASK

READY . . . SET . . . GO

What if your local newspaper ran the following ad: "EVERY STORE IN TOWN IS HAVING A SALE. EVERY ITEM IN EVERY STORE IS 90% OFF THE REGULAR RETAIL PRICE!" Every store in town was going to have this sale. 90% off every single item.

Every piece of furniture in the furniture stores: 90% off!

Every single item in the hardware store: 90% off!

Every item in the gift and specialty shops: 90% off!

Every single item in the large linen and bath stores: 90% off!

Every item in the department stores and large discount stores: 90% off!

A $100 item would sell for $10.

A $1,000 bedroom set would cost only $100.

A $500 patio set would sell for $50!

A $500 refrigerator would cost $50.

A $500 deep freeze would be only $50.

Would you go shopping that day?

I think there would be pandemonium in the streets! The highways would be packed with carloads of people trying to get into town for this fabulous sale. The parking lots would be jam-packed and the check out lines horrendous. You would probably have to rent trucks and vans to get all of your purchases home!

Well . . . this sale happens every week in your town and in every town all across the country. In some parts of the country this sale is held on a Wednesday; in other parts of the country the sales are on Thursday; and for sure, in every part of the country, these sales are happening on Friday, Saturday and Sunday.

I'm sure you've seen garage sale signs, yard sale, or estate sale signs all over your area. This is where you will find terrific bargain after bargain--from home furnishings to appliances, beautiful crystal and flatware, sterling silver to stainless steel. Why pay $40 for a Gallia crystal water goblet when you can buy it at a garage sale for $3.00? Why pay $1,200 for a 486 computer when you can buy one at a garage sale for $100?

Why pay $129 for a pocket-size Casio color TV when you can buy it for $15 at the local sales--brand new and in its original wrapping?

Do you really want to pay $800 for that new king-size mattress and box spring or would you rather pay $50? Brand new and factory sealed.

How about your kitchen appliances? They can really add up: $30 for that new vegetable steamer, $20 for that handy hand

blender, $19.95 for the mini-chopper, $24.95 for the crock pot and $35 for the electric skillet. All of these items I purchased for just $1.00 each--brand new and in their original boxes!

If you think garage sales are just filled with old junk--try again. Go to several garage sales in your neighborhood and in other neighborhoods. Soon, you will find many items that you've been wanting but just didn't have the extra money to spend.

If you're like most people today it's so easy to go shopping at the stores and just hand over your credit card to pay for your purchases. The hard part is at the end of the month when you get the bill. I was the same way, buying everything with a credit card until I reached my limit. Then you start using another credit card, right? So many people are finding themselves caught up in credit card debt and most of the purchases on the credit cards are probably for household items and furnishings. Why be in debt when you don't have to be? Why pay outrageous interest charges that are no longer tax deductible when you can be buying every single thing you could possibly want with just your change purse?

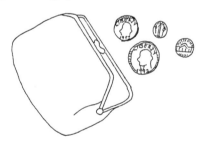

A NEW LIFESTYLE

This book will help you get rid of your debts and have a bigger savings account. You can buy all of your furnishings for every single room in your home. Not old trashy stuff, not some grandmother's hand-me-downs, but beautiful brand name furnishings and accessories. If you like to make things and are good at crafts, then you will enjoy learning how to make your own pieces of unique furniture. There are complete "how to" instructions in each section of this book that will walk you through what to look for at the sales, what to buy, how to mix and match, how to make and repair furnishings and accessories and how to elegantly outfit your entire home from top to bottom.

Garage sale~ing means living life debt free. No monthly payments for furniture, appliances and accessories. No more interest payments. No more credit card debt. You can throw your credit cards away, and say good-bye to debt.

With all of the extra money you will have each and every month, why not plan a great vacation, or build that vacation dream home you've been wanting for so long? You'll be able to furnish it completely and very inexpensively. Much of your building material and supplies, appliances and everything else you need can be purchased at local garage sales. Once you start sale~ing on a regular basis you'll probably need a much larger home anyway to hold all of your lovely new things.

You'll be able to afford one with all the money you're going to save by following the tips in this book!

Garage sale~ing is living life in abundance. Most of my sale~ing buddies and I have found a whole new way of living just by doing all of our shopping at garage sales. For one thing, life is much, much easier.

"Things" are not as important now because we have so many "things" in abundance. It's not a big deal if Junior breaks a glass or a dish--you'll find one to replace it this weekend for a nickel! You won't have to save for months to buy a new set of china or crystal. You'll find just what you're looking for at the sales for just a few dollars. Soon your cup and your cupboards will runneth over.

You won't have to take out a loan when the children want their own computer. You'll find plenty of them that will run the latest software, play the latest games and access the Internet for $100 or less. This book tells you exactly what to look for and how to find it.

If your TV isn't capable of getting cable but still has the best picture you've ever seen, no problem. Read the TV and Electronics chapter to find out how to make it into a cable TV with remote control for FREE!

When little Emily wants to start taking piano lessons and you've priced pianos, find a nice spinet or console piano for $200 or $300 at the sales. Why spend thousands of dollars just to get started? If Emily turns out to be a child prodigy, then you can go buy her a baby grand. You can also find these at the garage sales too! Even a Steinway!

You'll find yourself redecorating a lot more often, which is fun. You won't be stuck with a piece of furniture that you paid hundreds of dollars for only to get it home and decide you really don't like it. If you find you really don't like a garage sale purchase, you can either fix it up so you do like it or you can always sell it at your garage sale for exactly what you paid or maybe even more.

Once you become a regular sale~er you will start turning things over more often, meaning you might use something for a year, find something you like even better to replace it and sell the older item for what you paid. Once you get started shopping at garage sales and having sales of your own, your cash outlay becomes almost zero. If you re-sell the items that you purchase at a later date then your actual cost is zero. And think of the wonderful thing you are doing for the environment by using items again and again. You'll learn in this book how to use parts of one item and combine them with parts of another to make something really special. So many things are re-usable and recyclable if we just use their parts. You'll find that an old ugly lamp that you can buy for 50¢ makes a beautiful candleholder or flower-holder. An old chipped mirror can be re-cut and sized to fit an old frame that you find and fancy up with all the latest faux finishing techniques you'll learn to do in the Finishes chapter.

Start to live your life abundantly and have everything you want. Stop denying yourself beautiful treasures because they cost too much. You can now have everything you want and need with no debt or costly pay-ments.

Go to the designer showrooms often and pick out the style and finishes that you would like to have. Then start garage sale~ing. Follow the tips in this book and you will have those things right away.

PLAN AHEAD

As with any aspect of life, it pays to plan ahead. If you've had too many appliance repair bills for your dryer lately don't wait until it dies completely. Start shopping now for the replacement dryer. Once you find a dryer, put your old dryer in your own garage sale. Even if it's dead there are a lot of re-pairmen shopping the sales for appliances to repair and resell.

If you have some picture frames that you would like to have mirrored write down their measurements. The mirror doesn't have to have the exact dimensions. It can be cut to

fit. If you would like some different drapes or perhaps mini-blinds or fabric shades for your windows, write down the window di-mensions and carry them with you in your fanny pack.

You'll find a fanny pack is really convenient when you go garage sale~ing. It's much easier than a purse, which you could possi-bly lay down somewhere and forget. A fanny pack doesn't get in the way when you're digging through boxes and piles of things.

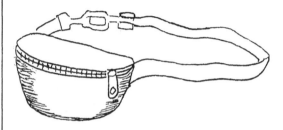

If you are thinking about fixing up your basement or building a vacation home and find great values--go ahead and buy them now. You will probably find that you have just about everything you need for that big remodeling project and can go ahead and get started on it now rather than a year or two down the road.

I knew our son was going to start college in a short time and by the time he was set to leave he had everything he would ever need. A microwave, a refrigerator, a Sony color TV, a VCR, sheets, towels, blankets--everything! By planning ahead, I had the luxury of being very choosy and got exactly what he wanted. It's as if he went to the department store and picked out the exact items he wanted. It pays to think ahead and plan ahead.

See Decorating Your Rooms chapter for more information on college dorm rooms.

HOW TO SALE

In the classified section of the newspapers are columns and columns of garage sale ads. I make a list of the sales that are close by and also look for any large community or neighborhood sales. Even if the community sales are far away, they are well worth the time and gas it takes to get there. Community sales are when entire neighborhoods or apartment complexes hold a garage sale. You can go to many more sales in a day this way. Some community sales have 50 to 100 garages open, which allows you to cover a lot of sales in a very short period of time.

Once I've read the paper and made a list of sales for that day, I then assign them a number by location and plot my course. If I plan to sale on Friday and Saturday, I sort out the sales by day--shopping the Friday, Saturday sales on Friday and the Saturday-only sales on Saturday. Not Rocket science . . . what I'm trying to say is you probably don't want to wait until Saturday to shop a sale that starts Friday. It will be pretty well picked

over. There should be plenty of Saturday-only sales for Saturdays! If there are a lot of sales, write out a page for Friday and a page for Saturday.

EARLY BIRDS

Everyone will tell you it's always good to arrive early and be one of the first sale~ers at a sale. This is true, but realize that you can't always be the first one at every sale, so don't let this discourage you. If you are one of the first to arrive at a sale, you can still try to bargain, but the majority of people stick to their asking price early in the morning and that's OK. If there is an item you really want and have been looking for it for some time, go for it--even if they won't come down in price

My sister-in-law, Nancy, had been looking for a specific kind and brand of lighted makeup mirror. We had looked for a while and found a couple for $1.00. Each of them had a minor flaw--one of the knobs was loose, the plastic was chipped on the bottom, it was always some little thing. Well, we found a perfect makeup mirror that looked brand new and the seller was asking $3.00. Nancy tried to bargain and offered the seller

$1.00 for it but the seller held firm. She walked away and was not going to get the mirror when I reasoned with her that she really, really wanted this makeup mirror. It was the exact brand and style that she wanted. It was in perfect condition and she would pay $24.95 at the store for it. I asked her, "If you found this makeup mirror at the store marked $3.00, would you buy it?" "Yes," she stated, "In a heartbeat!" She ended up going back and buying the mirror. Lucky for her it was still there.

It's fun to bargain and perfectly acceptable, just don't get caught up in it. Don't walk away from something you really want because of 50¢ or a dollar or two!

My friend, Jo Ann, and I were sale~ing one day and she found a beautiful antique inlaid wood dresser with a diamond dust mirror. I've seen these dressers priced at several hundred dollars and this one was only $65. It needed a little sanding to smooth out some rough spots but it was still a real bargain. She needed a dresser and she dearly loved it. We loaded it in the van and were off for more sale~ing. A few hours later we found an antique bed that had the exact same inlaid wood. It was a perfect match and she needed a bed too! The only problem was the $40 price tag. The bed was in very good condition . . . I guess it was just a case of being late in the day and having already spent $65 for the dresser. The seller would only come down to $30. We were willing to pay $20. He wouldn't budge so we walked to the car. I asked Jo Ann how badly she wanted the bed. After all, it did match the dresser perfectly and she did love it. Think of how long she might have to sale to find another one that matched her antique dresser as well as this one. You couldn't even buy a bed in the store that would match it for any price. The issue was $10. We ended up getting out of the van and buying the bed! It looks wonderful in her bedroom and matches the rest of her furnishings perfectly. She has no regrets!

PRICES

Take this book with you when you go sale~ing and use the appendix in the back as a reference on pricing.
The appendix in the back of this book is a listing of prices in the southwestern part of the United States. Prices will vary depending on the area. The retail column is probably low because I priced the items at discount stores and, in some cases, listed special sale prices as the retail price. The prices listed are the lowest I could find for that particular item. The garage sale column is the lowest I've seen the item actually marked at a sale, and Shelley's column is the price I've actually paid for a particular item.

All of the items listed in Shelley's best column were either brand new or in excellent condition.

DEALERS

For those of you who would like to take advantage of all the good stuff and terrific prices that you find at the sales but do not have the time to go sale~ing yourself, there are people who will do this for you. They are called dealers. They make their living by going to garage sales and buying the items that people are most interested in. Dealers then take their purchases and re-sell them at large community flea markets or co-op re-sell it stores. You will pay more for your items at dealer-operated markets than if you buy them yourself at sales, but the prices are still way below retail and certainly worth it when time is a precious commodity. Go to a few sales and you'll very quickly learn who the dealers are. If there is something specific you want, ask them if they have it or ask them if they could find it for you. This is their business and they should be glad to help!

ALWAYS ASK

A lot of sellers will ask you if there is anything special you are looking for. Sometimes they have so many items to sell that they stack them up and you might never find it or they just didn't have room to put items out. It may be something that they thought about possibly selling and forgot at the last minute. I've learned to ask for items that I'm looking for such as big rugs or maybe furniture. They either say "no" right away or "Well, I do have a bed or I do have a dresser or I do have a rug rolled up in the basement that I forgot about." It doesn't hurt to ask.

READY . . . SET . . . GO!

Pack a lunch. You don't want to take away from your valuable sale~ing time by having to stop and eat somewhere. Take something cool to drink. Sometimes you will find a sale that includes hot dogs and hamburgers, but you might not find them when hunger strikes. Someone is always selling pop at the sales and you will find several Kool-Aid and lemonade stands set up by the children. Cookies and doughnuts are a popular item at the sales and there are a lot of nice people who offer you free coffee in the mornings.

Speaking of nice people--in all the years and the hundreds and hundreds of garage sales that I have been to, I have encountered only one rude person. Sellers are usually glad to hold an item for you so you can go back and pick it up later. Sellers will help you carry things to your car and help load them in the car for you. They will go and look for missing parts of an item, take your phone number and call you back when they find it. They will always let you plug something in to try--or use their telephone to make a call. Most people are very friendly and helpful and, most of all, fun! A garage sale is a FUN experience. You'll have a happy, fun-filled day bargaining and buying all kinds of goodies so inexpensively. You will start to see the same people over and over again at the sales and make many new friends. They will even help you find what you're looking for. One of my favorite garage sale~ing acquaintances is Elsie. I see her every weekend and she always asks me if I've been to this sale or that sale and she lets me know where some good ones are. If the sales are crowded she will pick up lots of good things and ask me if I want them. If the clothing rack is crowded she will pull out the items she's interested in and all the other cute things to pass around to her friends. I look forward to seeing her every spring and summer.

Remember to make a list and plan ahead. Tell your sale~ing buddies what you're looking for and double your efforts. I promise, you will find everything you want and need to elegantly decorate and furnish your home.

Make yourself a "wants and needs" list with all the measurements you might need such as windows, door sizes, carpeting, mirrors, pictures and frames. Check your list with the appendix in this book to get an idea of what the items will cost. Keep the list in your car or fanny pack along with a tape measure. Most people have something to measure with at their sales, however if they are busy, it's easy to have your own tape measure so you can measure items yourself. Some items do not have to be the exact measurements to work for you, such as draperies or mirrors. There are many ways to make them work. This book is filled with tricks of the trade that show you how to make items that are either too large or too small work out just right!

NOTE: When measuring for blinds or pleated shades, make sure to check the length measurement. Some of them may be the correct width but they all vary in length.

CHAPTER TWO

DECORATING YOUR ROOMS

LIVING ROOM

DINING ROOM

BEDROOMS

BATHROOMS

KITCHEN

HOME OFFICE

LAUNDRY ROOM

DORM ROOM

It's easy to elegantly decorate every room in your home with garage sale bargains. Discovering "how to" decorate with garage sale finds was fun and enjoyable. By purchasing all of our items at the sales, learning the latest painting techniques, touching up with special finishes and switching a few furniture legs here and there, we were able to fill our home with lovely furnishings and accessories for pennies compared to what we'd have to pay at the designer showrooms. It is possible to duplicate the very expensive furniture and decorator items that you see in the showrooms and it's easy too! Turn your craft skills into decorating and furniture making skills. Everything you find at garage sales is so cheap it takes the fear out of trying.

I think most people believe if you decorate your home with garage sale bargains you'll end up with musty hand-me-downs, broken and chipped dishes, crates, rooms filled with plaid Herculon furniture, velvet paintings and orange glass lamps with a three-foot-high brown shade to go with the orange shag carpeting and avocado appliances! Nothing could be further from the truth! You will find beautiful antiques and decorator pieces at the sales too! Anything you need to furnish and accessorize your home is out there.

Start living life abundantly! You too can have 15 televisions, four freezers, three refrigerators, eight computers and brand name furniture purchased for $100 instead of $1,000! Your linen closets will be jampacked with exquisite linens and accessories fine enough for Buckingham Palace! You can have a dream kitchen stocked with every appliance made. Your table will be set with beautiful china dinnerware, hand cut crystal and sterling silver. The kitchen cupboards will be well stocked with everyday dishes, glassware, cooking utensils and bakeware. You will find more brass and copper pieces than you could possibly use. There are plenty of plants and decorator mirrors that cost $600 to $1,000 at the store. My $1,000 mirror was only $14! This book shows you how to find all of these treasures, fix them up so they're beautiful and furnish your entire home.

Unfortunately, I have very expensive taste and only the finest furnishings please me. I think that's one of the reasons my friends get such a kick out of hearing that I shop at garage sales. First, they don't believe it, knowing how picky I am. Second, they don't believe it when they see the rooms that I've decorated with garage sale purchases. Third, they really don't believe that I made or remade a lot of the items in the house! To me, real decorators don't buy a room--they create it!

If I added up the cost of everything I bought at garage sales versus the cost of these items in stores it would show a savings of tens of thousands of dollars. The computers alone would total five figures instead of the $50 to $100 we paid.

The rooms throughout our house are so full of treasures and we have so much of everything that we are thinking of moving to a bigger house. We can afford it with all the money we've saved by shopping at garage sales and you can too! This book shows you how! Maybe you want to build a dream vacation home with the money saved. Furnishing it will cost you next to nothing!

Come take a tour with me and see some of the wonderful treasures that I found, and how I turned them into something spectacular!

LIVING ROOM

Let's start with the living room. I hope you like it. You will, if you like French and fancy!

I found a Louis XIV chair with a cane back and lovely carved French legs, but it had terrible stained and torn orange velvet upholstery. The chair was only $10 and I knew I could fix it and make a beautiful piece. The wood was dark cherry and it was chipped and scratched. It was easy to fix the chipped areas by filling them with wood putty and sanding smooth. For very delicate wood carving, use an emery board to smooth over the rough spots. The cane on the back of the chair was in excellent condition.

Before the orange velvet went in the trash, I laid out the seat and tiny arm pad fabric on top of the new fabric I had chosen to use and cut it to match the old orange velvet pattern. It was just a matter of attaching the new fabric to the chair in the same manner that I had removed it. The batting and foam cushion were still in good shape so I reused them. I laid the new fabric over the seat cushion and staple gunned just as the old orange velvet had been. The old cording was striped of orange velvet and recovered with the new fabric. The cording was then glued with a hot glue gun around the outside edge of the chair seat exactly as the old cording had been. The tiny little arm cushions were also replaced in the same way. In just a few hours I had a beautiful Louis XIV chair that would have cost several hundred dollars in the stores.

See the Upholstering chapter for complete instructions.

I refinished the chair using a cream colored acrylic paint over the dark cherry and crackled it, cane and all.

See the Finishing chapter for a complete "how to" on different finishing techniques.

The end table next to the chair was an old cherry table that was badly damaged. However, the table had a wonderful cream and white marble top that was in excellent condition. I paid $10 for the table and finished it to match the chair.

The bottom shelf of the table holds lots of garage sale treasures: a $1.00 silver domed dish, a $2.00 glass lined sterling silver ice bucket complete with lid, 50¢ hand cut crystal bowls filled with potpourri and candy, crystal and gold candlesticks with beeswax candles that were only 5¢. The candlesticks are topped with small 25¢ black metal candle shades. The shades were brand new in their original packaging. They sell for $14 each in the store!

On the wall behind the couch are several pictures in heavy ornate frames. All were purchased at garage sales. Some were perfect--some were not. They are very easy to repair and make beautiful. I mixed and matched prints with frames and mats until I found what I truly wanted. A small 25¢ Renoir print that was already matted in red fit perfectly into a gold carved frame that I found a couple of weeks earlier for 50¢. A large Manet print went into a cream and gold leaf frame that I found for only $1.00!

The Manet print was in an awful black painted frame. But I liked the print and I could use the glass for another gold frame, so it was a good deal for $2.00.

See frames in the Accessories chapter.

On the other side of the Manet picture is a large cherub shelf that was already finished in real gold leaf. Sitting on this shelf are two silver candlesticks. They are real silver, and cost only $1.00 for the pair. Inside are two dark teal beeswax candles that were 10¢ and on top of the candles are the metal candle shades that are black and brass.

Every plant in the house came from a garage sale. There are several large Dracaena Marginatas that are over 8' tall. The largest one with three trunks was only $15. This plant would easily sell for $100 at the nursery. I have paid 25¢ for spider plants, aloe vera, ivy and philodendrons and $2.00-$3.00 for the larger type rubber trees, palm and ficus trees.

In one corner of the living room is a black Empire chair that was hand painted with gold leaf. This is a chair that dates from the Napoleonic period. When I found it, the seat was covered in an awful blue ripped vinyl.

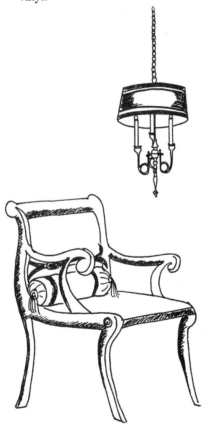

It was very easy to turn this chair upside down, unscrew the seat and recover it with a beautiful red moiré fabric that I found in a bridesmaid dress on a garage sale clothes rack for $1.00. The dress had a bad stain on the top front but the skirt had lots of useable fabric--plenty of fabric for the chair cover and matching pillows. The chair was only $15.

Beside the chair is an English style hunting lamp that hangs from a brass chain. It has three long candlesticks and is covered with a black and gold metal shade. I've seen this exact same lamp in the stores lately and it sells for $149. I paid $10!

In the hallway is a small cherry wood table that was actually a dressing table complete with mounted swivel mirror and matching bench. I removed the mirror portion and only use the table. The bench is being used upstairs in the master bathroom. The cherry dressing table with mirror and bench was only $15 and in perfect condition.

On the table are assorted pieces of hand cut crystal, a heavy bronze mirror, a crystal candy dish, a silver silent butler and a wonderful etched crystal globe lamp. Inside of the etched glass globe was a glass hurricane shade that was broken. That's probably why I got this beautiful lamp for only $2.00. I collect glass hurricane shades so I simply went downstairs to my collection and found a 25¢ glass shade that fit perfectly.

There are lots of marble topped cherry plant stands with garage sale plants sitting on top of them. Sometimes you will find these plant stands in pieces for only $1.00. It is very easy to glue the marble tops back on with epoxy glue.

On our sofa are piles and piles of richly covered down pillows--the expensive kind with lots of fringe and tassels.

See the pillow section in the Accessories chapter.

Across from the sofa is one of my favorite chairs. It is a down and feather filled club chair that I purchased for $1.00. Actually it was one of a pair of chairs. The chair fabric was so badly stained it looked like it was the centerpiece at a food fight! I knew they were once very expensive quality chairs, especially with the down cushions, so I happily carted them off. I upholstered the chair myself using a pair of garage sale drapes for the fabric. The drapes were quite large and altogether they contained over 18 yards of fabric. Such a lot of fabric for a pair of $5.00 drapes! They were a rich, silky

damask in a two-tone cream colored stripe. I ripped out the sewn in drapery pleating and took the large pieces of fabric to a bulk dry cleaner. The cleaning bill was only $6.00 for all the fabric. Had I not ripped out the sewn in pleats, I would have had to pay per pleat and this would have been quite expensive. The total cost for the two finished chairs was $13 including fabric and dry cleaning costs.

Next to the down filled club chair is a small tea table with inlaid wood. The inlaid wood is a flower and leaf pattern with different color stain on the tiny pieces of cut wood. The table has dainty French legs and the table top is edged in gold leaf scroll work. The table was only $8.00. This summer in Italy, I went to a store specializing in inlaid wood furniture and there was my table. The price in the store was $260! On the other side of the chair is a Florentine gold French table that was only $1.00. I saw a lot of this type table in Florence and Pisa.

At one end of the sofa is a floor lamp. It is not your usual style floor lamp with brass base and fabric shade. It is real copper verdigris with scrolled legs and three scrolled arms with etched hurricane lanterns sitting on top of the arms. At the base of the scroll work is hand painted Venetian glass. This is a very unusual and expensive piece. A one-of-a-kind item that you would not find very often. The seller told me she had it shipped over from Italy. I was thrilled to be its new owner for only $25!

DINING ROOM

One of the first furniture making projects I ever attempted was the marble topped buffet table in the dining room. It is one of my fondest treasures. I needed something to display all of the silver and crystal pieces that I was constantly finding at the sales. I had seen a marble topped, French leg buffet table in a decorator showroom for $2,800. As much as I loved it, there was no way I

could or would buy this elegant buffet--I knew I could make one just like it very easily. I just needed to find the right pieces. I started looking for four tall French legs, a table base and a top--hopefully, a marble top. The legs and base would be easy--it was the marble top that concerned me. I really never dreamed that I'd find a marble top that would be just the right size, so I planned on using just a plain piece of wood or a wooden coffee table top and marbleize it. Sure enough, after a few weekends of sale~ing, I had all the pieces that I would need from two separate pieces of furniture, including the marble top. The total I paid for the purchases needed to make the marble topped buffet table was only $23! I now have almost the same buffet that's on display in the showroom. It has the same antique crackle finish and beautiful cream marble top. I saved $2,777!

See the Making & Repairing Furniture chapter for a complete "how to."

On the buffet table sit hand cut crystal decanters that I love to fill with sherries and liqueurs. There are crystal glasses to match. They are the real thing--not pressed crystal, but hand cut and very expensive. So expensive that I even paid $5.00 for one of the decanters. Usually I pay $1.00 or $2.00 for the crystal decanters but this one was a $200 Waterford decanter! There are silver wine buckets, silver brandy snifter warmers and several pieces of unique antique silver. There are plenty of hand cut crystal bowls, crystal platters, pitchers and candy dishes. The silver wine bucket was only $2.00 and the other silver serving pieces usually run around $1.00 or $2.00 each. Even the champagne came from a garage sale. I purchased two bottles for only $2.00 apiece. When I went to the store to price the champagne, it was $25 a bottle!

In the center of the marble topped buffet table is a cloisonné vase filled with silk roses and baby's breath. The cloisonné vase was $1.00 and the silk roses and baby's breath totaled 35¢. Over the buffet is a very large mirror in an elaborate carved French frame. The mirror and frame are approximately 4' x 6'. The asking price for the mirror was $8.00 but I got it for $4.00. The fancy frame had an ugly oil painting of orange and yellow flowers. The seller wanted $20 for the painting and frame. All I really wanted was the frame, so he agreed to sell me just the frame for $10, feeling quite confident that someone would want those orange and yellow flowers! I had the $4.00 mirror cut to fit for FREE at the local glass shop. If you were to buy just the large, heavy plate mirror, it would cost over $100! My lovely mirror and fancy frame cost a total of $14.

The sconces on the sides of the mirror were just regular brass sconces with typical glass hurricane shades placed on top of the candleholders. They were $2.00 for the pair. I painted the brass candleholder stem with a black marbleized technique which gives them a rich, dressier look.

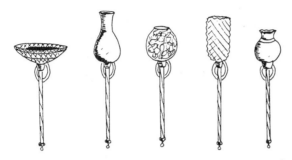

About a year later I found an old bathroom light fixture that I'm sure you have seen. This fixture has a round plate that is attached to the wall with chain draping out from the round plate and two glass globes hanging down from the end of the chain.

They should have paid me to take this old fixture away, but I did give them 50¢. I removed the three little screws that held the glass balls in place to see if the tops of the glass globes were chipped. They weren't. The glass globes are the crackled glass that you see so much of today. That is why I wanted them so badly. This new style crackled glass is expensive. I removed the old hurricane glass shades and set the round crackled glass globes in the brass and black marbleized sconces for an old-fashioned Victorian look. It's like having a new set of sconces just by changing the glass for only 50¢.

See the lamp section in the Accessories chapter for more ideas.

The dining room chairs are the traditional Queen Anne style. They were old and the wood was cracked, chipped and in bad shape. No problem--I was going to paint them anyway! The cracks and chips were filled with wood putty, allowed to dry and sanded smooth. I painted them an antique white color and gave them several coats of polyurethane. My set of six Queen Anne dining room chairs cost a total of $60 and, of course, the paint, wood putty and polyurethane came from garage sales too! The dining room table is plain, beveled glass sitting on top of glass bases at each end. It is actually quite modern but blends well with all the crystal and silver. Underneath the glass table is an authentic Persian rug.

See the rug section in the Accessories chapter for this story. It's too good to be true!

I made a table runner out of tapestry fabric that I bought for $10. There were over eight yards of the tapestry fabric and the exact tapestry pattern sells for over $30 a yard! I trimmed the table runner with gold filigree and attached a large silk tassel to each end. Most of the work was done with a glue gun. There is very little sewing involved.

On top of the tapestry table runner is a large ornate silver oval tray. Sitting on the tray is an assortment of silver candlesticks and a silver candle snuffer. The tray was $5.00 and the candlesticks and snuffer no more than $1.00 each. I also made a tapestry bell pull out of the same fabric. It is made much the same way as the table runner only I have a special trick that I use for the tops. Mine costs a few dollars. You will pay $60 in the stores. I like to make these and give them to my friends.

"How To"

TAPESTRY BELL PULL

Materials needed:
Tapestry fabric approximately 6" x 40" (finished size)
Silk moiré fabric, same dimensions
Trim (gimp*)
Large silk tassel
Large plastic potato chip bag clip (6" wide)
Stiffening product (Stiffy)
White glue
Fabric trim
Miniature silk roses
Primer
Gold spray paint
Brown stain

*See glossary

NOTE: For more information and decorating ideas for the clip, see the picture frame section in the Accessories chapter.

1 Separate the potato chip clip into two identical pieces. Prime one clip piece front and back.

2 Dip the fabric trim and silk roses into the stiffening product and saturate thoroughly. Let dry. Apply a coat of white glue over the front of the clip and arrange the trim and silk roses in a design of your choosing. (I like to arrange the roses in a ring around the top hole of the plastic clip.) Apply another coat of white glue over all the arranged fabric trim and miniature roses and allow to harden and dry thoroughly.

Continued . . .

THE GARAGE SALE DECORATOR'S BIBLE

3 Spray paint the decorated clip with gold paint and let dry. With a soft cloth, wipe brown stain over the gold to tone it down a bit. This will give you an antique look. Let dry. Spray with several coats of matte polyurethane, allowing to dry thoroughly between coats.

4 Lay the fabric, right sides together and trim the bottom portion into a large "V".

5 Stitch the fabric together, right sides together, leaving a 3" opening at the top flat seam. Turn the fabric inside out. Press the seams. Attach silk tassel to the bottom of the "V". Stitch the 3" opening closed either by hand or with the machine. You won't see this edge.

6 Attach the flat top edge of the fabric to the back bottom of the decorated clip with a hot glue gun. Lay something heavy on this edge while the glue sets.

OPTION

Do not cut the bottom of the bell pull into a "V". Leave it squared off and attach another decorated potato chip clip to the bottom the same way you did the top.

The china that I found has tiny blue and silver flowers trimmed with a silver rim. It's a complete service for eight and it was only $5.00 for the entire set. I found a set of silver-plated chargers to put under the plates. The four silver-plated chargers were $5.00.

There is an assortment of table cloths to choose from: Quaker Lace, Battenburg Lace or plain satin trimmed table cloths. None of these perfectly good table cloths cost more than $2.00 and of course there are lots of damask and linen napkins in every style and color that were either 10¢ or 25¢ apiece.

One of the most exciting finds ever was the Gallia crystal glassware. It was the exact same crystal that I had started collecting years ago. Unfortunately I had only two pieces of this crystal because it's hand cut and very expensive. I pulled up to a sale that was so junky looking, I almost drove on. I decided, since I was there to get out of the car and check it out anyway. There really wasn't much of anything, just junk packed in a lot of boxes. I opened one box sitting in a corner on the floor and in it was a set of glasses, crystal glasses, <u>my</u> crystal glasses, Gallia crystal glasses . . . Gallia crystal water goblets! *BE STILL MY HEART*! When I feebly asked, "How much for the glasses?" knowing full well she would tell me they're not for sale, she said, "How about $3.00 a glass?" There was a set of four water goblets--each one in perfect condition, still in the original wrapping and box where they were purchased. With my heart still pounding, I transported this wonderful treasure home and washed and admired them. Then, I went to the local department store and priced them . . . $40 PER GLASS. That's a total of $160 and I paid $12 for the entire set.

There are plants sitting around in porcelain vases and a beautiful crystal chandelier hanging over the table--all purchased at garage sales. I love the center medallions that you can buy and put on the ceiling over the chandeliers. Especially if your ceiling is painted a color other than white. These medallions really dress up the dining room and draw more attention to the lovely chandeliers. I found one that I liked at the home improvement store but it was $59. I found something at a garage sale that looks just as lovely and it was only $2.00!

Start looking at the wood picture frames to use for the center medallions. You can find several at any given sale. Most of the frames will either be square or rectangular. Sometimes you can find large ovals or a round frame. Either style shape will work. It's up to you. Make sure however, that the outer edges of the frame fit up flat against the wall so it will look right when placed on the ceiling. You do not want to use a frame for this project that angles out from the wall.

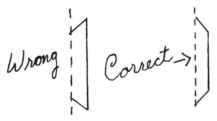

Paint the frame any color or antique it. Paint the area inside the frame a coordinating color or use gathered fabric. It's your choice and it's very easy and inexpensive.

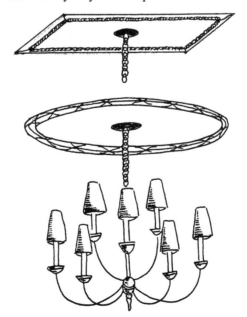

Just last week I found a sterling silver five-arm candelabra and a silver-plated chafing dish that sits up high on my favorite French style legs. I have so much silver and crystal that you'd think I spend a fortune in polish and cleaners. I buy them at garage sales too! Sometimes you can find them in the FREE box.

Another prize is the sterling silver coffee and tea service. It is a beautiful five-piece service complete with footed tray, sugar, creamer, tea and coffee pot. I'm not talking silver plate here . . . this set is solid sterling. It's so heavy that I can barely lift the set. It is the kind of silver service that I love with heavy, ornate carving. I found the set in an old paper bag at a sale and the seller was asking only $50. She said it was a wedding present and that she had never liked it. She just wasn't into silver or fancy things and wanted to get rid of it. I figured if she wanted to get rid of it so badly, she might take less. I asked her if she would take $25 for the set? Sure thing! This beautiful sterling silver tea and coffee set sells for around $800 retail. Everyone who sees the set admires it and asks me to find them one just like it! I have found several silver services for my friends and kept a few more for myself. The four-piece silver set I use for the guest bedroom was only $3.00! None however, are as lovely as my five-piece treasure.

BEDROOMS

Our master bedroom and the guest bedroom are decorated in a similar fashion. Everything in both bedrooms, floor to ceiling, came from garage sales. By describing these rooms in detail, I hope to give you some ideas on how easy it is to totally decorate, right down to the last detail with items purchased at garage sales.

The master bedroom and the guest bedroom have very high beds. You know--the kind you need a step stool to climb up into! If this look is for you, see the bed section in this chapter.

Each bed has a different style canopy. Each one is very elegant and luxurious and very easy to make.

See the canopy section in this chapter

My favorite piece of furniture in the master bedroom is an antique French bombe' chest that I found at an estate sale. It was in perfect condition and trimmed with real gold leaf. There is a cream and white carved marble top that matches the round shape of the chest. I had to pay $150 for this chest but it's easily worth $1,000!

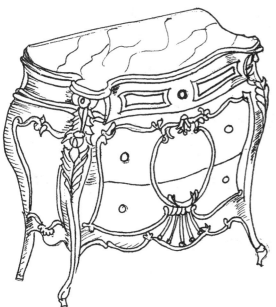

The French-style dressers and end tables are finished in an antique white with gold trim. They each have elaborate heavy carving on the drawers. The French double dresser in the guest bedroom was only $20 and in perfect condition. It was already finished in antique white so I didn't have to do a thing to it. The two-drawer end table was only $5.00. I needed to paint and antique the end table and trim it with gold to match the dresser. The mirror for the dresser was purchased at a later sale and it is a large oval with an ornate gold leaf frame. This frame was $5.00 and ready to hang--no repairs needed. The dresser drawers are lined with quilted drawer liner that I found for 25¢ a box. Tucked inside each drawer is one of the many sachet pillows that you can find for 5¢ -25¢.

Another easy way to make your dresser drawers smell wonderful is to tear out the perfume ad strips that you find in magazines. Open the strip and place it in a dresser drawer for a few weeks. You'll have so many of these strips piling up that you can change them often. It's a good way to see if you like a particular scent too!

On the dresser is a Battenburg lace doily which was 25¢ and a silver plated comb & brush set for 50¢. There are several crystal bowls that were only $1.00 each and they're filled with garage sale potpourri that was 25¢ for a brand new wonderful smelling bag! An onyx music box that was 25¢ and two crystal bedroom lamps sit on both sides of the dresser. I paid $2.00 for one of the crystal lamps, complete with shade. The other lamp I made out of pieces and it is one of my special favorites.

The glass base was bought separately for 50¢ and I found the beautiful glass scallop edged shade that was etched with tiny flowers in the bottom of a junk box. I couldn't believe it wasn't broken! I dug through the electrical parts box where I keep all of my lamp parts and found a finial to fit on top of the glass shade. I used cream colored silk fringe that I found on a 25¢ blouse and used tacky glue to glue the fringe around the scalloped edges of the glass shade for a Victorian look. The fringe is approximately 4" long. This type of lamp with the glass shade and silk fringe will cost around $100 at the store. Mine was only 75¢!

In each bedroom is a round skirted table that holds lots of garage sale treasures. The guest bedroom has a 24" round table that I bought for only 25¢. I made the table skirt out of a blue damask fabric that was $1.00

for seven yards of fabric! You will find lots of yard goods at the sales. There is a round glass top on the table that was only 50¢.

An easy way to make a round table skirt is to use a bedspread. Bedspreads are already sewn for you and are big and wide. All you have to do is fold and cut. This eliminates having to measure and sew seams like you have to do with fabric. If the bedspread has fringe on the bottom, cut it off. Cut out the round table skirt and reattach the fringe on the bottom of the skirt. If you don't want to sew the fringe on, try using tacky glue or a glue gun to attach the fringe. This is a very easy way to make the table skirt and you can find bedspreads in beautiful fabrics. A quilted bedspread works very well also. If you like a balloon look, gather up the bottom edges every 15 inches and secure with a clip on earring!

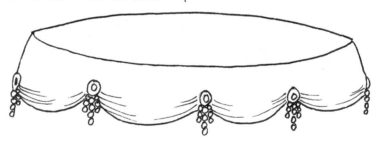

Table Topper with Earrings

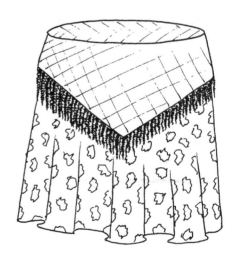

"How To"

MAKE ROUND TABLE SKIRT OUT OF BEDSPREAD

Materials needed:
Full size or larger bedspread
Scissors
Tacky glue
Decorative fringe (optional)
Cording or rope (optional)
String, marker & push pin

1 Lay the bedspread out flat on the floor.

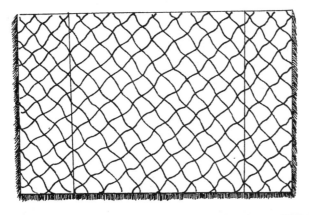

2 Fold in half, then fold in half again so you have a square. Determine the length of the skirt by measuring the diameter of the round table and the two sides from the table top edge to the floor. Add the side measurements together with the table diameter to get the total.

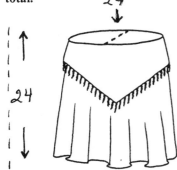

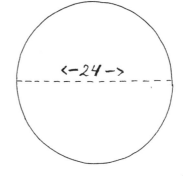

$$\begin{array}{r} 24 \\ 24 \\ 24 \\ \hline 72 \end{array}$$

Continued . . .

3 Tie a long string around a marker and press the end of the string into the top point of the fabric with a push pin.

4 On each side of the folded fabric measure down 1/2 the total number obtained in step 3 and draw a mark.

5 With the string and marker, draw an arc from one mark to the mark on the other side of the fabric.

6 Cut the fabric.

7 Hem or sew cording or reattach bedspread fringe by sewing or using glue.

Sitting on top of the round table is a small crystal Waterford quartz clock that cost $1.00. The same clock sells for $99 at the local department store. There are several different sizes and styles of picture frames filled with photos of family members. I especially like the silver-plated miniature frames. They were only $1.00 for three. Of course there is a favorite silver candlestick on the round table that was only 25¢ and a beautiful tulip shaped candle placed in the silver candlestick. The tulip-shaped candles were only 10¢ a pair. On top of the candlestick is a glass hurricane shade which was only 25¢. There's a crystal candy dish, $1.00 and several satin and lace potpourri pillows for 25¢. There is also a crystal and brass bedroom lamp that I assembled from garage sale lamp pieces. The total cost for the lamp was only 75¢.

See the lamp section in the Accessories chapter for a complete "how to" on making your own lamps.

The round table in the master bedroom is a lot larger. I needed a bigger table to hold so many beautiful things. The table is 36" in diameter and I thought finding a glass top that size was going to be difficult. It wasn't! I found an old bamboo coffee table with a very thick 36" round glass top. It even had two small bamboo stools that slid under the table. The entire set was only $10. All I really wanted was the glass top, so I sold the bamboo coffee table base at my garage sale for $8.00 and kept the two small bamboo stools, making the actual cost of the glass round only $2.00. At the store, a piece of 36" round glass this thick is $99!

I used a king-sized sheet that matches the bed canopy to cover the round table. On top of the sheet skirt I put a round white lace table cloth (25¢) and gathered up the lace with small silk roses at one side (5¢).

In one corner of the room is a dainty little French one-drawer chest that I found completely stripped down and ready to paint for just $5.00. The drawer handle was missing, so I went to my hardware box and found many handles to choose from. A lot of the odds and ends hardware pieces you can pick up in the FREE box at sales. It comes in handy to have a variety to choose from. You can easily change the look of your furnishings just by changing the pull handles or knobs. So pick these up if you find some you like, especially if they're FREE. Remember . . . you can always paint or finish them to match your decor. The little table was finished in an antique white and trimmed with gold to match the rest of the furniture.

Next to that table is a very large basket filled with lots of magazines. The basket was only $1.00. I saw the exact same basket at Pier I for $25! The room is also filled with lots of floor plants in FREE pots. All the plants came from garage sales too! Under the pots are brass plant stands with castors, which make them easy to move around. The brass plant stands were only 25¢.

On the walls are lots of pictures, all of which came from garage sales and they are in beautiful ornate gold leaf frames. Some of the frames were very plain that I fancied up. You can do this too! This book shows you how.

See the picture frame section in the Accessories chapter.

In the closet is a cherry wood luggage rack-- the kind that you see in hotels with the wide striped ribbons going across. I got the luggage rack for only $1.00!

The drapes in the bedroom are my favorite color--turquoise blue. They are antique satin drapes that cost $5.00 for two pair. They had just been freshly cleaned and were still in the cleaning bags on heavy hangers. They were very expensive drapes, lined and weighted. I would have bought these even if I didn't need them for the windows. You can use drapery material to re-upholster chairs, love seats and ottomans. Such a lot of fabric for only $5.00. All the curtain rods and traverse rods were either free or cost no more than $1.00. If you've ever moved into a new home and had to buy rods for every window you know how expensive they can be.

I found a beautiful love seat with the high Queen Anne style back and French carved legs. I plan on recovering the love seat and setting it at the end of the high bed in the guest bedroom, instead of a bench. There is also room for one of the those little French coffee tables that I have so many of in the basement. This will give me a place to set another silver coffee and tea service.

After the brand new $2.00 clock radio wakes up my guests, they can sip their morning coffee and turn on the $5.00 16-inch remote control, 115-channel cable color television. The $5.00 color television did not come with remote control, nor was it even capable of getting cable until I fixed it for FREE!

See "how to" make any TV a cable TV with remote control for FREE in the TV and Electronics chapter.

The television sits on an antique white wicker table that I purchased for $5.00. The 50¢ garage sale telephone and another $2.00 crystal lamp also sit on this table. On the bottom shelf of the antique wicker table are antique china cups and saucers for morning coffee and real damask linens that were only 10¢ a piece. Fresh flowers will be put in the FREE crystal bud vase when visitors arrive.

My guests will delight in thick bath towels, new bath towels that were only $1.00 apiece. The embellished, lace-trimmed hand towels that were 25¢ apiece will be placed on the crystal & gold hand towel holder that was 25¢. The brass base on the towel holder was beyond polishing, so I simply painted the brass an antique gold and it looks richer than the original brass. Guests will have lots of designer soaps, bath gels and salts to choose from. I usually pay 25¢ for a full box. I like to place the soaps in a basket that has dried flowers and ribbon tucked around the edges. You can find these baskets for 25¢ to 50¢. I think my guests will have everything they need to make themselves comfortable, right down to the white terry cloth robes hanging in the closet for their use! All together the entire guest bedroom, complete with furnishings, mattresses, bedroom linens, drapes and bathroom accessories totaled $131.25.

Mattress & Box spring.. 15.00	Crystal quartz clock........ 2.00	Gold mirror.................. 10.00
Mattress.......................... 5.00	Picture frame, large 2.00	Crystal lamps (4)........... 7.50
Bed frame 2.00	Picture frame (3) 1.00	Night stand, 2 drawer..... 5.00
Canopy 8.00	Silver candlestick.............25	Chest, 1 drawer 5.00
Sheets............................ 1.25	Tulip candle.....................25	Telephone.........................50
Pillow cases.................... 1.00	Hurricane shade...............25	Silver brush & comb.........50
Comforter, shams 8.00	Color TV......................... 5.00	Window drapes.............. 5.00
Mattress pad.....................25	Wicker table.................... 5.00	Luggage rack................. 1.00
Sleeping pillows.............. 2.00	Crystal candy dish.......... 1.00	Towels 5.00
Decorative pillows.......... 1.25	Potpourri pillow...............25	Towel holder 50
Velour blanket 1.00	Basket............................ 1.00	Shower curtain.............. 1.00
Knitted throw.................. 1.00	Plants, assorted............. 1.25	Bath soaps & gels.............25
Round table 25	Brass planters................. 1.00	Silver coffee service........ 3.00
Round glass top................25	Double dresser 20.00	China cups & saucers........50

BEDS

What's the most important part of any bedroom? The bed of course, both for comfort and beauty.

The bed is usually the largest piece of furniture in the bedroom and the focal point. I definitely feel a beautiful bed makes for a beautiful bedroom.

Ever since I was a young girl I have always admired and wanted to sleep in the very high beds. The kind that you see in history books and need a step stool to climb up into.

Unfortunately for me, I liked the style of my existing bed and it matched the rest of the bedroom furniture. To replace it with one of the high beds was out of my price range and there wasn't any way I could make the framing higher on the existing bed. One day when I was out garage sale~ing I realized how easy it would be to make my existing bed into a big high bed, and at a garage sale price. Here's how . . .

One of the items on my list of needs was a new set of box springs. Our bed is a king-size bed, so I needed two box springs. I had been looking at the twin-sized bedding sets. These will work also. If the twin mattress was bad - no problem. I just needed some decent box springs. The mattress that I had on the bed was only a few years old so I didn't really need a set. But, guess what I found? A brand new king-size mattress and box springs set--still factory sealed in the plastic wrap. It was just the right firmness and the asking price was only $100 for the entire set. This was easily a $700 king-size mattress set. When I offered the sellers $50 for the set, they said "OK".

When I thought about how much I paid a few years ago for the new mattress alone, this really was a bargain. But, what am I going to do with two new mattresses since the seller didn't want to split up the set?

#$%¢&*(¢%#

My mind was racing. It hit me like a brick wall. Where had my brain been all of this time? There was my big high bed that I had always wanted! The same beautiful high bed that was in all the decorator magazines and designer showrooms.

All I had to do was use two mattresses!

I put the new box springs in the existing bed frame, my old mattress on top of the box springs, and placed the new mattress on top. I knew it was destiny that I have my wonderful high bed! How simple and inexpensive. A "no brainer."

Just put two mattresses on the bed!

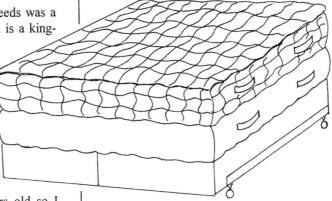

If you want a big high bed, just find yourself an extra mattress and place it on top of your existing mattress. No extra special framing required and great sleeping!

CANOPIES

The most beautiful bedrooms in the world usually have a canopy bed in them. Originally beds had canopies and draperies hung around them for warmth and if you could afford bed chamber servants--for privacy! Canopies truly make a bed the focal point of the room and they are very easy to make.

Canopies can be masculine or feminine in design depending on the style of canopy and the fabric used. Sheets are easy to use and so are the used draperies that you buy at the sales. Buy those draperies that you see if they're a color or pattern that you like or will like, or learn to like someday! There are lots of drapes at garage sales and they are very reasonably priced. You can pay anywhere from $5.00 to $10 on up for decorator prints, rich damask and antique silks.

Remember . . . all you want is the fabric. When making your purchasing decision, think of what you would pay per yard if you bought the fabric at a store. Garage sale drapes are quite a buy and all you want is the fabric, don't think of them as drapes--think of them as fabric--lots and lots of fabric.

Rip out the pleats in the drapes and take the fabric to a bulk dry cleaner for cleaning. This will be very inexpensive since you will not pay per pleat. Some drapes that you find will have already been cleaned and hanging in the plastic wrap. You'll have yards and yards of beautiful fabric to work with.

Let's make some bed canopies. Pick out the style you like and follow the instructions in the next few pages.

See Making & Repairing Furniture chapter to make an elegant bed canopy out of a coffee table.

HALF CROWN CANOPY
Page 44

FABRIC HALF CANOPY
Page 46

ROD POCKET CANOPY
Page 48

PICTURE FRAME CANOPY
See Fabric Half Canopy--Page 46

EASIEST CANOPY
Page 49

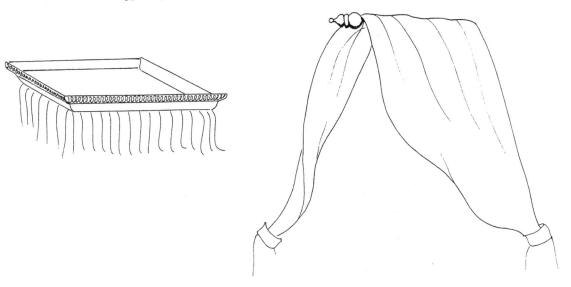

PLANT STAND CANOPY
Page 50

"How To"

HALF CROWN CANOPY

Materials needed:
Half round piece of wood approximately 24" diameter
Staple gun
Fabric
White sheets (optional)
2 Angle brackets ("L") shaped
2 Decorative tie backs or 2 cup hooks

1 Take a large piece of fabric and tack it on the wall behind your bed. Start at the top outside edges of the canopy and extend the fabric down behind the headboard. If you have a high ceiling or vaulted ceiling, decide how high the canopy should be and start the fabric at that height. The fabric can be flat against the wall or you can make gathers at the top so the fabric falls in folds. I prefer the gathered look for the half crown canopy.

The top portion of fabric will be tapered the
same size as the back of the canopy.
Extend the fabric about 2 inches on both
sides of the bed.

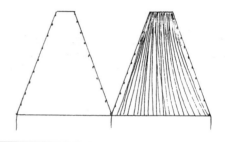

2 Cut a round table top in half or cut a piece of 1" plywood in a half circle. The round particle board tables that you see at the garage sales for 25¢ would work well.

3 Attach white sheeting fabric to the underside of the half circle by stapling. Line the inside of your fabric side panels with the white sheets that you are buying. If you are using drapes for the side panels they may already be lined. Hem the sides and bottom edges of the fabric side panels.

Continued . . .

4 Staple gun the long side pieces to the top side of the half round. Take one long side piece and staple it to the center of the round going all the way around to the back edge of the half round. Repeat this process with the other strip of long fabric.

5 Cut out fabric for crown design. I used a piece of fabric that was approximately 18" by 8 feet and scalloped it. To make the scallops, use a half round and draw on the fabric with a marker. You can use the other half of the round table top or a large skillet lid to make the scalloped edge.

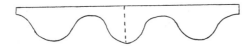

Mark the exact center of the fabric. Draw the first scallop center on this mark.

6 Make a mark or place a straight pin on the center straight edge. Hem the bottom, scalloped edge and the sides. Attach tassel trim or lace to the scalloped edge if desired.

7 Take the finished scalloped edge crown fabric and staple each end to the ends of the half round. Staple the center marked section to the center of the half round. Pleat up the fabric in between the end staples and the center staple. Staple the fabric all the way around the front section of the half round.

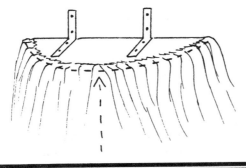

8 Attach to the wall with metal angle irons. Make strips of matching or coordinating fabric for tie backs or use braided cord.

"How To"

FABRIC HALF CANOPY

Materials needed:
Fabric
White sheets (optional)
Decorative trim (optional)
Staple gun
Firing strips or large picture frame
or
1/4" plywood sheet
2 decorative tie backs or 2 cup hooks

1 Make a frame the size of the desired canopy out of the firing strips. Stretch a piece of fabric (a white garage sale sheet will do nicely) over the frame and secure with staples. If using a large picture frame you can either cover it or let it show. Paint or finish the frame as desired.

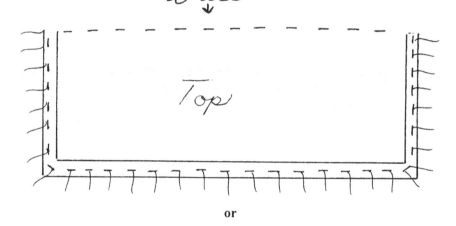

or

Cut a piece of plywood the size of the desired canopy. Cover one side of the plywood with plain white fabric, or paint the wood.

2 Attach fabric backing to the wall from both edges of the canopy frame down behind the headboard using small finishing nails. The fabric can be flat or gathered.

3 Cut two long rectangles of fabric, long enough to hang from the canopy to the floor. This fabric should be twice the width of the side of the wood piece or wood frame. These are the side panels.

Continued . . .

NOTE: Line the fabric side panels and topper with a garage sale white sheet. This will add weight to the fabric, allowing it to hang nicely and give the canopy a finished look.

4 Gather the fabric and staple to the top side edges of the frame or plywood piece.

5 Measure and cut the topper part of the canopy. Use either a balloon type valance or a scalloped edge type as in the half crown canopy. Measure the sides and front of the canopy frame or plywood section. Double or triple this measurement for the length of the fabric topper.

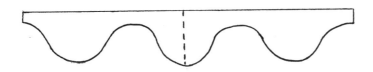

6 Hem and apply decorative trim to the bottom edge of canopy topper. Staple gun top edge of fabric around both sides and front of canopy frame or plywood piece. Make tie back strips out of matching or coordinating fabric. Attach the tie backs to the cup hooks.

Nail or screw canopy to the ceiling studs. Make sure it's securely attached to the studs.

NOTE: See the Making & Repairing Furniture chapter for a complete "how to" on making a beautiful wood canopy out of a coffee table.

"How To"

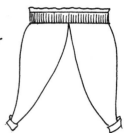

ROD POCKET CANOPY

Materials needed:
Wide curtain rod
Curtain rod hardware
Fabric
2 cup hooks or decorative tie backs

1 The curtain rod can be either 1/3 the width of the bed, 1/2 the width of the bed or up to the entire width of the bed, depending on the look you want. Just make sure it is the wide style rod.

2 Apply fabric backing to the wall using small finishing nails. Shape the fabric to fit from both edges of the rod and angle out to the outer edges of the bed.

3 Cut two lengths of fabric to hang from the rod all the way to the floor. You can allow extra length to puddle on the floor for a very rich look.

4 Sew the rod pockets in the top of the fabric allowing for at least a three-inch seam margin on the top.

   NOTE: Line the fabric with a coordinating fabric or a white garage sale sheet.

5 Insert the rod in the sewn pocket and gather the fabric onto the rod.

6 Attach the rod to the wall with appropriate hardware. Make tiebacks with matching or coordinating fabric or use braided cord. Attach to the cup hooks.

"How To"

EASIEST CANOPY

Materials needed:
"L" bracket
Round curtain rod*
Finial for curtain rod
Fabric
Lining fabric (garage sale sheet)
2 decorative tie backs or cup hooks

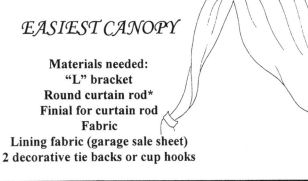

1 Attach "L" shaped bracket as high as you want the canopy and centered over the bed.

2 Cut the round rod to be approximately 16" to 20" in length. Paint or refinish the rod and finial. Slip round rod over the "L" shaped bracket. Attach the finial.

3 Sew fabric and lining into one very large rectangle--long enough to fall to the floor. You can make it even longer for a "puddle" effect. Lay the fabric over the round curtain rod and secure at the top of the bed with cup hooks or tie backs. You can make a small strip tie back out of matching or coordinating fabric or use braided cord.

"How To"

PLANT STAND CANOPY

Materials needed:
Large wrought iron planter stand
Brackets to secure the legs to the ceiling
or
Chain

1 Turn the planter upside down and attach the legs to the ceiling. You can center the plant stand over the bed or hang it towards the front of the bed. It's your choice.

Drape long sheers from the planter and swag to the four corners of the bed. For a half canopy effect, drape only to the sides.

2 There are many types of brackets that might work. If the planter legs have a curve, find a bracket with an arc in the middle.

It's very important to remember to secure the brackets to the ceiling studs. Sometimes this is not possible. Experiment with different sized brackets.

3 Chain will work every time with any kind of leg or holder. If your planter stand has three legs--use three strips of chain. You can always decorate the chain with tie wire and faux metal leaves. Use "S" hooks to attach the chain to the planter and cup hooks in the ceiling studs.

See faux leaf technique in the Accessories chapter.

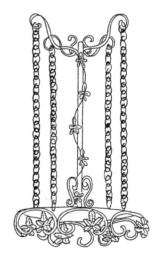

BEDDING

Buy all of your bedding at sales. New, beautiful bedding, not ripped, torn or stained, but beautiful 200 to 250 thread count sheets, silk, or satin sheet sets.

All of our bedding: sheets, dust ruffles, comforters, shams, pillows, feather beds--even the silk and lace sheets that I use for company in the guest bedroom were purchased at garage sales. Most of them were brand new.

You might not find an entire set at one time. That's OK. I found beautiful Battenburg lace pillow shams for $1.00 a pair at one sale, and later in the day I found a matching comforter for $8.00 at another sale.

The eyelet bed set that's on the day bed was all bought separately. Sometimes you can find an entire set (dust ruffle, comforter, shams) in very good condition, but it's very easy to find them piece by piece and probably at a lower price than if you bought them in a set. Learn to buy ahead and put your purchases away in the linen closet until you find a mate. You may find only one pillow sham. The matching sham might be badly stained, so just buy the good one at half price, you'll find the other soon. You will find a mate . . . I promise!

Big, beautiful blankets are plentiful. I've found several king-size blankets with lovely satin trim and wonderful warm wool blankets for winter. Velour blankets and electric blankets are found in every size and color.

Be imaginative when it comes to dust ruffles. You will see several white dust ruffles in a day's worth of sale~ing. The cost will be anywhere from 25¢ on up. I was in need of a king-size dust ruffle and after looking for a couple of weeks without finding one I finally decided to buy the full and queen size ruffles that were so plentiful and inexpensive--only 50¢ apiece!

It was easy to lay three separate white dust ruffles on top of the box springs. I had beautiful ruffles all the way around. No one can tell it's not a custom made bed ruffle! The dust ruffle (three dust ruffles) ended up costing only $1.50.

If you plan to use the double mattress technique, try using a double set of dust ruffles for a very feminine effect.

One ruffle (or several) is placed on the box springs as usual. Put down the first mattress. Place a garage sale fitted sheet on this mattress. Place another dust ruffle (or several) on top of this mattress. Finish with the final mattress. *BEAUTIFUL!*

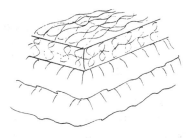

USE YOUR IMAGINATION AND MAKE THINGS WORK FOR YOU!

When buying garage sale sheets, always unfold them and check for rips and stains. Try to find the tag and check for size, content and thread count.

You can find many 200-thread count sheets. The higher the thread count, the better and softer the sheet. These are the sheets I prefer to have on the bed. I usually buy just white sheets unless I find a perfect shade that will match the bedroom decor. If you find clean, white sheets in any size, BUY THEM, especially flat sheets. You will be using these sheets for all kinds of projects around the house: drapery and curtain liners, dust covers, re-upholstering furniture, pillow liners, and ottomans. Keep your linen closet full of these wonderful sheets.

Think of your sheets as white fabric!

BEDSPREADS, COMFORTERS DUVETS

The beautiful Battenburg lace, king-size white duvet that I found for only $8.00 was spotlessly clean. Considering the fact that they sell for $89 and up, I couldn't resist buying it! The only thing wrong with the duvet was that some of the cording in the lace cut work was torn.

I went to the craft store and bought matching floss for only 20¢ and used a large needle to join one side of the fabric to the other with the floss to connect the cut work design. The design was again perfect!

This beautiful white Battenburg Lace king-sized duvet cost only $8.20, not $100.

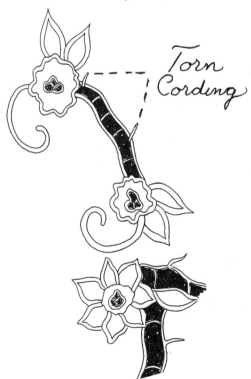

At another sale I found a satin comforter in a beautiful cream color. It was terribly soiled and very well worn. It did however have a wonderful satin and lace trim around the edges that was in excellent condition. The pillow shams that matched the comforter had the same satin and lace trim and they had never been used. I paid $2.00 for the comforter set and use the shams in the guest bedroom. I removed the satin and lace trim from the soiled comforter and sewed the trim on another satin comforter. The other comforter was my favorite shade of blue satin, but it was very plain. It was the exact shade of blue that I love and was brand new in its original wrapper. It was marked $5.00 and I got it for $2.00. After sewing the satin and lace trim around the edges, this inexpensive $2.00 comforter quickly become a very expensive looking elegant treasure for the bedroom.

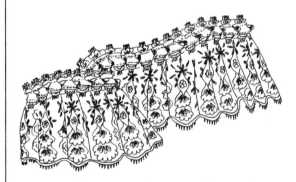

The old soiled comforter is now rolled up and stored in a 5¢ pillow case that I keep in the back of the van to help protect all of the treasures I buy when garage sale~ing.

DECORATING YOUR NEW BED

Now that you have that big high bed with wonderful soft sheets, dust ruffles, comforters, duvets and a lovely canopy--let's finish it completely with accessories.

Lay a dust ruffle or several dust ruffles on top of the box springs.

Put down the mattress.

Put a 25¢ garage sale fitted sheet on the mattress.

Lay a mattress pad on the top mattress. I found a king-size mattress pad that was brand new for only $1.00!

Make up the bed with sheets, blankets, and comforter.

Arrange the pillows.

Start with the European square pillows at the back of the bed next to the headboard. Prop them up straight or angle them with the pointed end up.
Prop the sleeping pillows next to the European pillows.

NOTE: Some people prefer to do this in reverse, especially if the sleeping pillows are not decorative. Either way is acceptable.

Now, start building out . . . layer after layer with decorator pillows in all different shapes and fabrics.

Remember all of the down and feather pillows that you've been buying and piling up in your closet and the boxes and boxes of beautiful fabric that you found on the clothes rack? Now is when you can really have fun decorating those pillows with all that beautiful fabric and trim!

I love satin and lace on my bed and if you've beaten me to the clothes rack, I'm sure you probably have a big box full by now!

See the Accessories chapter for a complete "how to" on making beautiful pillows.

At the bottom of the bed, lay a crocheted or knitted afghan or the designer throw that you made from the bridesmaid dresses. A rectangular crocheted tablecloth looks lovely lying out over the bottom edge of the comforter.

See the Accessories chapter for complete instructions on making a designer bed throw.

Place the upholstered bench that you made from a coffee table at the end of the bed and you've got a real designer bedroom for less than the price of ONE designer silk tasseled pillow!

See the Making & Repairing furniture chapter for instructions on making an upholstered bench.

A bed fit for a queen! My guests love to come visit and sleep in this bed as much as I love having them!

BATHROOMS

I decorate the bathrooms just as I would any other room of the house. They have upholstered chairs, benches, little footstools, shelves full of thick towels, plants, candlesticks and crystal bowls filled with wonderful smelling potpourri.

I love to make drapes, festoons, balloon shades or valances to hang over the top of the bathtub with drapes to match. Inside the tub is a clear shower curtain liner. Decorate the tub area just as you would a window in the living room.

The easiest way to drape the tub area is with an extension type rod that you can easily remove. There are so many different decorating ideas to choose from. Just remember to use the drapery fabric that you've been buying or try lace curtain panels and for sure, find that extension rod in the FREE box at the garage sales. You'll have a wonderful designer look for pennies.

All of the decorative type, embellished hand towels have been purchased at sales. It never ceases to amaze me that I find such wonderful things, brand-new, such as hand towels and wash clothes. You can find an entire set for just $1.00 at the sales.

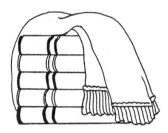

I used to place the lace-trimmed, embellished hand towels and wash cloths in the guest bathroom and main floor powder room, but now that the linen closet is filled with them, I use them every day. Why deprive yourself and save your beautiful things for special occasions when you have so much of everything for so very little cost? When I paid $10 each for these little embellished towels I wanted them to last a long time. Now that I find them for 25¢ to 50¢ apiece I can afford to treat myself every single day. You can too.

Another favorite bathroom treasure is the luxurious decorative soaps that you find. There are all different sizes and shapes-- large seashell soaps to small butterflies and spicy round ball soaps that come in many different colors. Sometimes I find these gift wrapped in a brand new package, never opened for just 50¢. Originally they would cost around $5.00 to $10 for the set. The larger gift wrapped sets complete with bubble bath, soaps, bath salts, cologne and body lotion will run anywhere from $1.00 to $2.00 at the garage sales. These sets are quite expensive in the stores.

I love to set all the bathroom amenities out in a garage sale pottery dish, crystal bowl or basket. The baskets that the soaps come in often make a nice display container. I'll definitely use the baskets for something else if I don't place the bathroom toiletries in them. The shelves in the cabinets are filled with designer shampoos, conditioners and lotions. If you don't already have tons of these from your own travels, you'll find lots of the miniature toiletries at the sales for 5¢ each or in the FREE box. They're wonderful for guests. Put together an assortment and if you are one of those people who travel a lot in your work and save these little miniatures, donate them to the retirement centers, or the women's abuse centers. They are very much needed and will be greatly appreciated. Pick these items up all summer long when garage sale~ing and store them in a big box just to give away. You'll never miss a nickel here or a nickel there.

When my guests and family step out of their showers and bubble baths they'll wrap big, thick, Egyptian cotton towels that I find brand new for $2.00 each! Small throw rugs can easily be found for $1.00. I prefer to carpet the entire bathroom area using carpet or a piece of carpet that I find at the sales for just a few dollars.

You'll also find plenty of hair dryers, curling irons, hot rollers, bathroom and tile cleaners, towel holders and racks--anything you will ever need to accessorize the perfect bathroom.

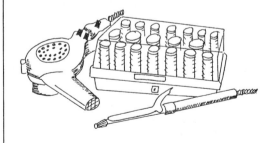

KITCHEN

When you start out with nothing, some of the first items you go out sale~ing for are kitchen items. I did have a set of dishes, everyday silverware and the usual array of kitchen tools but most of our small appliances were gone. Fortunately, just about any kitchen item you can imagine is found in abundance at the sales.

GADGETS

Spatulas, ladles, serving spoons, pasta servers, measuring cups, scoops, mashers, basters, knives, paring knives, steak knives, cleavers, lemon juicers, zesters, fondue forks, tongs, corn on the cob holders, shish kabob skewers, hooks, chip clips, party napkins, paper tablecloths, paper plates, toothpicks, spices, salt & pepper shakers, pepper mills--anything and everything for 5¢ or 10¢. Sometimes even FREE!

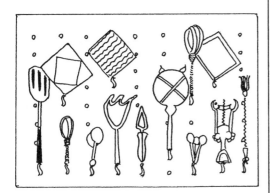

When you are out sale~ing you will see signs marked "SAMPLE SALES." These are where professional salespeople sell overstock or their display items. You can find brand new kitchen gadgets that do just about everything. I especially like all the kitchen gadget holders, the plastic coated wire shelving, tiered carousels, corner shelves, spice racks and lid holders. They really help organize the kitchen, laundry room and garage. It's easy to be very organized when you pay 10¢ to 25¢ for these items instead of a few dollars apiece!

Everyone has a plastic container cabinet filled with cottage cheese, sour cream and butter tubs. You know the ones that you just can't bear to throw away and clutter up your cabinets and end up falling out on the floor every time you open the cabinet. If you are a sale~er, pitch them or keep them in the garage for paints and crafts. You can find more than enough good quality Rubbermaid and Tupperware containers at the sales. Some new, some barely used for 5¢ and up. The most I've ever paid is 75¢ for a brand new three-piece set of the large Rubbermaid bowls with lids.

SMALL APPLIANCES

The new fun appliances that come out each year are plentiful at sales. I thought having a Tato Twister would be fun but I was unwilling to pay $19 for it at the store. I was glad to find one that was brand new complete with paperwork for only $2.00 The juice extractor I found was rated #1 in Consumer Magazine and the price was listed at $69. I found one that was brand new and selling for $15. Mini-choppers, blenders, mixers, hand mixers, crock pots, mini crock pots and microwaves are all at the sales in great quantities! When I find items that are brand new or nearly new I always ask sellers why they are selling them. They often tell me that they were Christmas presents or birthday presents that they really didn't want or just didn't have the time to use, so they would rather sell the items rather than have them take up space.

The heavy duty Sunbeam mixmaster complete with glass Pyrex mixing bowls was an unbelievable 50¢! The brand new Black & Decker toaster oven with mounting rack was sitting on a table marked $8.00. I had been wanting one of these for a long time and it was the almond color that I needed. It belonged to a young man who was sitting in the shade reading the paper. I asked him, "What is wrong with the toaster oven?" He said, "Nothing--it is brand new." He had never even plugged it in. "Why are you selling it?" I asked. He explained that he and his wife were separated and were going to get a divorce, so he went out and bought some things that he needed. He and his wife got back together, so now he didn't need the toaster oven. A happy ending for everyone. I got the new toaster oven and mounting rack for $5.00 and he got his wife back!

The Cuisinart is a good example of what sale~ing late in the day can do. It was hot and 4:00 p.m. Most of the sales had closed down. In fact, I was on my way home with the van loaded down full of bargains when I saw one more sign and decided to see if the sale was still open. It was open and pretty well picked over but there was a nice Cuisinart with all the different blades and attachments that I had been wanting. The seller was asking $25. It would easily sell for $129 new in the store. I asked to plug it in and test it out. It worked fine but I really didn't want to pay that much. I was tired and didn't really feel like bargaining and lucky for me, she was tired too! She said "Make an offer, I don't want to have the sale tomorrow and I really want to get rid of everything." "How about $5.00?" I asked. "SOLD!" She told me if there was anything else I wanted, feel free to just take it. She was ready to close the garage door and anything else sitting out would be put in the trash. I found lots of odds and end dishes for my son's college room, silverware, wrapping paper, ribbon, lots of nails and screws, curtain rods and flower pots! All FREE for the taking! There's a lot to be said about getting to the sales early, but there are still plenty of incredible bargains and free stuff at the end of the day.

The linen drawers in our kitchen are filled to overflowing with potholders, handle holders, oven mitts, place mats and napkins that cost 5¢ to 25¢--not used or stained, but brand new!

I love to find the large china serving platters. I found a very large white china platter trimmed in gold for just $1.00. Another platter was the popular clear glass. It is a very large oval platter and my girlfriend Jo Ann, who I was sale~ing with that day, had bought one just like it for $19 at a kitchen shop. The seller had the platter marked at $1.00. I guess the reason no one had bought it was because the name "JULIA" was etched on the bottom of the platter. I bought the platter for 50¢. After all, when it's filled with food no one will see the name!

The glass bottles and decanters that you find are wonderful to buy and fill with special oils or herbed vinegars. Buy them and fill them with your favorite recipes. They make wonderful gifts for your friends.

On our kitchen counter top is a 24" square marble chopping block that was only $2.00. They sell for around $30 in the kitchen shops. I've found several brand new wood chopping blocks for the counter and lots of decorative tiles and trivets.

POTS AND PANS

Pots and pans are plentiful at the sales. Not only were all of my pots and pans purchased at the sales but I've bought complete sets for my children. I bought a 10-piece set of Farberware for my daughter for only $8.00. Only a pot and a small skillet had been used, they were almost like new. I purchased some aluminum cleaner and polished them so they looked completely new. Now--if she can just learn to cook! I found a five-piece set of Calphalon, the large Dutch oven and lid, large skillet and small skillet with lid. The seller said she didn't care for it and sold the entire set for only $5.00! My favorite set of pots and pans is the pretty white enamel with flower and ivy design. The set consisted of Dutch oven with lid, two pots with lids, skillet and tea pot. All for just $5.00! You'll find plenty of cast iron cookware, skillets, griddles, kettles and pots. I never pay more than $1.00 for cast iron pieces. Buy cookie sheets, muffin tins, pie pans, cake pans, bundt pans, bread pans, either metal or glass, for 25¢ apiece.

CENTER ISLAND RACKS

Since my kitchen is full, really full of decorator items, I needed a nice place to display them. There is a center island in the kitchen so I decided to make a shelf to hang over the island. The metal racks that are in the stores and at garage sales were not big enough to hold all of the pieces that I had accumulated, plus they were over $100, so I decided to make my own!

I bought a piece of 10" x 60" fir shelving lumber and some shelf molding for a few dollars. I stained it oak and varnished it with 25¢ garage sale purchases. I attached four large cup hooks to each corner of the shelf and four more large cup hooks to the studs in the kitchen ceiling over the center island. The shelf is hung from the ceiling with a garage sale brass chain attached to all eight cup hooks. On the bottom side of the shelf I used a lot of smaller cup hooks to hold baskets, cooking utensils and decorator items. On top of the shelf sit more decorator items and unique cooking utensils, brass and copper.

There are all kinds of things you can use to make a rack over your center island. You can always go to the store and buy the metal ones or you'll find the exact same racks at garage sales. Round racks, rectangle racks or half round racks. You can hang things only from the sides of these racks and you're limited in size. If you've got stuff like I've got stuff, and if you keep garage sale~ing, you'll definitely have lots of stuff, and you will need something much larger.

My friend, Nan, used an antique ladder--the kind with the round wooden dowels. It's actually just a piece of ladder the same length as her center island. She found a blacksmith who forged wrought iron holders that were bolted into the ceiling on one end and then attached to the ends of the ladder. Chicken wire was stretched on top of the ladder so items could be placed on top. Pots and pans and collectibles were also hung from the ladder rungs and sides. The ladder could also be suspended from the ceiling using chain.

The size of the overhead rack really depends on the size of your center island. If it's square, it's nice to find a similar square shape. If it's rectangular, you would look for an oval or rectangular shape.

One Saturday afternoon while sale~ing I found a lovely wrought iron square patio table. The legs were curved and the table frame was very ornate. My favorite kind! It was missing the glass top but it was still a beautiful table and a real buy at $5.00!

I took the table home and put it outside on the deck. I was checking it over to see if it needed any repair or touch up paint. When I bent over to see the underside of the frame, I saw the most beautiful center island kitchen rack imaginable! Turn a table upside down!

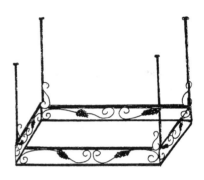

It is a very easy decorative type center island rack! Just about any patio table, end table or coffee table turned upside down can be a center island rack. A decorator's dream come true! Use the legs if they are long enough and a good style or remove the legs and use just the table top frame suspended from chain. It is basically already made for you. All you have to do is attach it to the ceiling. There are lots of wrought iron patio tables at the garage sales. Most of the time the glass is broken out so you can pick them up at a very good price--usually $1.00 to $5.00. You don't need the glass if you are going to use it for a center island rack. Just turn it upside down! Leave the center open or attach chicken wire with a staple gun or glue wood dowels several inches apart in the center opening and paint or stain to match the rest of the table. If your table is wrought iron and you don't care for black, paint it white or verdigris. Whatever pleases you. If you are using the legs, have your local blacksmith make iron brackets that will attach the bottom of the legs to the studs in your ceiling. These brackets should run around $3.00 to $5.00 apiece. Bolt the legs to your ceiling in the studwork and you have an instant, very beautiful and unique center island rack! If you saw the legs off, suspend the wrought iron frame with decorative chain.

Buy iron "S" hooks to hang over the edge or your blacksmith will make custom hooks for you.

You can also do the same thing with your wooden coffee tables or frames. Maybe you have an extra table frame lying around because we used the legs for an ottoman or bench. Just attach cup hooks to each corner of the frame and the ceiling and hang with chain. If the table has a piece of glass or cane or lattice work in the top, remove it so there is just open space. If your table has lattice in the center it might work. Just don't block out the kitchen lighting. You need the light to shine through. You can always put chicken wire or glue dowels across the center opening to hang things from. A wrought iron plant stand works well also. Just turn it upside down, attach the legs to the ceiling and hang beautiful pans and decorative accessories with "S" hooks.

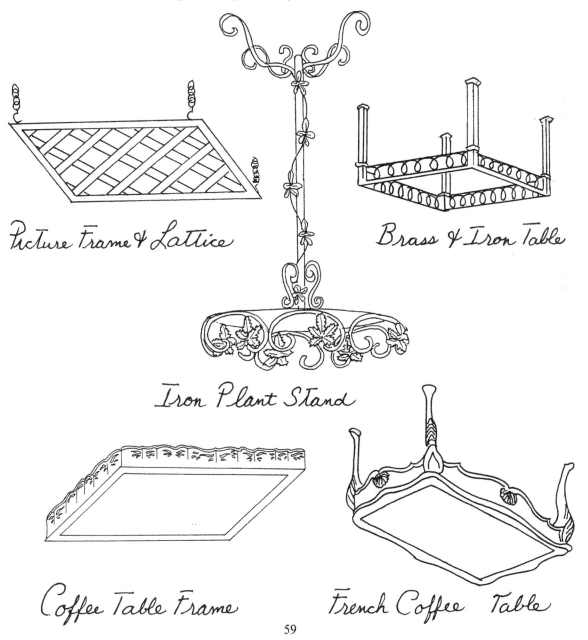

Picture Frame & Lattice

Brass & Iron Table

Iron Plant Stand

Coffee Table Frame

French Coffee Table

A quick word about chain. You can never have enough! I use it for all kinds of things throughout the house--hanging lamps or plants or simply to nail a long piece of brass or black chain to the kitchen wall. Using "S" hooks, attach brass and copper collectibles up and down the entire chain. Use brass chain or painted chain depending on your decorating style. It's an easy and inexpensive way to display your treasures. I have seen this treatment in a lot of showrooms.

I use chain for storage also, both in the garage and the basement.

See the Garage, Auto & Outdoor chapter for more information on storage.

After finishing the center island rack I still had more things that I wanted to display. I had been admiring the big black iron and brass baker's racks for a long time. Again, I promised myself "someday."

"Someday" happened at a local garage sale for only $150. It is one of the largest baker's racks made and I knew I had seen the exact same one at a designer showroom. I asked the seller if she would hold it for an hour because the showroom was close by and I thought I'd go look. When I got to the showroom, sure enough, it was still on the floor. It was on sale however, marked down to just $889 from $1,100. You better believe I got back to that sale really quickly and I gladly gave her $150 for the very large, ornate brass and black baker's rack.

I have on display several different sizes of soup tureens, a silver tea service, brass hurricane lamps, pieces of pottery, cookbooks, and French copper skillets--the kind that sell for $80 at Williams-Sonoma. I buy them for $1.00 each! There are lots of blue Delft pieces, baskets filled with dried flowers and garage sale candles.

Our kitchen table and chairs were not a set. The table is the old oak farm house style with big thick spindle legs and solid oak.

The chairs are the oak Windsor style. The table was $30 and the chairs just $5.00 apiece. Last week I found chairs that I like better. I need to recover them. The covering now is pretty bad, maybe that's why I got all four chairs for a total of $5.00! They are a padded style and I have just the right fabric upstairs in a box. The fabric came from a pair of garage sale drapes made out of Waverly decorator fabric.

I found our bar/counter stools at the neighborhood community sale. They were just what I wanted, light oak with a Windsor back and they swiveled--such a bargain at $10 apiece. The stools were bar height and I needed them to be counter height so we cut a few inches off the bottom of the legs and attached felt tipped pads for a perfect fit.

If you can't find counter stools, make your own. It's easy. You can find all kinds of chairs to mate with all kinds of stools. Remove the chair legs and attach the seat to the stool using wood screws. Place the screws underneath the seat portion of the stool and screw into the bottom of the chair seat. Do not screw all the way through!

With all the beautiful copper, brass and crockery on display the kitchen was starting to look like Country French. Just what I had always wanted. To really make it authentic, I needed to put brick on the walls. I was looking for a product called "Z" brick. It's real brick, but it's only a half inch thick. You apply adhesive and stick the bricks right on the wall. I was lucky to find boxes and boxes of "Z" brick at a sale, however, it was white brick and I wanted a used red brick. Since it was only $1.00 a box I bought it and laid the brick pieces out on sheets of newspaper and spray painted them with a brick color paint and black paint. It took about an hour to spray paint all of the brick and I had more than enough to brick the walls. The moral to the story is:

If you only look for exactly what you want, eventually you will find it . . . but, it might take a long time. Use your imagination and make things work for you. It didn't take long to spray paint the "Z" brick and I had exactly what I wanted to brick the kitchen for $10 instead of $100. Always think . . .

WHAT CAN I DO TO MAKE THIS WORK FOR ME?

HOME OFFICE

Or should I say home offices? We now have two offices in our home. At first, we dedicated only one area of the house for an office. We found a beautiful oak desk with two large filing drawers and thought it would be perfect. One filing drawer for him . . . one filing drawer for me.

It was fun to outfit the entire office with garage sale supplies: stapler, tape dispenser, brass and marble pen holders, plastic paper bins, beautiful leather bound desk sets, letter openers, electric pencil sharpener, desk lamps, telephone, speaker telephone, even boxes of envelopes, legal pads, computer paper, typing paper, and paper clips. Any-

thing you could possibly need for the home office is at the sales. I found an oak computer corner unit for $15 and an oak bookshelf to sit on top for only $5.00. It holds the computer, computer supplies and books.

We built floor-to-ceiling bookshelves on one wall for all the other books we had been collecting. I found a wonderful 19" Sony color TV for $20 and we quickly made it a cable TV with remote control for FREE.

See the TV and Electronics chapter.

A real conversation piece in the office is a beautiful lighted world globe in a cherry wood stand that I found for $5.00. It's one of those things that you've probably always wanted but never wanted to spend the money to buy. There are lots of garage sale plants and a very comfortable upholstered wing-back chair. I found a perfect double candled desk lamp, however my husband wasn't wild about the pink color! No problem. Remember, you can paint just about any surface so I black marbleized every part that was pink and replaced the pink shade with a 50¢ tailored black shade.

One of the smaller lamps on the built-in bookshelf was a heavy brass twin candlestick lamp. The shade was a unique shape but it was badly torn. Perhaps that's why I got the lamp for 25¢. It would be very difficult to find a shade with that peculiar shape so I cut off a piece of regular pleated shade material from another lamp shade that I had in the storage room and shaped it to fit the metal frame. I used seam binding to edge the top and bottom portions of the shade.

See lampshades in the Accessories chapter.

A favorite purchase for the office is our large brass and glass quartz world clock. It displays the time from all around the world. This very expensive clock was only $5.00.

This was truly an office to be proud of. There was just one problem--I quickly learned that my husband did not want to share. Remember those two file drawers, one for him and one for me? They quickly became two for him and none for me! The computer that we had bought to share, suddenly didn't have enough space on the disk for my things, plus I had to schedule computer time. I would spend hours looking for something I had set on the desk the day earlier. You know who put it somewhere out of <u>his</u> way! As you probably already know, and now I know, never share an office with your spouse!

So I was at it again! Diligently shopping the sales for more office equipment for MY home office. It didn't take long to find another EVEN BETTER!!!!! oak desk with a side return, credenza and <u>three file drawers!</u> The credenza provided lots of work space, built-in dividers and there was a fluorescent light built into the top portion.

It was only a matter of going downstairs to the storage room to pick out a telephone and one of the six computers we had put together by purchasing a monitor here, a CPU there, keyboards, RAM and all kinds of good computer peripherals.

See the Computer chapter.

There were desk lamps downstairs to choose from, drapes, a 19" color TV and a VCR with remote control. I found a wonderful stereo rack system with graphic equalizer, dual cassette recorder, turntable and speakers for $5.00 to go in the glass door stereo cabinet which was only $3.00. Of course I had to find another pencil sharpener, more file trays, a stapler, and another desk set. No problem.

Now we are both a lot happier. He has his office and I have mine. We each have our own computer, of course, and our own printers thanks to garage sales. My printer is a laser printer and he has a color desk jet printer.

Since we started shopping garage sales, our children have their own computers too! In fact we had so many computers that my husband decided to network the entire house so we could SHARE!

Oh well, it is handy to have a computer in every room--especially when you have two computer engineers and a computer science major living under one roof. Each office has an executive desk chair. I paid $10 for the chair in my husband's office. It is a high-backed executive chair with oak arms on a heavy duty base that swivels and rocks.

It was in very good shape and didn't need recovering or any repair work. This chair would easily sell for $199.

My high-backed executive desk chair was only $2.00. After I got it home and started using it I noticed the swivel rocker base was wobbly. We tried to repair it but the base was just shot. Soon I found another chair with a heavy duty base. The chair itself was ripped and torn and in very bad condition but the base worked well and that was all I really needed. I paid only $1.00 for the chair and simply attached the good chair seat to the new heavy duty base with a screw driver. Each chair sits on an office rubber mat that I found for $1.00 each, brand new! All of the diplomas, documents and certificates are out hanging on the wall exposed to the world in brass garage sale frames. The frames are all matching. I didn't find them all at once. It took a while, but not a long while to find these very popular brass and glass frames. Sometimes the glass was broken. No problem. I'd find several old black frames with the same size glass in the FREE boxes. In no time we both had a wonderful wall full of family history!

My husband's favorite garage sale find sits in his office: it's a clock that doesn't work! The lady from whom he bought the clock even told him that it didn't work!

She wanted $1.00 for this clock and he paid it without even bargaining.

What is so special about this clock is that it is made out of money. If you were to take the clear Lucite off the face of the clock you would find a Liberty silver dollar, eight dimes, a John F. Kennedy dollar and two quarters. She basically sold him $3.30 worth of money for $1.00!

Another favorite toy is his electronic, digital blood pressure machine. They sell for $90 at the store and I purchased it brand new for $5.00. Now he can take his blood pressure every day instead of going to the supermarket once a week!

One of my favorite finds for the home office is the large rectangular shaped ottoman that I bought brand new for only $5.00. It is quite large and you can buy it today in a furniture store for $149. I can't imagine why anyone would sell it, especially for $5.00, but I didn't stop to ask why.

LAUNDRY ROOM

Our laundry room is probably the best place to address buying large appliances at garage sales. When my two-year-old dryer that I bought retail died for the sixth time, I gave up and decided to start looking for one at the sales. I wanted to find one that would match the two-year-old washer that seemed to be working OK. What I did find a few weeks later at a garage sale was the very best brand washer & dryer made. It wasn't even one-year-old, however the lady was moving to a smaller home which only had room for a stackable washer/dryer. She had already sold the washer, but the dryer was still for sale and only $100 It was everything I wanted--the deluxe model and almond color. I bought it for $70! When I got it home I decided I would really like to have the matching washer and it was still available at the store since it was not even a year old. I went to the store's marked down outlet and bought the washer to match. I sold my existing washer at my own garage sale for the same price I paid for the new washer. It's been five years now with not even a hiccup from the dryer.

You will find every major appliance at sales and we've bought several items for ourselves and for our friends. I've bought refrigerators and we have three deep freezers! I can't remember how many freezers I've bought for friends. They range anywhere from $20 to $125, depending on the age and size. I feel comfortable buying a large appliance only if I can see it working. Sometimes refrigerators or freezers are in the basement or garage and they are not running. Usually if I'm interested, the seller is glad to plug them in and let them cool for a while. They are either selling them because they're empty nesters, it's a divorce situation or because they've bought something bigger.

Appliances are a big expense. Look around at the sales--I am sure you will find what will work for you and at a fraction of the cost. Yes, there is a lot of Harvest Gold and Avocado but it's very easy to turn them into a new decorator color with the new appliance spray paints. There are also plenty of the latest styles and colors out there too, especially almost-brand-new electric stoves. A lot of people are converting to gas and getting rid of their electric ranges and ovens. I went to a sale a few months ago and found a brand new GE range with self-cleaning oven for only $35. The sellers had just moved into a brand-new inventory home and the builder would not change out the appliances, so they did so at their own expense and sold the electric stove. I wanted to buy it to use in the vacation home we keep planning to build but I just didn't have a place to store it. Someone else would be very lucky that day.

If you are planning to build a vacation home or even to fix up your basement and want kitchen appliances, it's so easy to find everything you need at the sales. Dishwashers, microwaves, range hoods, combination range, oven and microwave, wall ovens, drop-in ovens, trash compactors, stainless steel sinks, laundry room sinks, gold plated bar sinks complete with faucets--washers and dryers, stackable washer and dryers--just about anything you can think of! I've seen lots of wall-mounted ironing boards--what a treat to have in the laundry room. On one wall in our laundry room is our handy dandy rechargeable rack. It holds a $2.00 dust vac, a heavy duty $1.00 flashlight and a $1.00 car vac. They're all plugged in, constantly recharging and ready to go. Of course there's a small color TV in the laundry room. I don't feel so deprived when I'm in there washing and ironing!

COLLEGE DORM ROOM

Sooner or later you will be faced with sending little Joey or Suzie off to college. Now that you've taken out a second mortgage on the house and have started a second job just to pay for tuition, room and board, you'll be handed a list of needs for their room. Every student must have his or her own microwave oven and a color television with VCR, a refrigerator to hold pop (SURE!), and the usual sheets, blankets, pillows, eating utensils, etc.

The college will gladly send you a price sheet to rent these necessities at quite a high price! I knew I could find everything my son needed at garage sales for less than one month's rental fee. There were several more

weeks left of sale~ing before he was to leave for college and I had a MISSION! Mission accomplished!

Within a few days, I found the small refrigerator. The seller was asking $25 and I bargained for $20. The microwave was brand new and still in the box. I checked the date on the back just to make sure and it was this year's date. The small microwave was just the perfect size for our son to take to college. The sellers were asking $20 for the microwave and I got it for $13. I wasn't too worried about finding a color television because we had plenty. Our televisions were all 19" or larger and he didn't have very much space so I was hoping to find a smaller television for him to take along. I found it! A Sony 15" color TV that I purchased for $15. I couldn't get a very clear picture in the seller's garage, so I was uncertain. I went ahead and bought it anyway since it was a Sony. Our television repair man will buy any Sony color TV for $25 just for the parts. I knew if I made a mistake, he would buy it for $25 and I would make $10. I needn't have worried because when I got it home, it worked perfectly. It had a beautiful color picture and it was just the right size for our son to take to college. We quickly turned it into a 115-channel cable ready TV with a remote control for FREE.

Everything that he needed and wanted for his dorm room we were able to find for under $40.

```
Refrigerator.......................$20.00
Microwave ..........................10.00
VCR.....................................5.00
Wool blanket........................1.00
Comforter............................0.50
Sheets & Pillowcases .............1.20
Towels ................................1.00
Silverware ...........................0.15
Kitchen Towels &
Potholders ...........................1.00
```

TOTAL **39.85**

CHAPTER THREE

ACCESSORIES

CANDLEHOLDERS

GLASS HURRICANES

PILLOWS

PICTURE FRAMES

MIRRORS

LAMPS & LAMPSHADES

CHANDELIERS

PLANTS

BOOKS

TELEPHONES

RUGS

WINDOW DECOR

Accessories are what makes a room exciting and your home uniquely yours! The little things you add make it personal and friendly and often say a lot about who you are!

This chapter is filled with tips on buying garage sale accessories and how to make your own treasures with bits and pieces of things that you will find.

Start by going to your designer showroom and pick out the accessories you'd love to have. Make a list and be sure to make a mental note of the price. Start sale~ing and soon you'll have all the things that you put down on your list for just a few dollars, not hundreds or thousands.

Assemble your own lamps or make your own candlesticks with bits and pieces of garage sale bargains. Customize your store-bought or garage sale drapes, and make decorator rods for FREE. Never pay retail again for picture frames, mix & match and make your own ornate frames. Fix up your own gift baskets with garage sale treasures and shrink wrap them yourself. This book shows you how. Make wonderful down toss pillows for $3.00 instead of paying $100 a pillow.

CANDLEHOLDERS

Candleholders are one of my favorite accessories. I love all sizes & shapes, so you can imagine how thrilling it is to find them at garage sales for 25¢ on up!

When you go to showrooms or walk through model homes you will see gorgeous candleholders in every room. Some of the candleholders you will find cost several hundred dollars. I decided with all of my existing candleholders and the bits & pieces that I have at home, it would be very easy to make the designer candleholders myself and save bunches of money. You can have something just as lovely as the candleholders in the showrooms for pennies. You'll learn how to make gorgeous designer candleholders out of crystal, fabric, wood, lamp bases and a variety of bits and pieces that you can find at garage sales. You can make them large enough to stand on the floor or exquisite enough to dress up the finest dining room table and all uniquely yours.

There will be all kinds, sizes and shapes-- brass, wood, glass. It doesn't matter what the bits and pieces are, just as long as you like the style and shape.

You can put almost any kind of finish on any kind of base. Don't worry if the parts are made of different materials.

Some finishing ideas are:

> Wood
>
> Crackle
>
> Granite
>
> Marble
>
> Verdigris
>
> Gold Leaf

See the Finishes chapter.

FAUX LEAF CANDLEHOLDER & ACCESSORIES

Let's make a plain candlestick into the new style wrought iron look finished in verdigris with leaves entwined all around the candlestick. (When finished it will look like forged metal.)

Find a garage sale candleholder, any size you want. I used a tall set about 18" high that was brass and cost $2.00 for the pair. The plainer the candlestick the better. Your decoration will be the twined faux metal leaves. Try to find a plain brass set of six candlesticks. I've seen lots of these sets at sales. Some of them were only 50¢ for the entire set. These candlesticks will make up into the ivy leaf candleholders very nicely.

My favorite finish for this type of candleholder is verdigris.

The twined leaf look can be an extra touch for several of your accessories--a plate holder, lamps, baskets, chain or chandeliers. Just use your imagination and start dressing up your accessories. Use the same technique for any of these items.

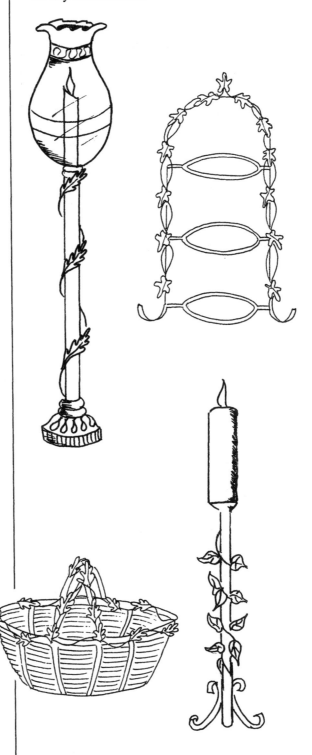

67

"How To"

FAUX METAL LEAF CANDLESTICK

Materials needed:
Candlestick
Fabric
Braided cording* or tie wire*
Stiffener (such as Stiffy*)
Glue gun

*See glossary

1 Trace an ivy leaf shape or any leaf shape from a real leaf, an artificial leaf, or use this pattern. Trace several of these leaves in different sizes.

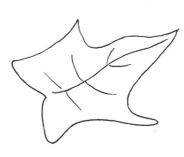 

2 Cut leaf shapes out of old fabric--the heavier the fabric, the better.

Use whatever you have on hand!

3 Cut a strip of braided cording or tie wire long enough to wrap around your candlestick base several times. The cording or wire will be your stem.

NOTE: If using braided cording--cut it a few inches longer than needed. After the cording has stiffened (see step 4), re-trim the ends at an angle. You won't have any frayed ends if you cut if after it's stiffened.

Continued . . .

4 Pour stiffening product into a plastic bag or plastic container. Add fabric leaves and cording--mix thoroughly. If using tie wire, just stiffen the fabric leaves.

5 Remove the leaves from the bag and pinch leaves at the base making a channel. Place the leaves on plastic wrap and let them dry thoroughly.

6 Loosely wrap the cord around the candlestick starting directly under the top lip and continue to wrap it around down to the bottom. Allow to dry thoroughly. If using tie wire, wrap this around the candlestick from top to bottom. Use a hot glue gun, glue the top and bottom of the cord or tie wire to the candlestick base. Glue the cord or tie wire at several places in the middle of the candlestick.

7 Paint the leaves the desired finish on both sides and let dry. Paint the entire candlestick including attached stiffened cord. *See the Finishes chapter.* Glue the stiffened and painted leaves to the cord or tie wire.

IT WILL LOOK JUST LIKE FORGED METAL!

"How To"

ANOTHER FAUX METAL LEAF TECHNIQUE

Materials needed:
Brown paper bag
White glue
Light weight wire (florist wire)
Candle
Tie wire*

*See glossary

1 Draw leaves in several different sizes on brown paper bag. Cut two identical leaves per size. Use the leaf patterns for the previous instructions--artificial or real leaves.

2 Apply a thick coat of glue to the paper bag leaves, lay a piece of wire on one glue-coated leaf and press the glue-coated matching leaf down on top. Let dry thoroughly.

3 Spread a thick layer of glue on the outer sides of the leaf. Hold the leaf over a lighted candle while turning it back and forth. It will darken and bubble. This is good!

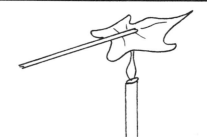

4 Wipe the darkened leaf on both sides with a soft cloth. Repeat these steps for each pair of leaves.

5 Spray paint the leaves with a mixture of gold and black or copper and black paint. With a soft cloth or foam brush, smear the paints together or finish in a verdigris. Paint a long piece of tie wire the same way. Let dry thoroughly.

6 Wrap the leaf wires around the tie wire and wrap the tie wire around the candlestick base, lamps, picture frames and more. Use your imagination!

TASSEL CANDLEHOLDERS

You can use different thicknesses of cording to create a variety of beautiful tasseled candleholders. Choose a cord width that is appropriate for the height and width of your candlestick (see illustration). Start by wrapping the cord around the base of the candlestick or you may tie the cord in a knot or bow and attach tassels to it. If you prefer, you may attach tassels to the underside of the candlestick rim with a hot glue gun (see illustrations).

This technique can also be used on your lamps. Notice the expensive lamps in stores with this type of look; however, their tassels and cording are cast in metal. When finished, your cord and tassel candleholders and lamps will look just like them. No one will know the difference!

Don't be afraid to experiment to create your own unique creations.

"How To"

TASSEL CANDLEHOLDERS

Materials needed:
Candleholder
Tassels
Braided cording
Stiffener (such as Stiffy*)
Glue gun

*See glossary

1 Pour stiffening product into a plastic bag or plastic container. Add tassels and cording and saturate thoroughly.

Lay out to dry on plastic wrap.

2 When cording is starting to get stiff, wrap it around the candlestick or tie it in a knot or bow and attach it to the candlestick base with hot glue gun.

Attach the tassels where desired.

NOTE: If the cording starts to unravel at the cut ends, apply more stiffener or white glue to seal back together. To avoid this problem, stiffen first, then cut to desired length.

3 Paint or choose a special finish or a combination of finishes when dry.

I like an "all over" metal effect like a burnished gold finish or pewter. *See the Finishing chapter.*

Feel free to stiffen any fabric items for your own unique designs.

LAMP BASE CANDLEHOLDERS

How many lamps of all shapes, styles and sizes do you find at garage sales? Most sales have several.

As lamps, some of them are pretty pathetic, but if you think of them as candlestick bases you can come up with some very beautiful and unusual designs. This is especially true of the larger, decorator style candlesticks that you find on buffet tables or coffee tables with large decorative candles in them.

Use your imagination and start to see these lamp bases as candlesticks with beautiful long tapers or thick, squatted beeswax candles sitting on top of the lamp bases.

For ideas, go to showrooms or walk through model homes. You'll come home with plenty of ideas! I like the look of crystal base lamps combined with brass pieces for elegance or the older, tall wooden base lamps that you can paint, stipple, frost, marbleize or cover with gold leaf. Combine some of these techniques to get just the look you want. Make them shorter or taller. You can even take parts of one and mix with another.

You decide what's best for your decor. You now will have so very much to choose from and of course . . .

Money is no object . . . especially when you will pay anywhere from 50¢ to $5.00.

A lamp base can be easily taken apart and given a different look by removing one or more of the pieces called "fittings." You can virtually create your own candleholder design by mixing these fittings, and finishing to match your decor. Place on top of the lamp based candleholders glass hurricanes, crystal vases, crystal bowls or glass shades. Try a wooden salad bowl--large or small. Glue

them to the top fitting and place a candle inside. *See page. 72.*

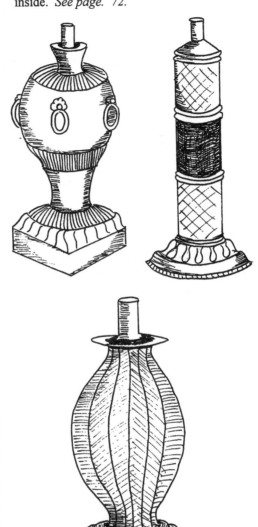

LAMP BASE "OBJETS D'ART"

Lamp bases also make unique "objets d' art." Notice all the unique shapes that are sitting on the coffee tables. They look like lamp fittings to me and I've made several out of lamp fittings for my friends. Finish them as desired.

"How To"
DISASSEMBLE A LAMP

1 Unscrew the top cap (the finial) to free the lamp shade. Remove the lamp shade and save it, to use later.

2 Remove the harp by squeezing in towards the light bulb area and pulling up on the two metal holders.

3 Remove the bottom cardboard circle (if applicable) from the base of the lamp. Loosen the hex nut at the center bottom of the lamp. Can you see that portions of the lamp base are moving? Note the separate individual pieces (fittings). It takes several separate fittings to build a lamp base.

Gently pull and turn the socket holder. There might even be writing on it that says "press here." It's a pressure point and if you press in at the exact spot, the socket and holder should snap right out. If you can't find the pressure point, use a screwdriver to help you "snap" it out. The socket and holder consist of a cardboard insulator, the plastic and metal socket and the brass socket cover. You will need all of these pieces again to reassemble your lamp.

4 Notice the two wires attached to the two screws at the base of the socket. Unscrew these.

5 You can now pull the electrical wiring out from the bottom of the lamp. Notice how all the "fittings" are stacked on top of each other on a metal pole.

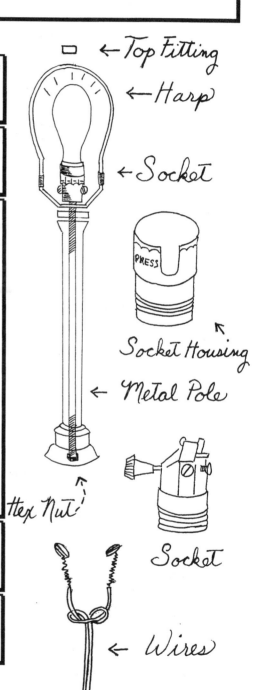

← Top Fitting
← Harp
← Socket
PRESS
Socket Housing
← Metal Pole
Hex Nut
Socket
← Wires

Now it's time to mix and match or reassemble and work with your "fittings" to get that perfect look.

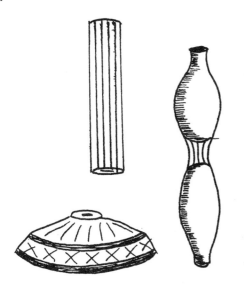

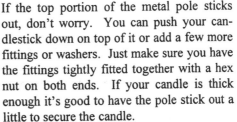

If your selection of "fittings" goes up to the top of the metal pole where the threads are, you can secure them tightly by screwing down a hex nut on the top and bottom of the metal pole.

If the top portion of the metal pole sticks out, don't worry. You can push your candlestick down on top of it or add a few more fittings or washers. Just make sure you have the fittings tightly fitted together with a hex nut on both ends. If your candle is thick enough it's good to have the pole stick out a little to secure the candle.

You may need to glue a nail upside down to the top fitting of your base to hold the candle in place. Make sure the nail has a big round flat head and a long thin point. Glue securely.

If your design of fittings leaves too much pole sticking out beyond the threaded area where you can't screw it tightly, remove the metal pole completely and use either epoxy glue or a hot glue gun to glue your fittings together without using the center metal pole. Remember, the center pole is to hold electrical wiring and since we've removed the wiring it really isn't necessary to use the center pole any more.

A cone-shaped brass fitting turned upside down makes a great candleholder for the top piece. Find a large cone-shaped fitting if you want to place a very large, thick candle on top or glue a large metal plate to hold a very large candle or use the upside-down nail to hold the candle in place.

Cone Fitting

Flat Fitting

MORE LAMP BASE CANDLEHOLDERS

What could be more grand and elegant than a candelabra candleholder. They are very easy to make using a lamp base and a multi-arm candleholder or chandelier. Mix and match lamp bases with chandelier tops to get the exact look you wish. Use wood and brass or brass and crystal. Interchange lamp fittings, make them taller or shorter . . . you are the designer. Follow the "how to" directions for "disassembling a lamp." Leave the center pole and tighten the hex nut at the bottom. Now start holding up multi-armed candleholders or chandeliers to get ideas. Readjust the lamp fittings if necessary to get the proper height and balance for the candleholder top you've chosen. Place crystal vases, crystal bowls, wooden salad bowls glass lamp shades and hurricanes on top of the lamp bases for your own unique, designer look. Follow the step-by-step instructions on the next page to make your own!

Lamp Base

Candelabra

Metal Bowl & Candleholder

Glass Lamp Shade Upside Down

Straight Hurricane

Crystal Vase &

Crystal Bowl

"How To"

CANDELABRA STYLE CANDLEHOLDERS

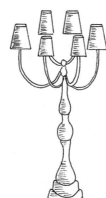

Materials needed:
Chandelier or multi-arm candleholder
Lamp base or several lamp bases
Candles
Miniature candleshades (optional)

See the lampshade section in this chapter for ideas.

1 Remove the electrical socket and cord from the lamp base. Follow instructions for Disassembling a Lamp.

2 If using an electric chandelier remove the electric wiring by unscrewing the bottom fitting. Remove the bottom cup section to expose the wiring. Unscrew the plastic wire nuts freeing up the electric wires. Untwist all the wires so they will pull out easier.

3 Remove the plastic candles from the top portion of the chandelier. There is probably a metal pole attached to each arm. Sometimes this is screwed in place--sometimes you can just pull it out. The metal pole and the electric wires will come out.

4 Notice the round threaded opening at the center bottom of the chandelier. This will screw down onto the top of the center metal lamp pole. You may need to add one or two more small fittings so there is a tight fit. Experiment--see what works. Screw it on tight and screw the hex nut at the lamp base very tight. Add candles. Top with miniature candleshades if you prefer.
Beautiful and one of a kind!

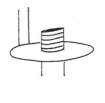

GLASS HURRICANES & GLOBES

Collect all the glass hurricane shades and glass and crystal globes you can find. You often see them in the FREE box or pay 10¢ to $1.00 for the larger ones. You will even find glass globes in fine cut crystal. A lot of the hurricane glass shades are made for chandeliers. Perhaps one was broken so the seller has decided to throw away the rest of them. Sometimes the glass shades are part of a sconce that no one wants. Simply un-screw the three tiny screws that are holding the glass shade in place and set the glass globes on top of your candlesticks.

I use the glass hurricanes in several different ways as you'll see throughout the book. Collect several of them so you will have an assortment of all different styles, sizes and shapes to choose from. Half the fun is hav-ing plenty of glass hurricanes so you can mix and match to find the perfect look! Set them on top of your candleholders or lamp bases. If you like the look of a glass shade on top of your new candleholder, find the one you like and don't worry if it doesn't fit. If the glass base of your hurricane globe is too big for your candlestick, attach a wider piece fitting for the glass to sit on. Glue the hurri-cane glass to the candleholder base. Epoxy, super glue, or E6000 work great!

One of my favor-ite uses for a large glass hurri-cane is to set it on the mantle and fill it full with long fireplace matches that have colored tips.

At the designer stores are plain glass hurri-canes which are covered with marbles and flat crystals. I duplicated the $89.00 designer hurricane for $1.89! Use a glue gun to at-tach the marbles and crystals.

I made a very large candlestick base out of lamp fittings and marbleized portions of the base and left some of the base the original polished brass fittings. I found a large crys-tal vase with a beautiful flower design and glued the center bottom of the vase to the top of the candlestick. The candlestick base was $1.50 and the crystal vase was only 50¢. I had seen a candlestick very similar to the one I made at a showroom for $289.

Glass vases and bowls work well too. You can set a beautiful crystal vase on top of your candlestick or lamp base. Use a good glue made for glass and metal to secure the crystal vase or bowl to the candlestick top or lamp base. You probably already have plenty of glass vases, but just in case you don't, check the FREE box. They are plenti-ful. Vases come in all different sizes and quality, so mix and match until you find what you're looking for.

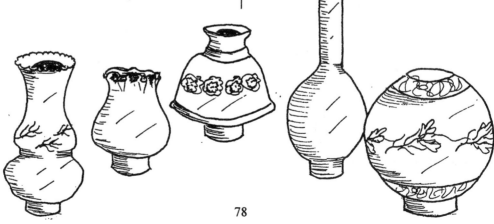

One of my favorite candlesticks (and probably the most dramatic in design) is made by assembling lamp fittings into a very tall thin shape. You will need a heavy base fitting so it won't topple over. Put a very long taper in this tall candlestick. I use tapers that are 36" high. Top the taper with small candle shades if you prefer or use this same shape candleholder and place a beautiful round ball of flowers on top. I guarantee compliments when you place these tall flower arrangements on your buffet table or if you have a high dining room ceiling, place two of these on the table. They are very luxurious and beautiful. If you want to use silk flowers, simply arrange them in a large styrofoam ball and use plenty of trailing greenery. Use heavy duty tape, like clear packing tape to tape the styrofoam ball to the top of the candlestick. If you plan to use live flowers and greenery, make the top fitting a large cone shape and glue a plastic container that will hold water to the top fitting.

The most important thing to remember in making this type of holder is that the bottom portion should be very heavy.

It's easy to mix and match these two designs. If you've made a flower holder and want to change it back into a candleholder, simply remove the large cone-shaped fitting on top and reattach the candle-shaped fitting back on top. It's very easy to change them. The top fitting for the candleholder may be taken from any type candleholder that will hold a taper candle.

Remember . . . brass and wood candleholders are usually fittings also. Collect them in every style and shape. You can glue the top taper fitting onto just about anything and turn it into a candleholder. In the showrooms I have seen an actual ram's horn that was made into a candleholder. Someone simply attached a top fitting from a silver candleholder to the horn. They sell for several hundred dollars. I haven't found a ram's horn at any garage sales yet but the idea is to use your imagination and you can very easily duplicate anything you see in designer showrooms.

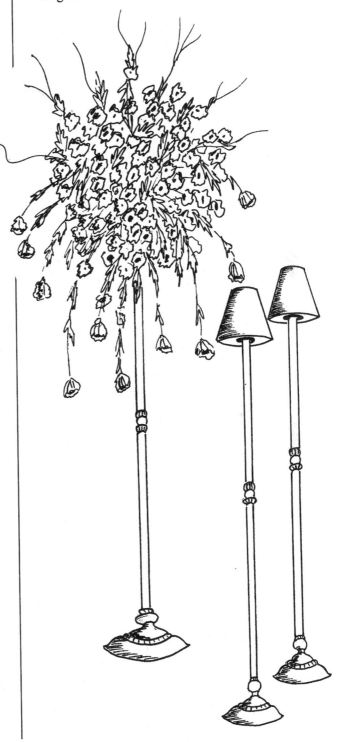

FINISHING LAMP BASES

You may want to use a lamp base exactly the way it is or you may want to customize it to match your decor.

Almost any lamp surface will accept a finish. You will need to prepare the surfaces first.

Wood: wipe down the lamp surface
with a deglosser*

Brass: BIN* primer-bonder --
cover the surface

Glass: BIN* primer-bonder
cover the surface

*See Glossary

NOTE: When taping off certain areas
I've found hotel shower
caps come in handy. They
stretch around difficult areas
and the stretch ends are easy
to tape.

Some finishing ideas are:

Wood: crackle finish

Glass: stone or granite

Brass: marbleized or partial
marble with brass or
gold or pewter.

See the Finishes chapter

Trim the lamp bases with rope, braided cord, stiffened tassels and wonderful garage sale jewelry. I like to glue a strand of colored stones or a thick gold necklace around the base. If you're using gold costume jewelry-- go ahead and stain it to tone it down a bit, then seal. Some of these thick strands of jewelry have wonderful designs. You can even glue a matching strand on the shade. You can work wonders to lamp bases and candlesticks with 25¢ pieces of garage sale jewelry.

CANDLE SHADES

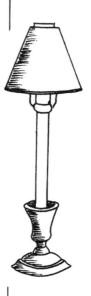

You've probably seen miniature metal lamp shades with the special metal base followers that fit down over a candle. You can find them in stores selling for $12.95 apiece. They add a very elegant and dressy touch to candleholders and candles. I found two brand new for 25¢ apiece. They were complete with the brass "followers."

Don't worry if the shades you find are not your preferred color. Spray paint them a solid color, marbleize or even stencil them.

I've seen several of these little lamp shades in the specialty shops--with special prices on them too! They are decorated with pearls, jewels, decoupage designs, silk fringe, tassels and even feathers. How very easy to glue these special touches onto a plain lamp shade yourself. Buy all of your jewel pieces and decorative trim at garage sales too. Use a little tacky glue to attach your trims and start accepting the compliments!

See the lamp shade section in this chapter for more ideas on the decorative type finishes available for miniature lampshades.

A favorite summer time treat is to place several candleholders and candles in the fireplace. Use all different sizes, styles and shapes. Light them all and enjoy the glow. Your fireplace will still be a focal point and your guests will love to gather round.

CANDLES

You will never be without candles to put in your beautiful candleholders if you shop at garage sales. You'll find brand new candles in all colors, sizes and shapes. Beeswax candles, long tapers, votive candles, tea lights, Christmas candles, Santa Claus candles, Easter candles and Halloween candles. You can usually find plenty of used candles in the FREE box if you want to melt them down and make your own candles or fire starters.

PILLOWS

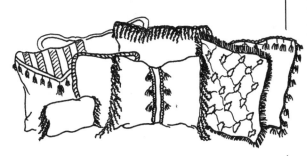

Pillows are a lot of fun to make and who doesn't love big fat pillows, especially those fluffy, soft, luxurious and very expensive down-filled and feather filled pillows-- (unless, of course, you're allergic)? These are such a fantastic buy when you purchase them at local garage sales. You'll find many pillows in all sizes and shapes for any room of the house.

This book shows you how to have the most wonderful, luxurious pillows for next to nothing with materials all purchased at garage sales.

If the pillows you find are not your color, no problem. If they are soiled or ripped, no problem. It's much better for you if they are soiled or ripped because they will cost you much less, maybe 25¢. And please don't fret over having to spend a lot of money for fabric to recover them. I'll also show you how to do that for pennies!

My favorite pillow is the down and feather filled pillow. These are the pillows that you can sink down into. Unfortunately these are the ones that cost a bundle. Have you ever priced down or feather filled pillow forms at your fabric store? For a small square pillow you will pay around $25 and they go up in price from there!

At garage sales never pay more than $1.00 for down pillows, small, medium or large!

I've even found several small square-shaped down toss pillows covered in awful fabric for just 25¢ apiece. You can recover the pillows or open them up and use the down and feathers to stuff into another pillow or stuff in furniture cushions.

See the Upholstering chapter.

The best buy is a king-size bed pillow--but as long as the pillow is down and feather, buy any of them that you can find. You will never have enough of these pillows when you see all of the wonderful things you can do with them.

Bed pillows are usually rectangular in shape, however, I prefer to use a square shape when making decorator pillows for the sofa and chairs, so first I have to make the bed pillows square. A king-size bed pillow will make two square pillows. A regular-size bed pillow will make one square pillow or, when rolled up lengthwise, it makes a wonderful neckroll pillow.

"How To"

SQUARE OFF DOWN BED PILLOWS

Materials needed:
Down bed pillow
Marker
Scissors
Tacky glue

1 **Measure and make a mark to make the pillow square.**

E.g., If the pillow measures 19" x 38" make a mark and cut exactly in half. If the pillow measures 20" x 36", make the mark on the longer side at 20" so you will have a 20" square pillow. Lay the pillow down just as you would sleep on it. Pound the pillow out flat so that all of the down settles evenly.

2 **Gently cut the pillow at the mark and stand the pillow on end so the down settles to the bottom.**

3 Glue the cut edges together using a tacky fabric glue so you don't have feathers flying all over. Stitch the glued edges together. You will have one or two very plump square pillows.

NOTE: If the feather pillow is on the thin side and not very full of feathers, you will only measure for one pillow to make it nice and full. You will need all the down and feathers at one end of the pillow.

COVERING YOUR PILLOWS

It wouldn't make much sense to get all of these bargain pillows at garage & estate sales and then have to go to the fabric store and pay a lot of money for beautiful fabrics to cover them. You can easily spend $25 a yard and more for silk damask, brocade or satin to cover your pillows.

Why go to the fabric store when you can find all of this beautiful fabric--yards and yards and yards of fabric for $1.00 or $2.00? Not just for one yard, but for several yards!

Where do you find these wonderful silk moiré, brocades, velvets, damask, satins and silks? The clothing rack at garage sales!

One of my favorite finds on the clothes rack was a faux leopard skin cape that was reversible to a bright red felt. I made several pillows and ottoman covers with the faux leopard and used the red felt to line silverware drawers in an antique buffet. I also use the red felt to glue pieces to lamp bases and large candlestick bases. Just one yard of the faux leopard sells for $59 at the fabric store. I paid $2.00 for the cape!

Look on the clothes racks at garage sales and you will find beautiful bridesmaid dresses, cocktail dresses and even bridal gowns in gorgeous, very expensive fabrics.

Start thinking of that clothes rack as your fabric boutique!

83

The bridesmaid dresses usually have a large gathered skirt with yards and yards of fabric in beautiful satins, silks and brocades. They have lots of decorative trim, lace, beadwork, ruffles, zippers, covered buttons and bows. A lot of your work is already done for you. Take advantage of these decorative touches when making your pillows and accessories.

I found a beautiful ice blue satin cocktail dress with a whole bodice of gathers. I simply cut the bodice portion into a square and cut another square out of the skirt portion of the dress for the back. It made a gorgeous pillow to place on the bed with very little effort or money--$1.00 for the dress, which I still have with yards and yards of fabric leftover, and 25¢ for the pillow!

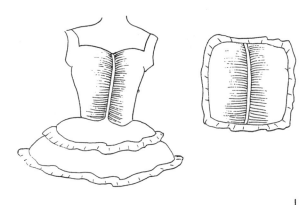

Look for old prom dresses or cocktail dresses. You can find wonderful silk or satin skirts and blouses. There are plenty of velvets available in skirts and dresses in every color. I always hope to find these articles of clothing with a little stain on them. That way you get the item for next to nothing and you have plenty of fabric left to make beautiful things. How about soft velvet drawstring pouches in various sizes to place Christmas gifts in? They can be very inexpensive and beautiful. The recipient of this lovely gift pouch will use it over and

over again. It will last a long time and hold many gifts.

Finding a wedding gown is a real treasure! Usually it's a divorce situation and an unwanted item. Wedding gowns usually have yards and yards of white or cream bridal satin, lace inserts, and beadwork. What a buy! You may pay anywhere from $10 to $50 for this treasure. I've seen them at garage sales for several hundred dollars too! Just keep looking and you will find one that has a bad stain or comes from a bad situation. This is where you will find one for a very good price. These bridal gowns are such a wonderful bargain when you consider what just one yard of that beautiful satin and lace would cost in the store.

A gathered skirt is also a good buy--it contains yards and yards of fabric. Satin and silk blouses make wonderful boudoir pillows, sachet pillows or potpourri pillows. A satin robe can make a lot of beautiful pillows. Chenille robes make fun pillows for the children's room, sun room or summer cottage and they are so very easy to make.

I've found beautiful little girls' velvet dresses with stains all down the front that were only 25¢. There was enough fabric in the back of the gathered skirt to make lots of little pillows and pouches. Usually these little dresses are loaded with beautiful decorative trim--lace, ruffles and tiny silk rosebuds. You can use all of this wonderful trim on your pillows, lampshades and for lots of other things you'll find in this book.

"How To"

SACHET & POTPOURRI PILLOWS

Materials needed:
Fabric
Decorative trim
Potpourri
Polyester pillow stuffing(optional)
Perfume (optional)

1 Cut the fabric into rectangles.

Small	5.5" x 7"
Medium	7" x 8.5"
Large	8.5" x 11"

2 Cut a piece of garage sale white pillow case the same size as the rectangle and stitch a separate bag to insert into your finished fabric. Keep one end open to insert potpourri or perfumed filling. Then stitch closed.

3 Fold under the long top edge of fabric and make a finished seam. Seam the sides and bottom, just like a miniature pillow case.

4 Insert the potpourri filled lining pouch. Tie the top end with a thick piece of braided cording and tassels.

OPTIONS

Sew lace on the top edge of the pillow or a tassel fringe.

Sew a casing on the top edge of pillow and insert a satin ribbon to gather and tie for a closure.

"How To"

MAKE A PILLOW FROM A BLOUSE

Materials needed:
Blouse, shirt or robe
Decorative trim
Pillow
Lining (optional)

1 Turn the clean blouse, shirt or robe inside out and lay flat on a table with the button side up.

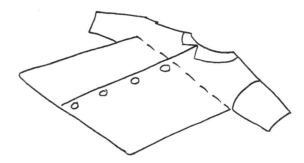

2 Cut out the size rectangle or square you desire for the pillow cover. If using a robe, make several at the same time.

3 Cut decorative trim the length of all four sides, plus 3 extra inches.

NOTE: Lay the trim on the fabric edges in between the two pieces of fabric. You won't be able to see the trim when stitching. Make sure the trim is facing the inside center when you stitch.

4 After you have stitched all four sides, reach inside and unbutton the buttons. Turn right side out and insert your pillow. Re-button.

NOTE: If using a finer fabric like silk or satin, make a lining from a 5¢ pillow case the same size as your pillow.

Don't forget to mix and match fabrics. Put a beautiful tapestry on one side of a pillow and velvet on the other. This way, by turning the pillow over, you'll have two different looks.

Look at the toss pillows in designer showrooms. See how the fabrics are mixed. Notice the new geometric pattern pillows that use scraps of gorgeous coordinating fabric backed with a rich velvet and trimmed with tassels or tassel fringe. These pillows are very expensive and you can easily make them with pieces of garage sale fabric and big fat down pillows.

NECKROLL PILLOWS

Neckroll pillows can be picked up for 25¢ to $1.00. Remember . . . don't be concerned about the covering. We'll be recovering them and it's so very easy.

Try a beautiful soft velvet for the middle of a neck roll pillow, with satin or moiré on each end.

Neckroll pillows can also be placed on each side of a sofa or placed in the back of chairs covered with a rich fabric and lots of trim and tassels on each end. They make a beautiful accessory for your furnishings.

LARGER PILLOWS

Larger pillows, usually the kind that are made for the back of a couch, are great to use as square European bed pillows. The European bed pillows are around 24" and they are square. Go to your linen store and see all the decorated beds filled with these square pillows placed next to the headboard. They can be covered or you can buy lovely, already made European shams for them. (Price the square European bed pillows when you're at the store and see just how expensive they are.)

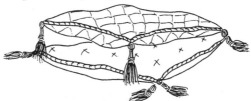

FLOOR PILLOWS

Buy floor pillows whenever you see them because they are usually filled with a sturdier type of stuffing. In my basement you will always find one of these pillows standing on end with one end cut open. This heavy duty stuffing is great for stuffing furniture and making benches and ottomans. At $1.00 per pillow for $25 worth of stuffing you can't go wrong--so keep an extra one on hand. That stuffing is going to come in handy for a lot of the projects you will find in this book.

DOWN FILLED FURNITURE

Do you love the look of down and feather filled furniture? You know, that pouf type of upholstered furniture or "fat" furniture? If you do, and if you have checked their prices lately, you probably said to yourself, "someday!"

Well . . . "someday" is NOW!

You can have that wonderful, luxurious pouf look by inserting those down pillows that you found at garage sales into your chair or sofa cushions.

Your zippered cushion covers should be on the loose side to accommodate this extra layer of down. If it is too tight or the fabric is too stiff you won't get the desired effect. You can put in a foam cushion that is not as thick as the one you have now. (I strongly suggest going to one of the finer furniture stores to look at and sit on the down furnish-ings before making any changes to your existing foam cushion.) Make sure you like this look and feel. If your cushions are square or rectangular you might already have a perfect fit with your down pillow or pillows.

Unzip the zippered cover and insert a pillow. Experiment to get just the right look--maybe one, maybe two or more pillows for the desired effect.

If your cushion is a "T" shape, make a "T" shaped casing out of a 25¢ garage sale sheet. By now you should have several of them in your linen closet. Place the down and feathers into this casing. Glue the unstitched portion together first using a tacky glue. Stitch the glued end and insert it into your "T" cushion. If your sofa cushion is one long rectangle shape, remove the foam inside the cushion covering and insert a down feather bed into it. Zip it back up and your done. What luxury!

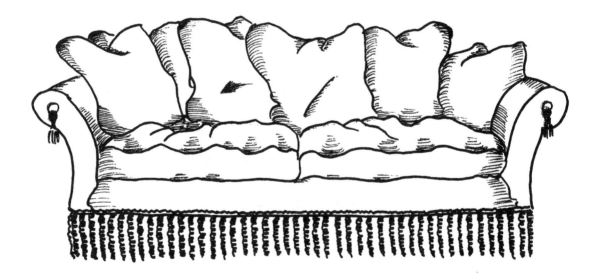

BED THROWS

I love the new style luxurious bed throws that you see in showrooms. They are usually made out of damask or moiré, sometimes with a panné velvet backing, trimmed in heavy braided cord with tassels. My favorite is a rich brocade on one side and a soft panné velvet on the other. They are so easy to make--you simply sew two pieces of fabric together. If you prefer your throw to be warmer and heavier, insert a layer of batting or a garage sale blanket that has been washed thoroughly.

Remember . . . you will never see the blanket so you don't have to worry about color or anything. Just make sure it's clean.

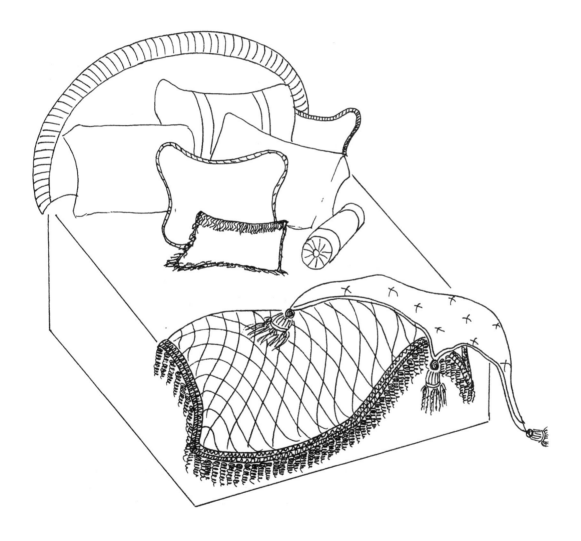

"How To"

BED THROWS

Materials needed:
Fabric
Bullion fringe* or braided cord
Tassels
Blanket (optional)
Batting (optional)
Upholstery needle

*See glossary

NOTE: This requires a heavy duty sewing machine because we are using several layers. Use a heavy duty needle also. See step 2 for an option.

1 Cut a length of buillon fringe or braided cord to go all the way around the rectangle, plus an extra two inches. Tape the edges of the bullion fringe with masking tape so they don't unravel.

2 If your machine is like mine and can't handle several layers of fabric, stitch the two pieces of outer fabric together along with the bullion fringe. Start your stitching at one corner. You want the bullion fringe to join at a corner. Leave approximately 12 inches unseamed so you can insert your blanket or batting.

3 Insert the piece of blanket or batting and stitch the opening closed just as you do when making a pillow.

> NOTE: When joining the two edges of bullion fringe, gently remove the masking tape and turn under each end for a finished look.

4 Since the blanket is lying loose inside the outer covering, you will need to use a heavy duty hand needle, like an upholstery needle. Measure every 18" or so and make an "X" type stitch through the fabric and blanket and tie off in a knot. This will hold the blanket in place.

Now . . . do yourself a favor and go to a designer shop and see the $395 price tag for your elegant throw!

PICTURE FRAMES

Picture frames are another favorite garage sale purchase that I just can't get enough of. The fancier and the more ornate, the better for me--of course, these are the most expensive type frames you can buy!

You can find the beautiful ornate, gold leaf frames at garage sales. I've found several at a cost of no more than $10 for the very large frames. The smaller ones I've gotten for an unbelievable 25¢.

If you are like me and really love the ornate, fancy style frames, I can show you easy ways to turn a plain wooden frame into the frame of your dreams!

Look in your sewing box or check for fabric trims on those bridesmaid dresses, drapes and comforters that you've been buying. Look for pieces of filigree, cording, flat lace, doilies or pieces of Battenburg lace.

Go to your fabric store and check the marked-down trim section. Don't worry about color, we will be painting or staining this trim. It can be purple or puce--it doesn't matter!

Lay the trims out on your plain picture frame in a design that's appealing to you.

For example, the cording or filigree can be put on the inside edge and the outside edge of the frame.

Remember the fabric leaves that we made and wrapped around our candlesticks and lamps at the beginning of this chapter? You can make fabric leaves, flowers, or designs and use the same techniques for your picture frames. Once the trims are saturated with white glue and left to dry on the picture frame, they feel just like carved wood.

Below is an example board filled with several types of trim that you might want to use.

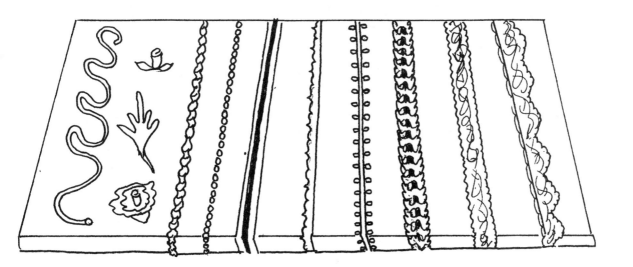

"How To"

PICTURE FRAMES WITH FABRIC TRIM

Materials needed:
Plain picture frame
Braided cord, filigree or lace
Fabric leaves, roses
White glue
Primer
Finish (your choice)

Make sure your frame is free of all grease and dirt. In fact, you might want to wipe it down with a deglosser first.

1 Apply stiffening product to fabric leaves or flowers if using and let dry.

2 Saturate cording, lace or filigree with white glue. The easiest way to do this is to put the glue into a small plastic food container or a plastic bag.

3 While wet, lay out the saturated strips of cording, lace or filigree on the frame in the design you wish. Wipe off the excess glue.

4 Miter* the edges of the fabric trim at the edges of the frame if you haven't already cut a mitered edge. Allow everything to dry thoroughly.

　　*See glossary

5 Attach the fabric leaves and flowers with a hot glue gun and coat them with white glue using a brush or dip them thoroughly in white glue, let dry, then attach with a hot glue gun.

6 After everything has dried, prime and finish as desired.

　　See Finishes chapter for ideas.

Ready for a bigger challenge?

Double framing makes it easy to cover a large wall with a small picture or mirror.

The two frames do not necessarily have to match--just make sure they look good together.

DOUBLE FRAMES

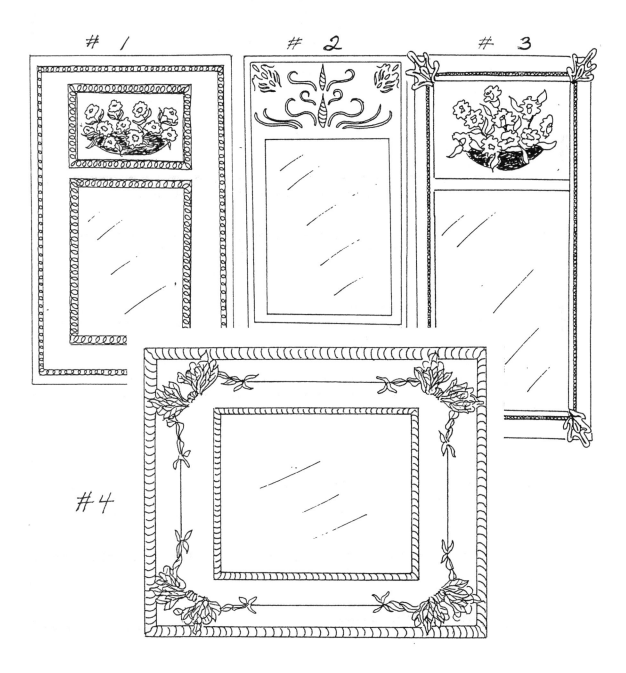

"How To"

DOUBLE FRAME #1

(See illustrations on previous page)

Materials Needed:
Large rectangle frame
2 small rectangle frames
Masonite or plywood
Fabric
Trim fabric
Wallpaper (optional)
Mirror

1 Decorate or repair your three frames as desired.
Note: The three frames do not necessarily have to match--they should just look good together.

2 Insert into the large frame a thin piece of Masonite or plywood that has been cut to fit the entire inside dimension of the frame.

3 Finish the three frames and the inserted piece of Masonite or plywood in your desired style, such as with gold leaf, paint, fabric, or wallpaper. You can make this as fancy as you want by using the techniques outlined in the picture frame section.

4 Insert the mirror into the bottom rectangle frame. Place the picture in the top rectangle frame.

5 Nail the frame with the mirror to the bottom portion of the large rectangular frame insert. Try to have the same amount of space between the bottom border and the side borders. Nail the top frame to the insert. The top portion of the frame can have the same size borders or smaller.

NOTE: The thin piece of plywood or Masonite can be cut to specifications at your local hardware store or if you're handy with a saw, GREAT!

I am comfortable with a saber saw and highly recommend picking one up at a sale and learning how to use it.

"How To"

DOUBLE FRAME #2 & #4
(See the illustrations)

Materials Needed:
Large rectangle frame
Smaller rectangle frame
Masonite or plywood
Chef's plastic pastry bag (option 3)
Nozzles and tips for pastry bag (option 3)
Fabric leaves and roses (option 1)
Decorative wood cut outs (option 2)
Wallpaper (optional)
Mirror

Follow instructions for Double Frame #1. Do steps 1, 2, 3 and the first part of 4.

There will not be a third top frame with a picture inserted.

The decorated top portion of this frame is done on the wood or Masonite insert.

FABRIC OPTION

Apply stiffened fabric leaves, roses and braided cord in a design of your choosing. (See faux metal candleholders in this chapter.) Attach them to the insert with a hot glue gun. Using a brush, apply a coat of white glue over the fabric trims to harden. Let dry.
Apply a primer such as BIN and finish as desired.

WOOD CUT OUT OPTION

Lay out a design of embossed wood cutouts
such as scrolls and wreaths on the insert.
Attach to the insert using a good wood glue.
Let dry and finish as desired.

PLASTER OPTION

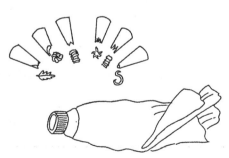

Mix sculpting plaster and pour into a chef's
pastry bag. Experiment with different tips
on a plain board until you get the look you want.
Trace design on paper and transfer the design
onto the insert. Go over the design with the
sculpting plaster. If you make a mistake, just
wipe it away and start again.

Let dry following manufacturer's direction. Finish as desired.

"How To"

DOUBLE FRAME #3

(See the illustration)

Materials Needed:
Tall, thin rectangular frame
Plain wood frame like a diploma frame (see note)
Masonite or plywood
Fabric
Mirror
Wood glue
Wood putty
Sandpaper
Glazing points *

*See Glossary

NOTE: The sides of this frame need to be longer than the inside width of the large frame.

1 Disassemble the small frame. Glue the two longer pieces of wood together at the outside edge using wood glue. Allow to dry.

Square off the mitered edges so they fit exactly into the width of the large frame. This inside strip of wood acts as a separator and will give us two frames in the large rectangle frame.

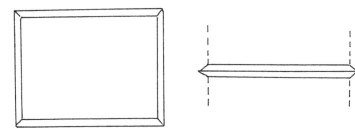

Smooth wood putty down the center seam, dry and sand smooth.

Continued . . .

2 Glue and tack the wood strip in the upper 1/3 or 1/4 portion of the large rectangle frame. Finish the frame and wood strip to match.

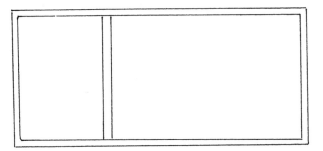

3 Cut the Masonite or wood to fit inside the top section of the frame.

4 Cover the wood or Masonite with a piece of fabric like a tapestry or use a beautiful picture. Center the fabric so the design is centered within the top portion of the frame.

5 Insert a piece of mirror in the bottom portion of the rectangular frame and secure with glazing points.*

NOTE: See the mirror section in this chapter for tips on buying all your mirror pieces at garage sales.

BEDROOM DRESSER MIRROR

I found a bedroom dresser mirror for only $3.00. It's been through several makeovers and I'd like to share some of them with you. It started out a dark walnut finish and it had a thin piece of plywood insert that was tacked to the top back of the frame. Notice the insert portion. The first makeover this mirror received was refinishing. I finished the entire mirror frame, insert and all, my usual antique white finish. I distressed it with a black walnut stain and flyspecked it. It looked great and matched the other furnishings in the room.

The second makeover came about when I started noticing the new style wrought iron decorating style trim. I had purchased several wrought iron hanging plant holders for 25¢ apiece. I used them to hang the flower baskets out on the deck. I had several that were still unopened and not being used. Some were black, some were brass, but they all had a fancy curved design so I decided to use them to give some of my furnishings the newer wrought iron look.

I removed the thin wood insert at the top of the mirror, found two iron plant holders that would fit, and attached them to the inside of the mirror frame. They were already painted a matte black. This instantly gave the mirror a completely different look!

When I tired of the iron and wood look, the mirror was ready for its third makeover. This time I needed an ornate, French style mirror for the entrance hall. I put the antique white wood insert back into the top of the frame. I had some wonderful braided cord that I picked up for 25¢ at the sales. I went to the craft store and purchased two embossed wood trims. One was a large olive wreath, the other was a tall carved Grecian urn shape. These two embossed trims were a total of $12. The braid was 25¢ and the original price of the framed mirror was only $3.00. What a gorgeous mirror for only $15.25!

The fourth makeover was done using three embossed wood trims--an urn shape and two fancy birds that I finished in antique gold leaf. The wood insert was painted black and the embossed trims glued to the insert. I painted two small pieces of screen molding antique gold and glued them on the black insert. The rest of the frame was finished in gold leaf and antiqued.

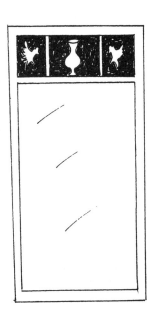
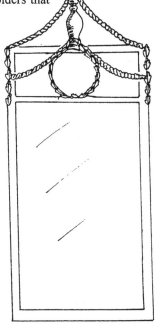
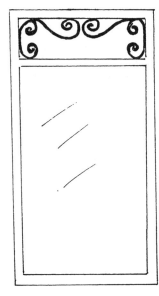

"How To"

ORNATE FRENCH MIRROR

Materials needed:
Framed dresser mirror
Thick plastic coated rope (available at hardware store)
Waxed paper or freezer paper
Embossed wood trim
Screen molding
Wood glue
Hot glue gun
Small finishing nails
Gold paint
Brown stain (optional)
Sealer

NOTE: When working with the braided rope, saturate with white glue first, then shape into the arc, place on waxed paper and let dry. Cut the rope extra long so you can cut to fit at an angle after the rope has stiffened hard. This will prevent any fraying at the ends.

1 Attach a piece of screen molding to the top center of the mirror frame with a couple of small nails. This should stick up high enough to hold the Grecian urn. Glue the embossed wood urn to the wood strip.

2 Tape a piece of large paper to the back of the mirror from the top wood strip to the top edge of the frame. Lay mirrored frame down on a flat surface. Draw your curved lines from the top of the wood strip to the top outside edge of the frame. Do this for both sides.

NOTE: I use freezer paper that has a slick side to it and a marker.

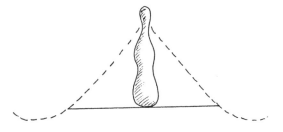

Continued . . .

3 Trim the braid the same size as the curved lines and saturate thoroughly with stiffening product. Lay the braid out on waxed paper in the same curved shape that you plan to use and let dry.

4 Paint the wood wreath and urn shapes with gold paint. Let dry. Rub brown stain over the gold with a soft cloth making sure to get in all the tiny crevices. Let dry and seal with a spray clear matte sealer. You may want a few coats of sealer. Allow to dry thoroughly between coats.

5 Attach the embossed wreath at the bottom center of the top portion of the frame with wood glue. Secure with 2 small finishing nails, one at the bottom and at the top of the wreath.

6 Paint the stiff braided cord with a primer like BIN. Let dry, then paint with gold, let dry and brush over the gold braid with stain. Let dry and spray a matte sealer over the braid. Use as many coats as needed, allowing to dry thoroughly between coats.

7 Lay the gold braid sections on top of the curved lines. Trim the ends at an angle and tuck the ends under the embossed wood pieces and glue to their back sides. You might also want to use a small finishing nail to secure the braid to the embossed wood.

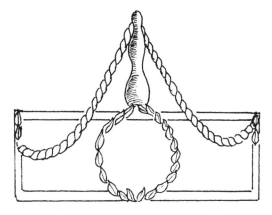

REPAIRING FRAMES

Plain wooden frames are easily repaired with wood glue and clamps. Unless it's a family heirloom, I usually don't bother repairing plain frames because they are so plentiful and inexpensive at garage sales.

The frames that I do repair are the very ornate and expensive frames--especially frames with a lot of scroll work. Many times you will find these beautiful very expensive frames at sales for only $1.00 or $2.00 because they are chipped. Most of these chips are easily repaired. I like to use dimensional fabric paint that is available at craft and hobby shops to repair these built-up pieces of scrollwork and intricate designs. Dimensional fabric paint builds up. It is three dimensional and you can apply layer after layer to build up quite high.

The dimensional paint comes in handy little tubes with a tip. There are several kinds of tips you can buy to attach to the tubes of dimensional paint, much like the cake decorating kits with different tips that you can use to make almost any kind of design. You can also use a chef's pastry bag filled with sculpting plaster for the larger broken pieces. Experiment with the different tips to get the design you want.

If a piece of scrollwork is extensively damaged it might be necessary to attach a small piece of balsa wood with wood glue to the damaged area. This way you have a base upon which to start building up your damaged design.

If the glass is broken in a frame, know that you will find the right piece of glass to fit in another frame. Sometimes you will find frames where the glass is broken in the FREE box. This is not a problem if you like the frame. You are sure to find another frame complete with glass that will fit perfectly. I've bought several picture frames that I didn't care for just to get the glass. It's easy to cut glass to size. Sometimes I buy very large frames that may be old, badly damaged, or plastic that is beyond repair, however, they have good pieces of glass. The price might be 50¢ to $1.00. This is a good deal for a big piece of glass that I can cut down and fit into several frames.

If you are going to start buying glass, storing it and cutting it yourself, PLEASE BE VERY CAREFUL.

Store the glass pieces together on a piece of garage sale carpet. Separate the glass pieces with large pieces of cardboard or more carpet.

When you handle glass, wear thick gloves and work goggles.

CUTTING GLASS

You can buy a glass cutter at any hardware store for under $2.00 or find one at a garage sale for 25¢.

Mark the glass to be cut with a marker or crayon. Use anything that will wash off. Lay a piece of heavy duty garage sale carpet under it. Press down firmly on the glass with your glass cutter and score all the way down your mark. Once you start your cut, don't stop and start again--it needs to be one continuous score. You will hear a noise that lets you know the glass is being cut, however, you won't actually see the glass separating and cutting. After you have scored all the way down the side to be cut, use both hands and snap the extra portion of glass down. The glass should now separate and you have your cut piece.

Save the extra piece of glass to use later for another project.

PLEASE BE VERY CAREFUL!

PICTURES AND PRINTS

Many of the frames that you find are made for an oil painting and not a paper print. Some people prefer the look of an oil painting to a picture with glass.

Paper prints are more readily available than paintings or copies of paintings. If you order a copy suitable for framing without glass you will find it to be quite expensive. A paper print that is 11" x 14" might run $10. To get the same picture on canvas or cardboard with a matte, textured finish runs around $100.

I've found an easy way to give an inexpensive paper print a textured finish. It will look just like the reproduced textured prints and, if you prefer, you can age it very easily for a very old, antique look.

Start with a small paper print to experiment and see if you like this look.

Apply spray adhesive, Mod Podge, or rubber cement to the back of the print and adhere it to a piece of heavy cardboard (not corrugated), a canvas board or any flat surface. Remember there will be no matting around this picture, so make sure the actual print extends to the end of the cardboard or canvas board and will fit exactly into your frame.

Apply a thick coat of Mod Podge to the entire print with a small (1" brush) using irregular brush strokes. You want these brush strokes to show--you do not want a smooth finish. Allow to dry following manufacturer's directions. You can also do this same process with a Gel Medium product available at craft and hobby stores.

For an antique look squeeze a small amount of oil pigment from a tube onto a cloth. Oil pigment tubes can be found at an artist's supply store. I like a burnt sienna oil pigment for an antique look. Start at one cor-

ner, using a clean cloth and very lightly rub a small amount of oil pigment out as far as you can over the print. Apply more pigment in another location and continue doing this until the entire print has been lightly wiped over. Make sure it is a very light application so the print shows through.

By doing this to your paper print you remove the sheen of the paper and add brush strokes, making the print suitable for framing without glass. It looks more like an oil painting.

Another exciting technique is to apply a coat of lacquer to the entire print. Let dry thoroughly. Follow with a coat of yellow school glue over the lacquered print. Allow the glue to set for about 15 minutes, then apply another coat of lacquer on top. This technique will give your print an aged cracked appearance.

Prints of high quality artwork are easily found on calendars, notebooks, in magazines and in the newspaper. If you have several small frames ready to fill, check these sources for some beautiful artwork. For smaller pictures, I just cut them out and put them in a frame with a mat and glass and they're lovely.

Some of the pictures in our family room were actually place mats. Have you seen the boxes of thick cardboard placemats with lovely pastoral scenes, flowers or English hunting scenes? They frame up beautifully!

There is always a colored border surrounding the picture which gives the picture an instant mat. Frame the picture placemats just as they are, or, put another mat around the colored border for a double matted look.

I found a wonderful box of four 15" x 18" English hunting scene placemats bordered in white with a gold leaf edge, followed by a 3" wide dark red border. It took only two weeks to find four identical brass frames complete with glass at the sales. I paid 50¢

for a couple of the frames and $1.00 each for the other two. I bought four black mats at the store and altogether the box of four placemats, brass frames with glass and black mats was a grand total of $14! You can buy the exact same English hunting scene pictures in the same brass frames at department stores and specialty shops. They sell for $79 apiece!

Start using your imagination!

PICTURE FRAME MATS

You can even find mats for your frames at sales. I usually buy any I find, even if they are not the right color, especially since they only cost 5¢ or 25¢, It's easy to stipple them with a sponge and light coats of paint or you can cover them with wallpaper or fabric to match your decor.

To make a custom mat lay wallpaper or fabric wrong side up on a flat surface. Apply tacky glue or use a spray adhesive on the entire mat. Place the glued side of the cardboard mat on top of the fabric or wallpaper. Smooth out any bubbles or ripples. You want a flat, smooth surface. In the center of the mat, draw a large "X" on the fabric or paper with a marker. Cut the "X" and fold back to the edge of the mat. Cut off the excess paper or fabric and use a tacky glue, spray adhesive or rubber cement to adhere the remaining fabric or wallpaper to the back of the mat. Press down firmly, allow it to dry, and then place it inside your frame.

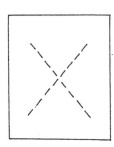 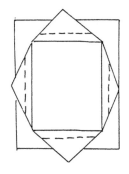

MIRRORS

Nothing opens up and brightens your rooms as much as a beautiful piece of mirror.

Hang mirrors in decorator frames over the buffet, the fireplace, an entrance hallway, or over the console table that you will learn how to make in the coffee table section. Mirror an entire wall if you like and get all the mirrors you need at garage sales for just a few dollars. Even a mirror that has a chip on the edge is no problem. You can get a good deal on mirrors with chipped edges-- sometimes you can even get them for FREE.

I have all sizes and shapes of mirrors stored up against the wall in the basement. I look for the largest pieces of mirror I can find, but, of course, if the price is right I'll take the small ones too! The larger pieces of mirror usually come out of bathrooms that were remodeled or off of mirrored walls or doors. Remember that a mirror can be cut to specifications and the larger the piece of mirror, the more you have to work with.

Most glass companies will cut your mirror FREE OF CHARGE as long as it is a simple straight cut. If they charge it is usually a very reasonable $1.00 per cut.

If you already have a frame for the mirror, take your piece of mirror and your frame to a glass company. They will do the measuring for you and lay the mirror in your frame. They may even carry it out to the car for you!

The most expensive piece of mirror I ever bought was only $10 for a piece 60" x 50". It was in perfect condition and, I might add, very heavy! To buy a piece of heavy plate glass mirror this large would have cost over $150!

There are small niches in the walls of my home where I usually put a flower arrangement or a statue. I like to find pieces of mirror at the sales and have them cut to fit the back and sides of the niche FREE at a glass company and insert the mirror into the niche. This "mirrors" or "reflects" the statue or flowers that are sitting in the niche. A lot of new homes are using corner niches or flat niches. Mirror them with pieces of garage sale mirror for a very dramatic look.

I've bought so many beautiful large frames that are sitting in the basement waiting for something to go in them. Nothing is as beautiful as a mirror in these large ornate frames. (Check the prices of these ornate framed mirrors when you go to showrooms-- you'd better sit down!)

I found a beautiful French carved wooden frame, quite large, 40" x 50" for $10. I had a piece of mirror in the basement that I had gotten for $4.00 and took the frame and mirror to a glass company. This beautiful framed mirror cost $14, but would easily sell for over $400 in the store.

One of the decorator treatments that I admire is a picture hanging in front of a large expanse of mirror. You can do this by hanging the picture right in front of the mirror with gold cord or use rope or chain. Paint your chain if you prefer or cover it with a gathered piece of fabric to match your decor. Sew a long thin tube and gather it over the old rope or chain. Attach the chain to the ceiling and to the top edges of the picture frame. (Remember all that chain I've been telling you to get at the sales?) By now you should have boxes and boxes of all sizes. Cover the chandelier cord or chain with fabric too!

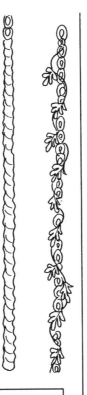

LAMPS & LAMPSHADES

My friend, Jo Ann, thinks I must have been locked in a dark closet during my childhood because I buy two or three lamps in a day's worth of sale~ing!

I love them as lamps, but I also use all of the lamp parts to make other things like candleholders, sconces, and candelabras. I also like to make my own style lamps out of bits and pieces of other lamps.

Why buy a lamp in the store when you have so much to choose from at the sales? I've even bought a pair of Stiffel lamps at $2.00 for the pair!

Don't worry if the shades are not right, we'll be buying lots of these to mix and match for less than $1.00 apiece.

My friend, Sherri, was having a garage sale and showed me her things. She had a lovely very large gold leaf lamp that she gave me for FREE. Lucky me! It had a very nice shade but I really didn't care for it. I told her to keep the shade and sell it for $2.00, so we were both happy. I took my new lamp home and put a black shade on it that I had found for $1.00. The look of the gold lamp is changed completely. I hope Sherri doesn't want it back! It pays to experiment and mix and match with all the different accessories that hopefully you've started collecting.

I have crystal lamps in our bedrooms and bright brass lamps in the family room with rich black shades. There are delicately carved gold leaf lamps, twin arm lamps, English hunting style, Austrian crystal candelabras, swing-arm, floor lamps, Victorian lamps, and hurricane lamps that were all purchased at the sales.

Lamps that had a glass shade or a hurricane which was broken were bought for less than 50¢. If you've been collecting the glass globes and hurricanes highlighted in the candleholder section, all you have to do is find one that you like and place it on your new 50¢ lamp.

The small candlestick lights that you see at Christmas time are perfect little lamps for those nooks and crannies or placed on a small tea table or as a bookshelf light. I put a small lampshade on the candlestick light bulb and it looks like a decorator lamp. You can find these little shades at garage sales for 25¢. They usually come in a white or cream color. Don't hesitate to dye or paint the lamp shades. Use any fabric dye. There is a good cold water dye available at craft & hobby shops.

See the lampshade section to learn more about dying and decorating lampshades.

Place several little lamps in your bookcases and on your shelves to highlight all of the garage sale treasures that you will be collecting. One of the taller (20") candlestick lamps I found was a mauve color with brass trim, complete with a little metal mauve shade. I spray-painted the mauve black, both candlestick and shade.

Just as with making candleholders, you can take your lamps apart and use fittings and pieces from other lamps to make something unique.

A very popular style lamp today is the tall (approximately 48") lamp. These lamps are usually tall and thin in shape and are placed alongside a mirror or on a buffet table. Because of the unique size of these lamps, they are usually found only in designer showrooms and are very expensive. Why pay several hundred dollars when you can make your own for just a few dollars! Find a threaded center lamp rod or buy one at the hardware store. These are usually threaded all the way up the rod. Start building your lamp base with your selection of fittings, add any decorative trim like tassels or fabric decorations, finish as desired, and top with a beautiful lamp shade that you decorated or made yourself.

See How To Disassemble A Lamp in this chapter for complete instructions.

WALL LAMPS & SCONCES

Wall lamps and sconces can add beautiful decorator touches to any room. Some wall lamps look just like regular lamps with a regular lampshade. Others have beautiful crystal hurricanes. No matter which style of wall light you choose, you don't want to have an unsightly cord hanging down the wall. What an eye sore! I've got just the solution to this problem and you can probably find it for FREE at garage sales. Use the center extension section of a curtain rod to place over the unsightly cord. Place the rod directly underneath the back plate of your lamp or sconce and insert the wire into the

curtain rod going straight down the wall and plug in. Glue the curtain rod straight down against the wall, hiding the cord. Paint the curtain rod extension the same color as your wall or wallpaper the curtain rod with the same paper that you have on the wall. Make sure to properly align the pattern on the wallpaper. No one will notice this nifty way of hiding that unsightly electrical cord.

LAMPSHADES

If you've ever priced lampshades at the store, you know--depending on size, shape and color--they can run $10-$20-$30-$40 on up! I like the black shades, which are even more expensive.

Most of the shades you find at garage sales will be white or cream color. If you want another color, dye the shade, paint the shade, or remove the fabric from its metal frame and make your own. Collect lampshades in all sizes and shapes. When you start bringing those lamp bases home, it's fun to have several different style lampshades to choose from. They start at 10¢ a shade and go up to around $2.00. Look for them in the FREE box too! If the shade is all soiled or torn but the frame is the perfect size, go ahead and get it. It's easy to add new fabric. Anyone can do it!

Change the look of any room just by changing your lampshades.

"How To"

PAINT, STAIN, or DYE LAMPSHADES

Materials needed:
Stain or paint
Paint brush or rag or sponge
Fabric dye

1 Using a rag or sponge, apply a thin layer of stain starting at both the top and bottom edges of the shade and working in towards the center. This will give your shade an antique look.

2 Painting works best on the stiff cardboard style shades. Don't get the shade too saturated. <u>Paint with a light touch</u> by using a sponge. Stippling works very well on lamp shades. Paint decorator touches and designs on the shades or add flowers, cording or fringe.

3 Dissolve dye in a plastic container large enough to hold the lampshade lengthwise. Dip the lampshade in the dye and turn it to coat. Keep turning the lampshade to get a uniform color. For a deeper color, allow the lampshade to rest in the dye until achieving desired color.

"How To"

MAKE YOUR OWN LAMPSHADES

RIBBON

Materials Needed:
Lampshade frame
Very wide ribbon
Seam binding
Decorative trim

1 Remove the old lampshade covering from the metal frame.

2 Wrap ribbon under top edge of frame and secure with tacky glue.

3 Wrap ribbon around length of shade continuously overlapping it until you've reached your starting point. Make sure you are pulling the ribbon snugly around the frame.

4 Apply decorative trim around the top and bottom edges of the lamp shade.

"How To"

MAKE YOUR OWN LAMPSHADES

FABRIC LAMPSHADE

Materials needed:
Lampshade frame
Fabric or lace
Seam binding
Decorative trim

1 Lay your fabric or lace out flat on a table and place the lampshade on its side on one end of the fabric.

2 Roll the lampshade in its natural arc to complete one whole revolution. While rolling the lampshade in its arc, hold a marker to the top frame and mark the fabric. Repeat this step while holding a marker to the bottom frame and going around the same arc.

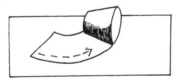

3 Cut out your pattern leaving an extra 3/4" for a seam at the sides and at the top and bottom.

4 Press under a 1/4" seam at the side.

5 Attach the fabric to the frame with tacky glue, turning the fabric around the top and bottom edge of the frame. Glue down the side seam. Make sure the fabric is pulled tight.

6 Trim with seam binding or decorative trim.

"How To"

MAKE YOUR OWN LAMPSHADES

PLEATED FABRIC

Materials Needed:
Lampshade frame
Pleated shade fabric removed from larger lamp shade
Tacky glue

1 Remove the pleated fabric from a larger shade. If you can't remove it, cut a straight line in the fabric next to the metal frame. Then cut down the side and remove it that way. Now you have your piece of pleated shade material to use on your frame.

2 Cut the pleated fabric with an extra 1/2" of fabric at the top and bottom of your chosen frame.

3 Wrap the pleated fabric around the metal frame and cut off any excess fabric at side seam. Allow an extra 1/2" for the side seam.

4 Glue the side seam with tacky glue. Then glue the fabric to the top and bottom of frame, and wrap the fabric around the frame edge and secure with tacky glue and let dry.

5 Trim the top and bottom edges with seam binding or decorative trim.

"How To"

COVER "ODD" SHAPED LAMPSHADES

Materials Needed:
Pencil
Aluminum foil
Fabric
Tacky glue
Decorative trim

If your lampshade has an odd shape or has scalloped edges, you will need to make a pattern for each section of the shade.

A section is defined by the wire frame running down the sides.

A square shade may have 4 sections.

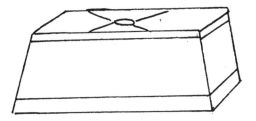

A round shade may have 6 sections.

Continued . . .

1 Lay a piece of heavy duty aluminum foil over one section.

Take the side of a pencil and rub it over the wire frames to get a pattern for the section.

Do this for each different-sized section. If all the sections are the same size, you need to do this only once.

2 Next, cut out the foil along the raised rubbing marks. This is your pattern. Lay the pattern on your piece of fabric and cut it out. Do this for each section until you have enough fabric pieces for each section. It is not necessary to cut extra fabric for a seam allowance.

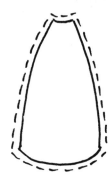

3 Attach each fabric section one by one to the metal frames with tacky glue and let dry.

4 Attach decorative trim over seamed sections and around the top and bottom edges of the lampshade frame, or glue silk fringe on the bottom edge.

OPTIONS:

Cover alternating panels with fabric AND lace or cover all panels with fabric, covered with lace.

See OPTIONS, page 115 for decorative trim ideas.

"How To"

LACE LAMPSHADES

Materials needed:
Miniature or full size lampshade frame
Lace fabric
Tacky glue
Stiffening product* (Stiffy)
Aluminum foil
Pencil
*See glossary

1 Remove the fabric from the lamp shade.

2 Make a pattern of each metal section by placing aluminum foil over the section and rubbing hard with a pencil edge along the metal borders. See page 112.

3 I like to use scallop-edged lace. Place the pattern on the center design portion of the lace with the scalloped edge centered on each pattern piece. Allow the scalloped edge to fall over the bottom metal frame of the lamp shade frame.

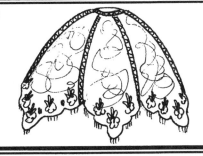

NOTE: You can use one piece of lace and wrap around the lampshade if you prefer.

4 Saturate with stiffening product and allow to dry partially. Attach each piece of lace to the metal frame with tacky glue before the ace has completely stiffened. Glue decorative trim over the cut edges of the lace and around the top edge of the shade.

OPTION
Roll the scalloped point up and around a pencil or tissue paper roll and let stiffen. Attach a small silk rose bud and silk ribbon with tacky glue to the top edge of the rolled lace on each scallop.

MINIATURE LAMPSHADES

Have you seen the very expensive jeweled, miniature lampshades that sell for over $100 apiece? They are very popular right now. The fabric is removed from the shades and strings of colored crystals are wrapped entirely around the lampshade frame.

You will find lots of plain miniature shades at garage sales for 25¢. Jewelry is an easy way to give your lampshades an exquisite look. Earrings can be pushed through the fabric and secured with an earring back or attach clip on earrings to the bottom and top edges. An old-fashioned jeweled sweater clasp can be draped in many different designs. Try using matching brooches or earrings with a string of crystals or pearls swagged between them. Start looking through the jewelry at the sales and collecting strands of pearls, crystals, jewelry pieces and feathers to cover the shades. You can make these beautiful shades for only $1.00! I'll show you how!

Gold Stretch Bracelet & Earrings

Baby Lace Headband

Pearls

Pearl Choker & Earrings

Sweater Clasp

Pheasant Feathers

"How To"

JEWELED MINIATURE LAMPSHADES

Materials needed:
Miniature lampshade metal frame
Strings of pearls or crystals
Hot glue gun

1 Remove the fabric from the lamp shade frame. Use pearls or crystals all the same size. You will need very long strands. If you are combining multiple strands of jewels you will need to cut off the clasp and apply a small dab of hot glue to the end of the strand so the pearls or crystals will not fall off the string. Do this for each strand you use.

2 Starting at the bottom or top edge of the metal frame, attach one end of your pearls or crystals to the edge of the frame with the glue gun.

Start wrapping the jewels around the metal frame horizontally and glue at each metal section. Keep wrapping the jeweled strand snugly around the metal frame. Keep the rows of jewels directly against each other. Do not overlap the rows, just keep them lying flat against each other without any spacing between the rows.

When you reach the top edge of the metal frame, secure the jewelry strand with hot glue, especially at the end.

OPTIONS:

Use a different type of jewel for the top and bottom rows.

Glue silk fringe around the bottom edge.

Glue separate jewels on top of the jewel strands.

Glue lace & jeweled appliqués on top of the jewel strands.

Thread loose beads or crystals on wire, wrap and glue around the lamp shade frame.

Push earrings through the beads and secure with an earring back or attach clip on earrings to the bottom and top edges.

Drape a jeweled sweater clasp to the shade or use matching brooches or earrings with a string of crystals or pearls swaged between them. Attach the string of crystals or pearls to the back of the brooches or earrings with a hot glue gun.

"How To"

MINIATURE LACE LAMPSHADES

Materials needed:
Miniature lamp frame
Lace stretch tights--women's or children's
Decorative trim
Jewelry or feathers
Baby lace headband

NOTE: I purchased the miniature shade for 25¢ and a jacket trimmed in lace and silk fringe and lace tights for only 10¢. Altogether this beautiful shade took about two minutes to make and cost only 60¢.

1 Remove fabric from the miniature lamp frame.

2 Cut off the foot portion of the lace tights at the ankle. Pull down and stretch the lace leg over the miniature lampshade frame. Adjust to fit.

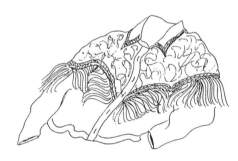 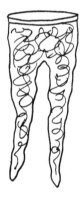 

3 Cut off excess at top edge of lamp shade, leaving approximately 1/4" to glue under the bottom and top edges of the lamp shade.

4 Apply decorative trim, silk fringe, a string of pearls or stretch the baby headbands around the top and bottom edges of the lampshade and adhere with tacky glue.

OPTIONS:

See page 105 for a complete list of optional decorative trims.

CHANDELIERS

When we think about chandeliers, the room that always comes to mind is the dining room. If you shop garage sales you can afford to have lovely chandeliers anywhere. They don't always have to be centered and bolted to the ceiling. You can swag a beautiful crystal chandelier over a fabric-covered round table in the corner of your bedroom, living room or study. I've paid $2.00 up to $5.00 for beautiful crystal chandeliers!

Chandeliers come in all styles, made from crystal, brass, porcelain, glass and metal. There are numerous things you can do with the chandeliers that you find.

If the chandelier has little white candlesticks that are turning yellow--spray paint them a glistening, gloss white.

If the little white candlesticks are cracked, cover them with white contact paper or use a piece of your wallpaper to wrap around each one for a dressier effect. If you have wallpaper with a border--wrap some border pieces around the little candlesticks for a coordinated look.

If the chandelier is missing teardrops or crystal cups, you will find lots of extras at sales or there are fine lamp stores that carry these parts.

If a brass chandelier is tarnished beyond repair, don't hesitate to paint it or gild it a beautiful antique gold or pewter or the very popular verdigris. Paint it white and trim in peach and mint green for a southwestern look. Wrap fabric leaves attached to tie wire all around the chandelier arms or glue fabric roses on them.

See the candleholder section for more information.

Attach the small fabric lampshades that you can find for 25¢ to the light bulbs.

Dye those shades to match your decor or remove the fabric and cover the shade frame with a fabric of your choosing. I love the look of a tiny plaid shades on brass chandeliers. This looks great in a library or den.

Remember the chain that hangs the chandelier can be covered with a gathered sheath of matching fabric.

You can also remove the short chain and add a long swag chain to hang it in the corner of a room over a table.

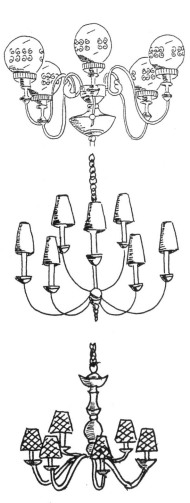

CANDELABRAS

Would you like a candelabra to match your chandelier or to place on the piano--just like Liberace?

If you could buy these candelabras they would be very expensive. They are very hard to find, even in the finest stores. The last time I saw a crystal candelabra at a store was in San Francisco several years ago and it sold for $1,000! I made one just like it for $8.00!!!!

You can use these same instructions to make any style candelabra you like. My favorite is an elegant crystal candelabra with crystal beads and teardrops mounted on a crystal and gold base. Choose any style chandelier you like and mate it with a lamp base or a floor lamp base. You can top them with the miniature lampshades to get another type of look or wrap the faux metal leaves all around and finish in a verdigris. Remember to mix and match lamp base fittings if you like, and mix and match finishes.

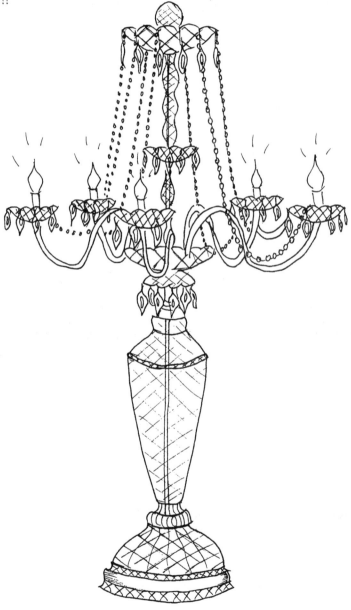

"How To"

MAKE A CANDELABRA

Materials needed:
Chandelier
Lamp base
Pliers
Screwdriver
Wire cutters
or
Craft knife

OVERVIEW:

All lamps and chandeliers have a hollow center rod for support and to hold the electrical wiring. What we're going to do is mate the lamp base with the chandelier by attaching their electrical wiring and hollow center tubes together.

NOTE: If you want to paint or finish any portion of the chandelier or lamp base, do it now before proceeding further.

Make sure the lamp base is large enough and sturdy enough (heavier) to balance out and hold the chandelier once it's attached. A chandelier can be quite top heavy. Make floor style candelabra or stop the fittings at the dotted line and attach a heavy bottom fitting for a tabletop candelabra.

1 Loosen the hex nut at the bottom of the lamp base to allow for a little "play" in the lamp wiring.

2 Next, remove the light bulb socket. The socket is typically a dark brown plastic called BakeLite and is encased in a brass housing. Disassemble the brass housing by locating the crimping on the exterior of the brass socket. The crimping is where the brass bulb housing will separate. You can remove it by pressing together firmly and pulling up and out. If it does not remove easily, use a screwdriver and pliers to help set it free. The housing will separate at the crimped part. You will hear it click free.

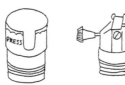

Continued . . .

3 The top part of the removed brass should slip up and can be set aside. Grasp the brown plastic part and pull up, pulling some lamp cord up with it. Pull up approximately 3 inches of the electric cord and remove the two wires that are attached to the socket with a screwdriver.

Save the entire socket in your electrical parts box.

The base part of the socket should screw up and off the hollow center rod. Sometimes there is a screw on the side that must be loosened. The lamp base will be a hollow support rod with male threads extending and electric wires protruding out the hollow opening.

4 Remove any washers at the top of the lamp pole and possibly the top fitting. You should see at least 1/2 inch of threads extending on the center rod.

5 Strip the wires back approximately one inch using a wire stripper or a craft knife.

The lamp base is now ready to accept the chandelier top.

6 Proceed to the chandelier and loosen any nuts at the bottom so the fittings will move around a bit.

You will be working only with the center stem portion of the chandelier. You do not need to do anything at all to the arm portions of the chandelier.

7 Remove any bottom fittings and the large round bottom cupola at the bottom of the chandelier to expose the electrical wires, which will come from the top down to a junction point at the bottom. Attach the round bottom cupola to the top of the lamp base rod leaving at least 1/4" to 1/2 " of threads exposed. This is the rounded cup that holds the electrical wiring and wire nuts.

Continued . . .

Leave the top plate or lid for the cupola on the chandelier.
You will see two wire nuts with several wires twisted inside them.

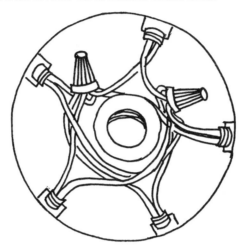

If your chandelier has 6 arms, there will be three wires running into each wire nut.
If your chandelier has 8 arms, there will be 4 wires running into each wire nut and so on . . .

8 Lay the lamp and the chandelier on their sides so they will fit together. The bottom portion of the chandelier will be lying at the top of the lamp base.

Do not remove the wire nuts or the clump of wires. Find the one wire that was attached to the ceiling and pull down through the center of the chandelier so the copper strands are coming out the bottom center. This is the one and only wire that needs to be mated with the lamp base wire. It may be necessary to expose more copper strands by stripping more of the plastic coating.

Mate the copper strands together and twist securely. Wrap electrical tape securely around the twisted wires to hold together. Wrap completely, leaving no copper strands exposed.

NOTE: You can buy electrical wire connectors instead of using electrical tape.

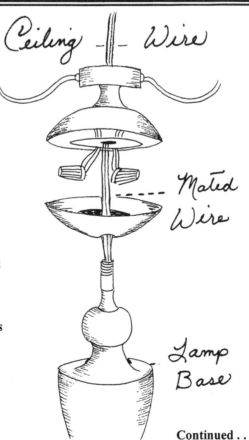

Ceiling — Wire

Mated Wire

Lamp Base

Continued . . .

With the lamp base and chandelier lying on their sides, gently pull the electrical cord from the bottom of the lamp base. Be careful not to pull the connected chandelier and lamp base wiring apart.

NOTE: The following steps will require assistance from someone--neighbors or relatives or innocent passers-by are suggested!

9 Attach the chandelier base to the lamp base by inserting the lamp base into the threaded opening at the base of the chandelier.

You need someone to hold the chandelier while you twist the threaded metal pole of the lamp base up into the bottom of the chandelier.

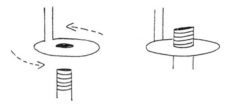

Make sure the lamp and chandelier are threaded together securely.

10 Replace the hex nut on the bottom of the lamp base. Screw tightly making sure all of the lamp fittings are tight. Plug it in! If you like, add the small lamp shades to the chandelier bulbs.

SWAG LAMPS

No matter what condition I find swag lights in, I usually buy them just for the chain, electric switch and plug.

My husband thought I was out of my mind when I brought home an old ripped and torn cardboard swag lamp. It cost 25¢ and had a wonderful long brass chain and cord with switch. These swag lamp kits (chain, wiring and switch) cost $14.95 retail.

Every time I find one this inexpensive I buy it. Sometimes I'll use only the chain as you will see when reading throughout the book. There are a lot of uses for chain.

When you take the swag lights apart, store the swag kit (chain, wiring, switch and plug) in your electrical parts box because they'll come in handy.

PLANTS

Our home is filled with beautiful greenery in every room and every plant in the house was purchased at a garage sale. There are wonderful multi-trunk Dracaena Marginatas that are over 8 feet tall and cost only $15 apiece. They easily sell for $100 at a nursery.

I've paid 25¢ for spider plants, aloe vera, ivy or philodendrons; $3.00 for the larger floor type plants (rubber trees, palm and ficus trees).

I found a very large ficus tree at a sale and can understand why the owners wanted to sell it. The tree was probably overtaking their home! It was 8 feet tall and about 6 feet wide. They wanted $10 for it, but I got it for $6.00! I learned several years ago, from a master gardener friend, that the trunks of these trees can be braided & shaped into an actual tree, rather than a ficus bush. When I went to the nursery I saw exactly what he meant. The larger size ficus that were braided were almost twice as expensive as the regular trees.

The branches on these trees are very flexible, allowing you to braid them just as you would your hair. You can braid up a couple of feet or more, depending on the highest branch. This way, you have one nice, long stalk with the branches bursting out the top in the shape of a real tree. In time, the trunks actually start to graft together into one large trunk. I've recommended this technique to all my friends and neighbors and no one has lost a tree yet! It makes for a nicer plant and it's much more manageable too.

I place the larger plants on heavy-duty plastic or brass stands with castors. This makes them a lot easier to move around. These stands cost only 25¢ to $1.00 at the sales.

Tucked in behind the larger plants are plastic containers that have spotlights in them. You can put a Gro-light in them if you prefer. Set the lights on the floor behind the plant containers and angle them up through the plant. This gives a dramatic shadow lighting effect. These light stands cost 25¢ to 50¢ complete with a spotlight or Gro-light. Gro-lights alone are $6.95 for the 150 watt. I have a whole shelf filled with Gro-lights that cost no more than 25-50¢.

Remember to get all your light bulbs at sales. Spotlights, flood lights, grow lights, fluorescent lights, chandelier bulbs, night lights, appliance bulbs--you'll find them all!

BOOKS

Most of the books in our numerous book-shelves were purchased at garage sales. We're avid readers and someday we hope to get to read all of the wonderful classics and best sellers that we find. The hardbound books normally sell for $1.00 per book. Paperbacks can range anywhere from 10 for $1.00 to 50¢ apiece. My favorites are the hardbound books which display nicely on the bookshelves.

My greatest book buy was a set of classics-- the kind that are bound in leather with gold leaf pages and silk book marker. The inside covers are lined in silk moiré fabric and the titles are embossed gold leaf. I'm sure you've seen these collector's edition books. They are very expensive!

One day I drove up to a sale that I call a "box" sale. Nothing was really out on display--there were just boxes and boxes of "stuff." In several boxes underneath all the old clothes were the beautiful collector edition books. I asked the seller how much he wanted for the books and he replied $5.00 a book. I asked him how much for the entire collection. He replied $1.00 a book! I went through every box and counted out every single, wonderful book. There were actually 95 of these treasures!

When I got the books home, my children (who are book lovers also) helped me unpack them and dust them off. If you were to purchase these books they would easily sell for $40 apiece. My arithmetic comes to $3,800 if I were to order these books.

To our surprise and amazement, when we were going through all of the wonderful books, we found several first editions that were signed by the author!

I wish Voltaire and Plato had signed their books!

TELEPHONES

There's a telephone in every room of our house, garage and basement. We also have shelves of phones "to be used" stored in the basement. When the children go off to college or need an extra phone for their computers, they go downstairs and pick out what they need. There are all kinds of phones to be found at garage sales. Every size, shape, color and style. The best phones to look for are the ones made by an operating utility: Western Electric, Pacific Bell, or AT&T. Turn the phones over or look in the handset for the brand.

You can tell the difference between these phones and the off-brands just by picking them up and feeling their weight. My husband likes to joke that these phones were built to survive a nuclear blast!

Plug the phones in and make sure you get a dial tone. Most sellers are very cooperative and allow you to plug in phones or anything electrical to test them out. You can expect to pay anywhere from 50¢ to $5.00 for good telephones. I paid $5.00 for a telephone complete with built in speaker and automatic re-dial. Cordless telephones are easily found at the sales too! Again, make sure you test them out.

TELEPHONE SPEAKERS, INTERCOMS & ANSWERING MACHINES

Expect to pay around $2.00 for either the speakers or intercom sets. I've seen them priced higher but they are so plentiful there is no need to pay more. You take your chances with answering machines. Make sure it's a newer model and hopefully in the original box with instructions. I never pay more than a few dollars for any answering machine.

RUGS

You will find throw rugs, bathroom sets, large area rugs, oriental rugs and even wall-to-wall carpet at the sales. We even found a whole house full of very expensive cream carpet. There was a large roll of carpet lying on the driveway at a sale so it was very easy to roll it out and check for dirt and stains. The lady selling the carpet said they had never had any pets because her children had severe allergies. In fact, they were so allergic that they had to remove the carpet in the entire house and replace it with wood floors. That's why she was selling the carpet. She took me inside the house and there were carpet people removing the rest of the matching carpet. We bought the large roll of carpet for $5.00 and the lady told me if I wanted the rest of the carpet I could have it for FREE if I would come back and get it later that afternoon.

I had been looking for a nice piece of carpet to lay down in the basement. This $5.00 carpet purchase was the catalyst to finish the basement into a large rec room. I had more than enough beautiful carpet for the entire basement!

PERSIAN & ORIENTAL RUGS

Our three very expensive Persian rugs were the result of one Saturday morning garage sale. While driving to the grocery store, we passed a sale that was just opening up and I recognized some small Persian rugs out on the grass. It was the only time I've ever jumped out of a moving car!

They were small rugs, approximately 3 x 5 feet. The seller said they were purchased in Iran when they lived there several years ago. They were Baluchi prayer rugs and she wanted $15.00 apiece for them. They weren't exactly my color but I recognized them to be valuable and could perhaps resell them. That afternoon I took them to my friendly Persian rug dealer and he confirmed their history.

For years I had been wanting an authentic Persian rug to place under the dining room table and because of these small $15 garage sale rugs, my dreams were going to come true! The rug dealer gave me a $1,200 credit for my four Baluchi rugs and for a few hundred dollars more, I got three large handmade wool rugs. A Bokhara for the family room, a Tabriz for under the dining room table, and a carved Chinese rug for the living room. My thanks to the lady who sold me $1,200 worth of rugs for $60!

A LITTLE "RUG" KNOWLEDGE

A person can write a whole book on rugs and there are several good ones in the library. If you are into rugs as I am--browse through one of these books or go to your local Oriental & Persian rug dealer for an education. You will learn a lot about quality, knots per inch, wools, single knot, double knot, dyes and patterns.

There are so many different patterns and it's best to actually see them to decide what you like.

One of the easiest ways to tell a quality rug is to flip it over. It should have the same design and colors on the back as it does on the front. If you see a webbing you know that it is machine made. Also, look at the fringe. If you can see that the fringe was stitched on, it was machine made. The fringe on a handmade rug is actually an extension of the rug. There is no seam.

At the turn of the century, it was very popular to actually turn rugs over and display the underneath side of the rug because it gives more of a tapestry effect. I've seen this done today in the hot summer months.

If you find a rug at a sale that is slightly damaged or soiled you can have these rugs repaired and cleaned or turn them over and use the underside.

I would recommend calling a Persian rug dealer and having him or her recommend a cleaner. Do not take them to a local dry cleaner and do not vacuum the rugs with your beater bar. They will last a lot longer.

How long will one of these beautiful rugs last? A single knotted rug--20 to 30 years. A double knotted rug--longer than you and I added together!

WINDOW DECOR

All of your window treatments, drapes, curtains, mini-blinds, pleated shades, shutters, Plantation shutters, vertical blinds, lace panels or sheers can be found at garage sales. If you are in need of window coverings, I recommend that you take measurements of your windows and tuck them in your fanny pack. That way when you find the mini-blinds or draperies that you've been looking for, you will know for sure that they will fit.

DRAPERIES

Whether your choice is formal with elegant draped swags and cascades, a tailored cornice, country muslin, lace or ruffled Priscillas--everything you can imagine is at the sales. Sometimes the drapes will be dirty and need cleaning, often times they will have been freshly cleaned and still in the dry cleaning bags with a selling price far less than the cleaning price.

I've found several drapes, freshly cleaned, ready to take home and hang. This is especially useful if you have just moved into a new house and would like to have your windows covered but you're not quite sure what kind of window treatment you prefer. You will only spend a few dollars to have the privacy you want and when you decide exactly what it is you want, sell the drapes you've been using at your own garage sale. You can probably get the same price you paid, which means they won't have cost you a penny! Some of the drapes you find may be damaged with a hole in them or stains running along the bottom or sides that you know will not come out with cleaning. If they are a color or print that you really like, go ahead and buy them. The price will be next to nothing and there are several things you can do with them. First of all, you might not need the entire drape to cover your window so if the ends are ripped or stained you may be able to cut the bad portion off and use the rest. If the bottom edges are stained, cut them off and attach long bullion fringe to the bottom. If the fabric is a floral, cut a coordinating strip of a plain colored drape or fabric and put a border around the sides and the bottom. If the fabric is plain, add a floral border or another color border.

See the Upholstering chapter and the pillow section in the Accessories chapter.

There are so many wonderful things you can make out of yards and yards of drapery fabric, including your own designer drapes. Strolling through decorator showrooms and designer showcase homes is one of my favorite pastimes and I always come home with plenty of ideas.

The latest trend in drapes is the "no sew" variety. They are just very long rectangle pieces of fabric that are hung on brackets or pulled through large rings. They simply fall into place. This technique can be used for a casual decor or made to be extremely formal. Several different treatments can all be achieved using different sizes of rectangle fabric pieces. It's easy to dress up a plain rectangle fabric piece with designer trim and tassels. One of my favorite, very expensive looks is to sew bullion fringe on the outer edges of the rectangles and drape several of them over a decorator rod.

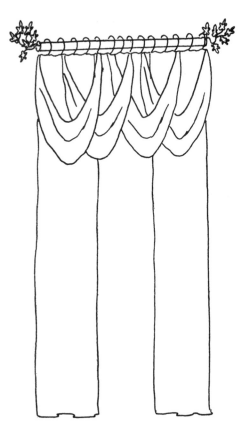

I like to hang lace panels or priscillas on a spring rod over the bathtub for a feminine or old-fashioned look or use a sheer muslin panel for country. A designer treatment is to simply sew a wide strip of fabric into a long tube and gather it up tightly onto the spring rod. This can be either formal or casual depending on the type fabric you choose. Wrap a piece of heavy duty cording around the fabric covered rod for even more detail. There are so many easy and decorative window treatments that can be done with garage sale drapes and curtains.

DRAPERY AND CURTAIN RODS

Find all of your curtain and drapery rods at the sales. Traverse rods, one way rods, curtain rods, curtain rod extensions, or even the decorator round brass rods. I've found most of my rods in the FREE box! It's certainly worth a day of garage sale~ing just to find all the rods you need. Have you priced them lately?

One of my favorite finds is the round traverse rod with finials at both ends. Finding them at the sales is easy. They are usually dark brown and out of date but it's very easy to update them by using one of the faux finishing painting techniques.

See the Finishes chapter.

One of the techniques that I like to use is attaching tie wire and faux metal leaves to each end of the drapery finials. Twist and turn the wire into any design you like. You can extend the wire out to the sides, up to the top, or flowing down the sides of the drapes. Follow the instructions to make this decorator touch.

"How To"

DRAPERY ROD TRIM

Materials needed:
Tie wire
Heavy fabric
Stiffening product
White glue (optional)
Paint
Hot glue gun

NOTE: Use leaf patterns in the candlestick section of the Accessories chapter.

1 Finish the drapery rod and finials as desired.

2 Cut out fabric leaves and saturate with stiffening product or white glue. Lay the leaves out on a piece of plastic wrap and let dry. Paint the leaves black, then smear copper paint and different shades of green for a verdigris finish or paint the leaves black and smear with gold paint or copper paint. Use any type of paint finish you prefer to make the leaves look like metal--gold leaf, antique gold, silver--the choice is yours. Paint the tie wire to match by dragging through puddles of paint. Allow everything to dry thoroughly. Attach the leaves to the tie wire with a hot glue gun.

3 Make another identical one for the other side of the drapery rod.

4 Wrap one end of the tie wire around one end of the drapery rod. Bend tie wire into any design you like.

5 Repeat step 4 for the other end of the drapery rod.

FINIALS & TASSEL HOLDERS

You will pay quite a lot of money for hand painted finials and tassels. In fact I found a designer store full of decorator tassels for $89.00 each. They are easy to make using finials that you find on garage sale drapery rods or lamp fittings. Hand paint them using the techniques on page 198.

"How To"

FINIALS & TASSEL HOLDERS

Materials needed:
Lamp fittings or Drapery rod finials
Tassels & decorative trim
Primer and paint
Glue

1 Make your own tassels or buy a basic tassel and then add the decorative touches.

2 Prime the drapery rod finial and paint in a design of your choice.

or

Assemble the lamp fittings to be used. Mix and match any kind--any style. The top fitting can be a ring type or any type. Don't worry about the hole in the top--the silk braid will come out the top hole. The bottom fitting should be a cup type and it should be as large as the tassel diameter.

3 Glue the lamp fittings together, let dry, prime and finish as desired. Some finishing ideas are gold leaf, crackle or mix several finishing techniques to match your decor. I like the hand painted and high gloss tassel holders best. Try the hand painting techniques on page 198.

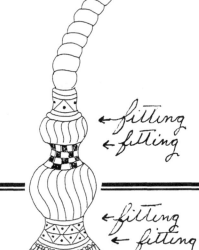

← fitting
← fitting

← fitting
← fitting

CHAPTER FOUR

MAKING & REPAIRING FURNITURE

TOOLS

COFFEE TABLE FURNITURE

    HALF CONSOLE TABLE
    DINING ROOM BUFFET
    BEDROOM BENCH
    COFFEE TABLE OTTOMAN
    SOFA TABLE STOOLS
    BED CANOPY

OTTOMANS
    "POUF"
    "TUFFETS"

HUTCHES & SIDEBOARDS

HALL TREE

CANING

O nce in a while you will find the perfect piece of furniture you want for a particular room. A dining room buffet, a breakfast hutch, a chaise lounge, or a bedroom set. It's just the right style, color, size and everything else you've ever wanted.

Once in awhile I find that perfect piece of furniture, but not very often--just once in a while.

There's no reason to wait it out until you find that perfect piece. You can make your own perfect piece of furniture out of all the furnishings and bits and pieces and parts of furnishings that are available at garage sales.

When you read through this chapter, you'll discover as I did, how easy it is to make a lot of furnishings out of pieces of existing furniture. I could never begin to make furniture from scratch. I wouldn't know how or where to begin. But if I use a piece of this, like a table top and a piece of that, maybe some coffee table legs, a little glue here and there, and a few nails, most of the work is already done for me.

Best of all, if you mess up, it didn't cost very much to try. On your next attempt, you will definitely know what not to do, and how to do it better.

Wood furniture pieces are very forgiving. A wrong nail here or there, a few misplaced drilled holes are easily repaired. The only real mess up is when you saw a piece off that shouldn't have been! This mistake can be pretty permanent, well, it's almost permanent. Sometimes you can put it back together again. It's always worth a try.

TOOLS

<u>Measuring and marking are very important</u>. I can't stress these two things enough. You'll want to find a "T" square to help with measuring and marking. I found a large one at a sale for $1.00. You'll also need a tape measure, a yard stick, wood glue, clamps, a staple gun, hammer, screw drivers, saws, and a very good saw blade.

I like to use a saber saw* (jig saw) when woodworking. I feel I have more control with a saber saw. When cutting wood pieces, make sure you have a guide on the saw. The guide will help in cutting a straight line and it is a lot easier to control the sawing process. A general wood cutting blade with finer teeth should give you a nice, smooth cut without chips. Use a 2 and 3/4" blade that has 20 teeth per inch.

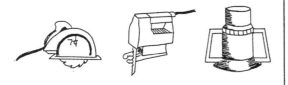

If you choose to use a circular saw, there are a lot of things you need to consider before making a cut. You need to purchase a good quality carbide tipped, 40 or 60 tooth plywood blade with a narrow kerf*. Each tip of your blade has a kerf on it, and the kerf determines the cutting diameter.

A carbide tipped blade cuts sharper and makes a better cut. It lasts longer too, however, such blades usually have a wider kerf. Make sure you use a saw blade with a narrow kerf.

Either one of these blades should work well going with the grain or across the grain with no chipping according to the local woodworker's shop.

I measure, measure again, then re-measure whether I'm working with wood or fabric. It's well worth the time and I've learned to do this because of past mistakes.

When working with wood or fabric, make a mark like this.

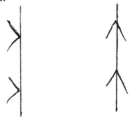

Measure and make this mark all across the piece to cut or saw, then draw a line through the center point of each mark.

My first experience with woodworking was repairing a coffee table that was in seven different pieces. Either a herd of wild elephants stampeded through this lady's home, or perhaps it was her two little boys! I think it was the fancy carved French legs lying under piles of cardboard boxes that first caught my eye. After removing all of the boxes that were piled on top, I found the rest of what had been a beautiful and very expensive name brand coffee table, but, it was in seven pieces and had an asking price of $10! EXCUSE ME? $10?

Had the table been in one piece, she could have easily asked five times that price, but all broken up and with the top glass missing, I don't think so! She finally settled for $2.00. It was worth trying to repair for $2.00. I needed a coffee table and this was my style of table. My husband's words when I brought the table home were, "Did a herd of wild elephants stampede through the house?"

With a little wood glue and some clamps, the table was put back together in one piece. It turned out to be a beautiful table with the fancy, carved French legs that I love with hand carved flowers and leaves all around the frame of the table. I really didn't want a glass top for this table and decided to use a plain piece of wood and try one of the new marbleizing kits. I ended up buying a piece of Masonite to put on top because it was the right thickness to lay in the top grooves. It cost a lot less than plywood too! I finished the Masonite to look like beige marble and the rest of the table to resemble what they call "200-year-old pine." It's a beautiful distressed golden brown color and a very popular and expensive type of wood. A very expensive look for the $2.00 elephant table!

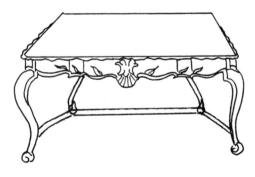

I'm lazy when it comes to stripping furniture. However, if I find a beautiful antique piece, I will do whatever it takes to restore it to the original wood finish.

Most finishes are paintable and it is very easy to make painted surfaces look just like real wood. I prefer to use this technique unless it's an antique.

See the Finishes chapter.

COFFEE TABLE FURNITURE

Since that first attempt with the elephant table several years ago I've gone through a lot of coffee tables with fancy carved French legs. You will see them all over our house. Not necessarily as coffee tables, but as benches, ottomans, bed canopies, parts of breakfronts, hutches and buffets. If you took a good look around our house, you would find coffee table parts in every room.

HALF CONSOLE TABLE

Use a rectangular or square coffee table to make the half console tables that you find in European palaces and very grand homes. Hang one of the long mirror pieces that you buy at sales on the wall over the table and you have an elegant entrance piece for just a few dollars.

Use any style coffee table, modern, Italian, traditional, French--whatever you prefer. This "how to" will work with any style coffee table.

To make a smaller width console table, cut at one end of the table. Measure and make your cut depending on how far you want the table to stick out into the room or hallway.

The smaller console tables measure approximately 10 inches out and the bigger tables 12 inches or more. To make a longer width console table, use a rectangular coffee table and cut the table in half lengthwise. A long mirror approximately the same width as the console table should be hung over the table. The ideal mirror extends all the way down to the top edge of the console table and up about six feet high or higher. The mirror should be at least as tall as a person. If your wall is very high, the mirror should be even larger. I have found several pieces of mirror this large. A lot of people are removing the large sheet mirror from their bathrooms and putting in a smaller oval framed mirror. Sometimes mirror has been removed from a wall or from doors. It could possibly be chipped. Remember . . . you can have the chipped section cut away.

If you choose the smaller width table, you can get by with a thinner mirror. A door mirror would work very well. You can always make the mirror look bigger by making a double frame with an extra piece of wood around the mirror.

See the frame section in the Accessories chapter.

If you find a door mirror that is chipped, take it to your local glass company and have it trimmed, then make the frame.

If you choose the wider size console table, obviously you need a wider piece of mirror. It's nice to have the mirror and frame as wide as the console table itself. If you can't find a piece of mirror that is tall enough, use the same technique as above, a double frame with the extra piece of wood insert around the mirror. The wood insert at the top can be extra high with some type of decoration for the top piece. A tapestry across the top would be lovely or an old world print, even another piece of mirror. You can make this work.

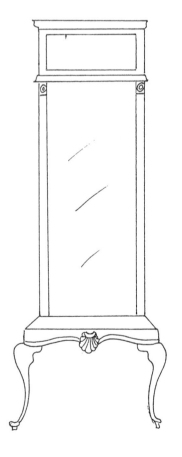
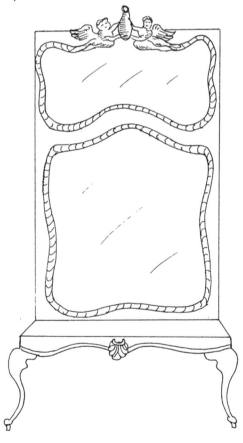

"How To"

HALF CONSOLE TABLE

Materials needed:
Rectangular or square coffee table
Circular or saber saw
Special blade (see Tools in this chapter)
Tape measure
Pencil
Screwdriver
"L" shaped brackets

1 Decide how far you want the table to extend out from the wall. Make your marks and draw the line across the underside of the table and along the side table frame.

2 Cut both side frame portions first, then cut the table top following the marked line.

3 Sand the cut edges smooth and finish as desired. Attach to the wall with iron angle brackets.

DINING ROOM BUFFET
TABLE
&
BEDROOM BENCH

On my garage sale list of wants and needs was a dining room buffet table. I was finding so many pieces of crystal and silver at the sales that I needed furniture to display all of it.

For years I had wanted a long upholstered bench to put at the end of our king-size bed. Now that I had the big high bed that I always wanted, a bench for the end of the bed was a necessity because I couldn't easily sit on the end of the bed to put my shoes on in the morning!

I had seen both items that I wanted in the showrooms, but the dining room buffet with the marble top was almost $3,000 and to have a bench long enough to accommodate the king-size bed would have to be custom made for around $800. I did see a lot of smaller benches at the showrooms--about half the size I needed, but even these smaller benches upholstered in the type of fabric I wanted would be $300 to $400. Both of these items were much more than I could afford!

My dream of having a dining room buffet table and a king-size bed bench came true for only $28 instead of $3,800!

In just one weekend of garage sale~ing I found all the furniture pieces that I needed to make the marble-topped dining room buffet and the fancy bench for the foot of the bed.

All I needed were three pieces of garage sale furniture.

THE THREE PIECES OF FURNITURE
THAT I USED WERE:

1. A walnut dining room table with French legs.

The top of the old walnut dining room table
was bashed in. More elephants I guess! The
frame was still in good shape and it had the
curved French legs that I wanted. This table
was only $15.

2. A marble-topped coffee table.

The marble was an ivory Travertine and it
was in perfect condition. The table frame
was an Italian style and in usable condition.
The legs were cone-shaped wood and brass
that I would probably use later for another
project. I paid only $8.00 for the table.

3. A small bench with four carved French legs.

This bench was in very bad condition. It
was in several pieces and the top wood was
cracked completely through. The legs were
already removed and lying under the bench
seat. I'm so glad I picked up the old bench
top to see what was underneath. I found
four very beautiful ornate carved French legs
with ball and claw feet. I paid $5.00 for the
bench.

For the dining room buffet I used the dining
room table frame and legs and the marble
top from the coffee table. For the bedroom
bench I used the coffee table frame and the
fancy carved ball and claw French legs from
the old bench.

In one weekend I assembled and finished
both pieces.

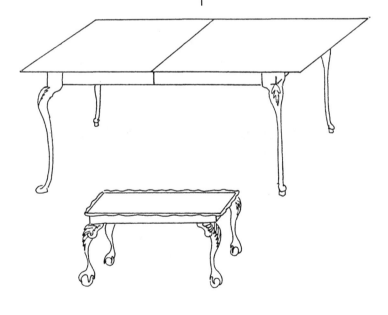

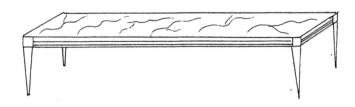

"How To"

DISASSEMBLE A TABLE

Materials needed:
Screwdriver (flathead and Phillips)
Claw tool* (optional)

NOTE: Most tables--dining room tables, coffee tables, table bases--are put together as illustrated below.

1 Turn the table upside down. The legs are removed by removing the large bolt or screw in the center of the angled pieces of wood. There are four smaller screws attaching the angled pieces of wood to the frame. Unscrew the legs from the angle bracket. Unscrew the angle brackets from the frame.

2 Notice the small wood blocks holding the frame to the table top. Unscrew these. The table frame may also be glued to the table top. Use a claw tool to pry the frame free from the table top.

Save and label each part as you remove it.

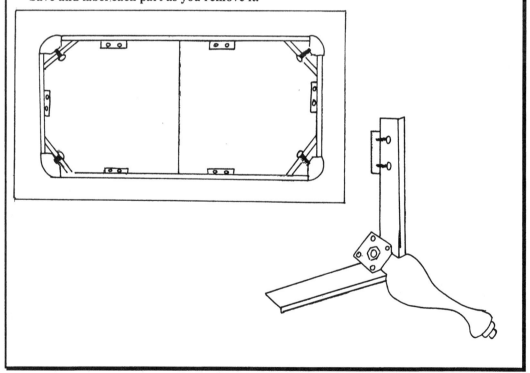

"How To"

MARBLE TOPPED DINING ROOM BUFFET
or
SOFA TABLE

Materials needed:
Old dining room table or coffee table frame and four long legs
Coffee table top or rectangular piece of plywood
Edge molding if using plywood top
Screwdriver
Saw
Glue
Hammer and nails
Embossed wood pieces

1 Turn the table upside down and see how it is put together. You want to take it apart and use just the frame and the legs. It's really easy to take apart once you see how it's put together. See "How To" Disassemble a Table.

2 In the corners of the frame are angled pieces of wood that hold the legs in place. The legs are removed by removing the large bolt or screw in the center of the angled piece of wood. There are four smaller screws attaching this angled piece of wood to the frame. Leave the angled pieces of wood attached to the frame. Just remove the legs.

Measure the frame so that it will fit under the marble top. (You can use any kind of wooden top.) I wanted the marble top to extend over the frame a couple of inches all the way around.

The length of the old table frame was just the right size. The width needed to be made smaller.

Continued . . .

139

3 To make the table narrower, make two cuts in each side section of the frame, and glue and nail a center block of wood into the inside of the frame at the cut.

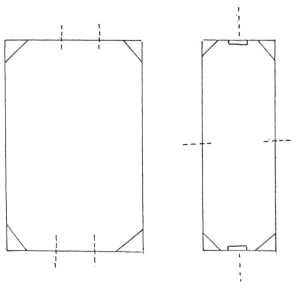

NOTE: If you are using a coffee table frame, you will need a rectangle frame or cut down a square coffee table in the same manner as the dining room table.

4 Reattach the legs by screwing them back into the corner sections. To cover the cut portion of the frame, glue a wooden motif on each side cut and the center front. I used a wooden shell motif. You could also fill the cut seam with plastic wood and sand.

5 I refinished the dark walnut table frame and legs with a cream crackle and set the marble top right on top of the frame.

SO EASY!

"How To"

BEDROOM BENCH

Materials needed:
Frame (old coffee table)
4 legs (old bench legs)
or
a coffee table with rectangular top
Plywood or table top
Fabric
Cording or decorative trim (optional)
3", 4", 5" or 6" upholstery foam
Batting
Electric knife

To make the bench I used a marble-topped coffee table frame and legs that came from an old $5.00 bench.

Ball and claw bench legs were attached to the frame with one long screw that was embedded in the top of the legs. The long screw went into a solid wooden block at each corner of the frame. Luckily the bench legs that I removed had the same long wooden screw at the top of them.

They fit perfectly!

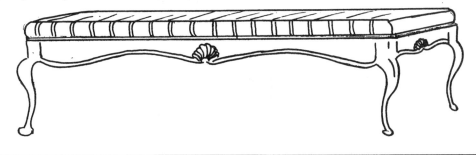

1 Pour wood glue onto the leg screw and screw it into the corner of each frame and let dry thoroughly. When making the final turn, make sure the legs are positioned properly.

Continued . . .

BENCH COVERING

2 Cut a 1" piece of plywood to fit on top of the coffee table frame, or use a coffee table top, or use an existing rectangle coffee table frame complete with legs and just remove the wood table top for covering. The wooden top can extend over the edges of the frame, however for benches I prefer that the wooden top is the exact same dimension as the wood frame. The following directions are for a bench top the exact same dimensions as the frame.

3 Lay a piece of garage sale foam, either 3" or 4" or more (your preference) thick, on the wood top and cut the foam to fit the plywood. A garage sale electric knife works great for cutting foam. The foam should extend to each end of the cut plywood.

Use a good glue or spray adhesive to attach the foam to the plywood or wood top.

4 Lay out a large piece of fabric. Place the large piece of batting on top of the fabric. Place the wood table top with the foam lying on top of the batting. The batting and fabric should be approximately 8" to 10" wider all the way around so it will wrap up and around the sides and over the foam and plywood or wood table. Staple gun the fabric and batting to the underside of the plywood starting in the center of each side and working toward the outside corners. Make a fold at the corners and staple.

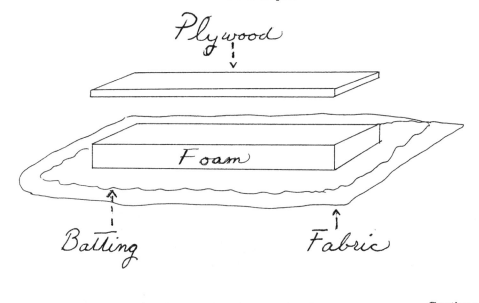

Plywood

Foam

Batting

Fabric

Continued . . .

5 Add cording or tasseled fringe if desired. If you choose cording, sew the cording with matching fabric or use already made braided cord and staple gun it to the edge of the bench frame or staple to the outer edge of the foam-covered wood. Use the same procedure for tassel fringe or staple one large tassel on each of the four corners before attaching the finished seat.

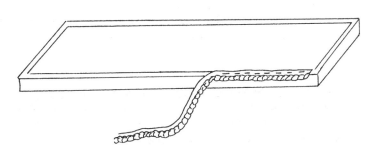

6 Drill a hole in the corner brackets of the frame. Lay the finished bench top on the frame and make a mark on the bottom through the drilled hole. Drill a small starter hole in the bottom of the bench top. Lay the bench top back on the frame and insert a screw into the drilled corner brackets up, into the bench top. Use a screw long enough to penetrate the bottom of the plywood but not so long that it comes out the top of the plywood. OUCH!

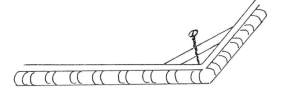

NOTE: Your table frame and legs may be different than this frame and legs. The other style frame and legs is explained in "How To Disassemble A Table" and "How To Make A Sofa Table." See these instructions if you have a different style frame and leg assembly.

"How To"

A QUICK AND EASY BED BENCH

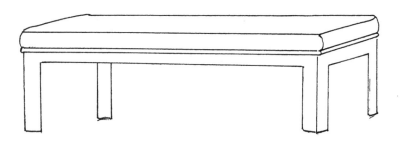

Materials needed:
Straight, block-legged coffee table
1/4" piece of plywood cut in a rectangle*
3" foam for top cushion
Batting
Fabric
Staple gun
Tacky glue, spray adhesive or rubber cement
Electric knife

*The plywood rectangle should measure four to six inches smaller on all four sides than the coffee table top.

The entire coffee table including legs will be covered with fabric. If the legs of the coffee table are removable--remove them and cover the legs separately with the same fabric.

Continued . . .

1 Measure the length and width of the legs and cut fabric with an extra 1/2" or 3/4" of fabric for the top, bottom and side seam. Use spray adhesive, tacky glue or rubber cement to adhere the fabric to the entire leg. If the leg has grooves in it, press the fabric down into the grooves using your fingers, a pencil or a heavy piece of cardboard.

2 Apply tacky glue, spray adhesive or rubber cement to the coffee table frame. Cover the top and sides of the coffee table with fabric using tacky glue, spray adhesive or rubber cement. Wrap the corners--similar to wrapping a present.

Leave enough extra fabric to turn under the edges of the table and glue or staple gun to the inside of the table frame

3 Cut a piece of foam the exact same size as the coffee table top with an electric knife. Center the smaller cut piece of plywood over the foam and glue together. Lay out the fabric covering wrong side up. Lay the batting on top of the fabric. Snugly wrap the fabric and batting around the foam and staple gun to the smaller wood piece. Staple in the center of each side and work out smoothly to each corner, folding over at the corners.

4 Center the foam cushion seat on top of the coffee table top and secure underneath with small 1/4" or 3/8" wood screws.

"How To"

COFFEE TABLE OTTOMAN

Materials needed:
Coffee table (I prefer French legs)
Fabric
3", 4" or 5" foam
Batting
Cording (optional)
Claw tool*

***See glossary**

NOTE: Usually coffee table tops extend out over the frame. You want the top of the ottoman to match the frame proportions exactly. If you are not going to reuse the coffee table top for another project, just cut the outer edges off to match the frame dimensions. The top should sit on top of the frame and match the outside edges.

1 Turn the coffee table upside down and remove the table top. Usually there are small wooden blocks with screws next to the inside table frame. Sometimes the table tops are glued on and need to be pried off with a claw tool. Do this carefully. If there are wooden blocks, unscrew them from the frame portion and leave them attached to the table top if you can. If they are in the way of cutting the top to size, remove them and save for later.

Continued . . .

2 You will probably want to cut the frame and make it smaller. Do this after removing the table top and legs. Cut the frame down at each side so as not to disturb the center design on the frame if there is one. Cut the top to match the frame dimensions or use a piece of plywood or particle board approximately 1" thick. Use small wooden blocks to reattach the cut portions of the frame. Make sure the small wood blocks are at the top edge of the frame. Reattach the legs and apply wood putty to the cut seam if needed.

3 Cut a piece of 3" or 4" foam to match the top piece of wood. Use a garage sale electric knife to cut the foam.

OPTION: For a rounded top edge, cut the top edge of the foam with the electric knife at an angle.

Attach the foam to the wood with tacky glue or spray adhesive. Lay out your fabric wrong side up. Lay batting over the fabric and staple gun to the underside of the top wood. Staple in the center of each side to secure the fabric, then staple out to each corner, folding over at the corners.

If you are going to use cording, stitch the cording now. Cut a piece of cording and a strip of fabric to cover the cording. The cording should wrap all around the edge of the table frame.

Staple gun the cording to the outer edge of the table frame or at the bottom edge of the foam seat. I prefer to staple it to the edge of the table frame.

4 Lay the upholstered top down on the frame; make sure the cording shows around the outer edge and secure the top to the frame by screwing the small wood blocks to the underside of the table top.

"How To"

SOFA TABLE STOOLS

Materials needed:
End table
Fabric
Foam
Batting
Cording (optional)
Claw Tool

1 Follow the exact same steps for Coffee Table Ottoman.

Instead of using a coffee table, use end tables that have higher legs. This is the right height for benches to slide under sofa tables. Buy a pair of old end tables and you have sofa table stools.

"How To"

COFFEE TABLE CANOPY

Materials needed:
Fabric
Staple gun
Rectangle French coffee table
Cove molding*
Quarter round molding* (optional)

***See glossary**

If you've read the coffee table section in this chapter, you already know how many things you can make with coffee tables and all of their parts. You can make a half canopy out of a coffee table with or without the wooden top section.

To make the wooden half canopy, find a French-style coffee table or a table with some carving on the table frame. Turn the table upside down and remove the legs by unscrewing. Save the legs, you will use them for a project later.

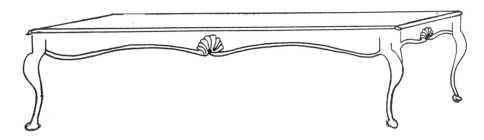

Attach the fabric backing to the wall the same width as the coffee table and extend down past your headboard. Nail the fabric to the wall with small finishing nails. The back fabric can either be smooth or gathered.

Now you have several options.   **OPTIONS**   **"A"**   **"B"**   **"C"**

MY FAVORITE IS OPTION "A".

Any of the options will give you basically the same look. The only difference is in the assembly of the coffee table frame.

Continued . . .

OPTIONS:

A Remove the frame from the table top by unscrewing the small wood blocks that are attached to the top and the sides. Remove the corner leg brackets and the legs. Save all of the parts. Fit the edges of the frame together. Glue the frame and nail the frame together using finishing nails. You need only three sides of the coffee table frame--the front and the two sides, but it's OK to use the entire frame. If the table frame is very ornate you may want to save it to use for something else.

B Follow the instructions for option "A" and connect the frame by using <u>angle brackets</u>. Use a piece of cove molding to fill the outside corner space. You can use quarter round molding if you can find a piece wide enough to fit the open space. Cut the bottom of the molding to match the bottom of the frame.

Quarter   *Cove*

C Remove only the table legs. Do not remove the table top. Insert and glue a large piece of cove molding into the section where the legs were removed. Cut the bottom of the molding to match the bottom of the table frame.

Continued . . .

1 You can use the table top or leave it off. If the table top extends more than three inches from the frame it's best to leave it off. Finish as desired and screw the coffee table frame to your ceiling. Make sure you attach the frame to the stud work in the ceiling.

2 If you choose not to use the table top, attach the small wood blocks to the top edge of the table frame with wood screws. Attach the wood blocks to the ceiling with long wood screws. Make sure you screw into a stud and not just the ceiling plaster.

Use a plain gathered piece of fabric for the front and side portions of the canopy, a balloon or Austrian style topper, along with the table and side fabric panels.
Staple gun the topper valance along the inside sides and front of the wood frame. Staple gun long rectangles of fabric (sheets or garage sale draperies) along the sides of the inside portion of the coffee table frame.

"How To"

HEADBOARD

Materials needed:
2 six-panel doors (each door should be 1/2 the width of the bed)
3 strips of fluted molding, sometimes called casing (door height)
3/4" x 2" strip of wood (double door width)
Crown molding
2 matching outside crown corners and 3 wood rosettes (optional)
2---1 x 3's (door height)
Wood glue
←- 3 heavy duty metal straps & screws
Saw
Finishing nails

I know you've seen this wonderful bed in either magazines or stores. It sells for over $2,000 and I can show you how to make it for under $200 if using brand new doors. If you can find two matching six-panel doors at garage sales--then you can probably make it for under $50!

1 Lay the doors out on a large flat surface with the door knob hole on the outside. Apply a coat of wood glue to the inside edges of the doors and press together tightly. Screw a metal strap bracket to the top, middle and bottom of the door backs to hold them together. Let the wood glue dry.

Turn the double doors over to the right side. Nail a 1 x 3 to the outside edges of the doors. Cut the plain piece of wood so it matches the exact top width of the double doors plus the 1 x 3's. Attach the piece of plain wood all the way across the top using wood glue and finishing nails. Let dry.

2 Attach the three wood rosettes to each end and the center top directly under the thin strip of wood. Use wood glue and finishing nails. There should not be any space between the rosettes and the wood strip. Attach the three strips of fluted molding to the front outside edge, covering the door knob hole and attach a strip of fluted molding down the center seam, making sure the fluted molding fits right under the rosettes. Use wood glue and finishing nails to attach the molding.

3 Attach crown molding to the top plain wood molding, bringing it around the sides. Use the optional pre-cut outside corner crown molding if you do not want to miter the crown molding yourself. Attach the molding with finishing nails.

4 Finish as desired. *See the Finishing chapter for ideas.*

Attach this magnificent headboard to the wall. Make a matching footboard using the bottom portion of six panel doors or cut the bottom portion off of your headboard doors. Attach 2 x 4's to the bottom of the headboard to achieve the right height. Lay a flat board across the top of the footboard and secure with wood glue and finishing nails. Attach the headboard to the footboard with wood boards the size of your mattress.

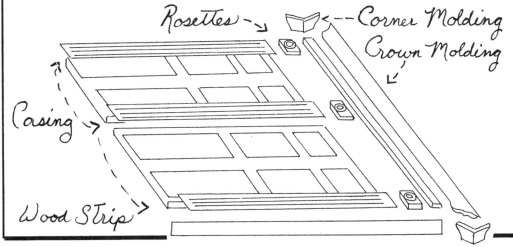

Rosettes →   ←-- Corner Molding

Crown Molding

Casing →

Wood Strip →

COFFEE TABLE SHELF

COFFEE TABLE VALANCES

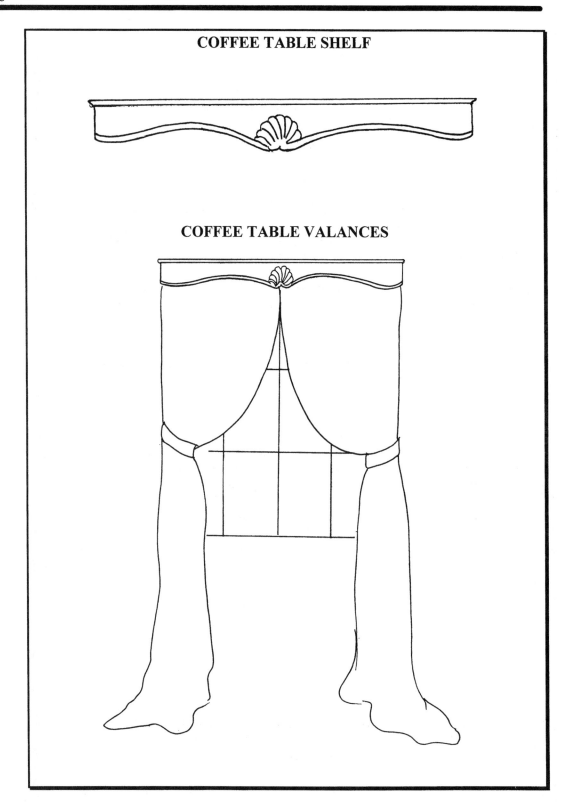

"How To"

COFFEE TABLE SHELF
OR
COFFEE TABLE WINDOW VALANCES

Materials needed:
Coffee table with nice frame (I prefer French)
Saw
Wood cutting blade**
Wood glue
2 small iron angle brackets
2 larger iron angle brackets
Screwdriver

*See glossary
**See the tools section in this chapter

1 Turn the coffee table upside down and remove the legs. Unscrew the small wood blocks from the table frame and table top. Remove the top. See "How To" Disassemble A Table in this chapter.

2 Cut the sides of the coffee table frame in half. If you want to get two matching valances or shelves--the frame will need to be cut in half.

3 Attach the long or front frame to the two cut side pieces of frame with wood glue and angle brackets.

4 Cut the coffee table top in half lengthwise or smaller if you wish. Make sure it's the right dimensions to sit on the new size half frame.

5 Reattach the small wood blocks to the inside frame and the cut table top.

6 Sand any rough edges and finish as desired. *See the Finishes chapter.*

7 Attach to the wall with large angle brackets at each end of the old table frame.

CABINET OR CHEST BASE

Turn a plain ordinary cabinet or chest into a decorator piece by putting fancy legs under it or attach a coffee table frame with legs to the bottom of the chest or cabinet. Use either a wood table or wrought iron.

FOOTSTOOLS

Just as we made the bed bench you can make several different styles of footstools and ottomans with small coffee table legs and frames. Remember . . . you can always cut the frame down to any size and reattach the legs.

Follow the directions for the bed bench. You may want to place a thick down & feather pillow on top of the foam for a luxurious look and feel.

There are lots of little square tables that are just the right size to make dressing table benches or benches to place under sofa tables. Cover the wood tops with foam, batting and staple gun fabric over all.

If you prefer the straight or blocked table leg, consider covering the entire frame and legs with the same fabric used on top. Adhere to the frame and legs with a spray adhesive, tacky glue or rubber cement. Keep your eye on the clothing rack and stock up on garage sale drapes!

An old piano bench makes a great bed bench. It even has storage! Put a padded seat on top. Glue fabric to the entire bench or finish as you desire. Mix and match legs.

ALWAYS ASK . . .

WHAT CAN I DO WITH THIS?

WHAT CAN I MAKE OUT OF THIS?

HOW CAN I MAKE THIS WORK FOR ME?

UPDATING COFFEE TABLES

Every designer showroom is filled with wood and iron furniture. It's a new look and one that is very easy to do. You can dress up your plain wood coffee tables, end tables, shelves or mirrors with fancy metal plant holders that you find for 25¢ at sales. You may need to paint the plant holders black or verdigris or any style finish that looks good to you. Your furniture and accessories will have a whole new look!

OTTOMANS

There is a resurgence of wonderful ottomans in every size, shape, and style. They were very popular in the 50s and 60s and very expensive. They are even more popular today and a lot more expensive. Depending on the fabric used, ottomans can run over $1,000. You can mail order the small ones starting around $100.

I've made several different style ottomans for our home and for my friends. One of my favorites is a "pouf" ottoman!

"POUF" OTTOMAN

I had been wanting a "pouf" ottoman for a long time and had priced several in decorator showrooms. I knew exactly what I wanted and felt confident that I could easily make one, but first, I had to find either an old round ottoman or something round to use as a base.

One day I found it--a 30" round ottoman with wonderful heavy duty castors. It was covered in an old greasy avocado green vinyl. You've probably seen one of these before. I tried to purchase it for 50¢ but I could tell the elderly gentlemen seller was emotionally attached to it. I ended up paying the full $1.00 price! The castors alone were worth $10! When my husband saw it, he thought I had lost my mind and all this garage sale~ing had finally affected my brain. What in the world could I possibly do with such an ugly, horrible avocado vinyl ottoman? He was amazed and pleasantly surprised. I took a utility knife and removed the ugly green vinyl to see exactly how the ottoman frame was put together. .The first step is to unscrew the castors from the bottom of the ottoman. Remove the bottom dust cover--it is probably attached with staples. You will probably see a sisal cord or rope stapled to the bottom piece of wood. This cord holds the top center button in place. Remove the staples and pull the top center ottoman button off along with the sisal cord. You will reuse these.

Remember . . . it's important to take things apart to see how they are made, then, it's much easier to put them back together again. Make a list of all the supplies you will need to put it back together again, label each piece and the order in which it was removed.

Once you remove the outer fabric from the round ottomans you will probably find two round pieces of wood, one on the bottom and one on the top portion. Inserted between the two pieces of wood rounds are wood strips that hold the two wood rounds together. Sometimes the center is filled with straw. Each ottoman is made differently. The instructions below will work for wood ottomans or ottomans filled with straw.

I've found that the easiest way to cover round pouf ottomans is to cut another round piece of wood the same diameter as the bottom wood round. A thin 1/4" thick piece of plywood will do nicely.

We will remake the ottoman in two pieces using the new wood round to make the round top cap portion and simply recover the existing bottom portion with new fabric and lots of special trim.

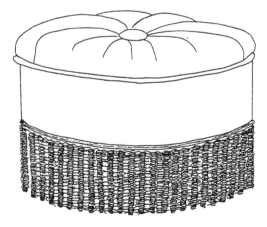

"How To"

POUF OTTOMAN

Materials needed:
Old round ottoman
Fabric
1 or 2 wood rounds (same dimensions as bottom wood round)
Staple gun
Glue gun
Screwdriver
Drill
Cording, decorative trim
Bullion fringe*
Stuffing or polyester fiber
Batting

*See glossary

1 Measure the bottom wood round on the existing ottoman and cut another wood round the same diameter. A 1/4" piece of plywood will do just fine. Drill a small hole in the exact center of this wood round.

2 Cut a strip of fabric the circumference of the round wooden circle plus 2" for a side seam allowance and an extra 3" on both the top and bottom. Cut a piece of batting the same size without the seam allowance. Turn the raw edge of the side seam fabric under. Lay the batting over the fabric and staple to the underside of the bottom piece of wood round and to the top side of the middle piece of wood round. If there was no top piece of wood--just straw then lay the extra wood round down on the straw with some glue squeezed all over it. The glue will keep the wood round from shifting. Make sure all wood rounds have the small center hole. No sewing involved here, just stapling.

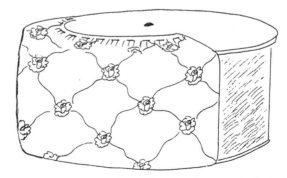

Continued . . .

3 Cut another strip of fabric the circumference of the round wooden circle plus 2" for a side seam allowance. Measure 1/2 the diameter of the wood. round and add 12 inches. This is the width of your fabric for the round "pouf" cap. Staple gun one edge of the fabric to the bottom of the extra wood round.

E.g.,If the diameter is 30,"
   one half is 15"
   15" + 12" is <u>27.</u>"

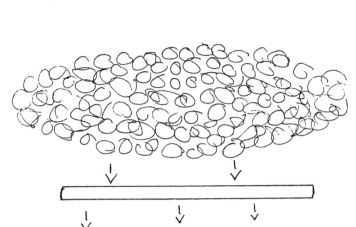

4 Before attaching the top cap wood round to the ottoman's top wood round, attach fabric covered cording or decorative fringe to the top wooden edge of the ottoman. Attach the top cap by reaching down through the top fabric sleeve and screw the two wood rounds tightly together. The top cap portion should now be firmly attached with the cording or decorative fringe falling around the edges. The top portion of fabric will be an open sleeve that you will fill with foam and stuffing.

5 Cut a piece of 1", 2" or 3" foam to match the diameter of the wood round. Put tacky glue or spray adhesive of the top of the wood round and lay the foam piece on top. Let dry.

6 Stuff the sleeve with heavy duty stuffing or polyester fiber. I hope you have one of those garage sale floor pillows in your basement just filled with wonderful heavy duty stuffing.
(*See the pillow section in the Accessories chapter.*)
Stuff the fabric sleeve full, fuller, then stuff in some more.

Continued . . .

7 Hold fabric sleeve up straight and pin at the four corners. Staple each corner top at the center of the top round. **LEAVE THE CENTER HOLE OPEN. DO NOT STAPLE FABRIC OVER THE CENTER HOLE.** For each quarter section, staple in equidistant pleats. Staple all the way around the center hole leaving the hole open. You may need help for this. You want the top cap to be taut and stuffed very, very full. How full depends on how big you want this top cap to be. If you have too much fabric at the top, making the cap portion too big, cut it down to your liking. You want a nice rounded top and the extra 12" of fabric just may be too much. It's better to cut fabric off than to be short!

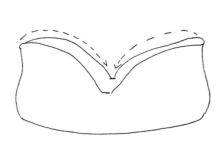 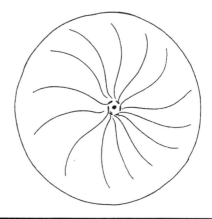

8 Cover the large center button with matching fabric by cutting a circle slightly larger than the button. Attach the fabric with a glue gun. Let dry thoroughly.

9 Thread the center button with the long piece of sisal. Attach the doubled sisal cord to a long piece of heavy wire--long enough to go through the ottoman and out the bottom hole. Pull the sisal cord and button as tight as you can. The button should completely cover the center staples. Staple gun the sisal cord to the bottom wood round.

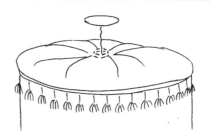

10 Reattach the bottom dust cover with staples and reattach the bottom castors. Attach bullion fringe to the lower portion of the ottoman with a glue gun or make a tailored pleated skirt or a gathered skirt.

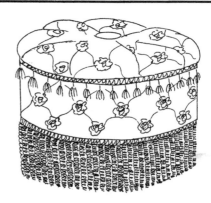

TUFFETS

Tuffets are a lot of fun to make and so very easy. Tuffets are the little stools that you can use for resting your feet, to sit upon, to climb into those great big high beds, or to lay a glass slipper on! Tuffets come in all different sizes, shapes, and styles. You will probably want to have a different style tuffet for every room. All of the tuffet parts can be found at garage sales.

For the "Pouf" tuffet I use the round table tops that are on the round particle board tables with three legs--the kind that you cover with a skirt. I find these tables all the time at sales for 25¢ or 50¢. Unscrew the legs and use them later for another project.

It's easy to find little stools at sales that are really beat up. They probably will have four old-fashioned cone-shaped legs. This would make a great step stool for that big high bed. Cover the top with foam, batting and an elegant fabric. Make a tailored skirt to hide the legs or glue elegant bullion fringe around the top edge of the seat. I found a wonderful piece of flowered needlepoint at a sale. It was an old-fashioned Victorian Cabbage Rose pattern and a small part of the edge was not finished. The large piece of needlework was lovingly wrapped in plastic and had a price sticker of 50¢. The seller was an elderly gentleman and he told me his wife had passed away many years ago and he finally decided it was time to get rid of some things, including this lovely needlepoint that his wife never got to finish. I put it down not wanting him to part with it but he insisted that I take it and wanted to know what I would do with it. I told him that someday I would put it on a beautiful stool or just the right antique chair. It's still wrapped up in plastic waiting for something very special.

The "Cinderella" slipper tuffet I bought for $2.00 at a sale. It was a perfect square shape and had beautiful little gold French legs. I removed the awful lime green corduroy and replaced it with a more suitable fabric. I planned to reassemble the tuffet just as I do with everything I take apart. But it soon became a real pain and I found a much better, easier way to recover this tuffet. The following instructions show you the easier way and will give you the exact same results! Use plenty of imagination when making tuffets. They are easy and fun and use the fabric that you find in garage sale dresses. I especially like to use lots of fancy trims, fringe and tassels on the tuffets.

ROUND "POUF" TUFFET

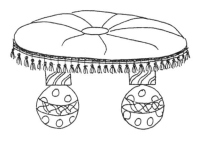

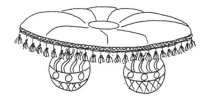

CINDERELLA TUFFET

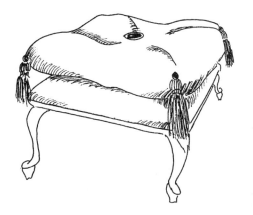

"How To"

ROUND "POUF" TUFFET
SHELLEY'S TUFFET

Materials needed:
4 Fence post tops (newels)
4 small wood salad bowls
4-4" lag bolts or wood screws
1-20" diameter wood round (plywood or particle board)
2-5" wood rounds
sisal (cord)
thick piece of 22" diameter foam
batting and fabric
primer, craft paint & polyurethane

Staple gun, glue gun, crescent wrench or screwdriver
Drill, electric knife

NOTE: All of the items needed to make the "pouf" tuffet were found at sales. The total cost of the tuffet including fabric and trim was $6.00! This designer style tuffet is $800 at the design shops.

1 Drill a center hole in large wood round and in one small wood round. Drill a center hole in the 4 salad bowls and fence post tops (if needed). The fence post tops should already have a hole in them.

Lay the salad bowls on top of the large wood round in a square. Insert a pencil in the center holes and make a mark. Drill through the large wood round at each of the 4 marks. If your fence post tops have a screw in them, use pliers and remove. Drill 2 holes, 2 inches apart in the extra small wood round.

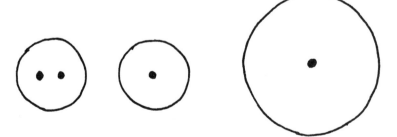

Continued . . .

2 Prime and paint fence post tops and salad bowls. I used purple and gray stripes for the salad bowls, black and cream checkerboard pattern on the upper section of the fence post tops and cream with pink dots for the ball part.

Polyurethane several coats on the painted surfaces for a shiny, porcelain type finish.

3 Insert 4" screws or bolts into the 4 drilled holes in the large wood round and attach the salad bowl and fence post top to the underside
Tighten the screws or the bolts.
This is your base.

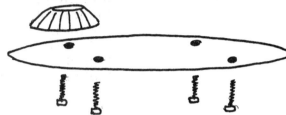

Lay large wood round with feet attached upside down on top of the foam.
Draw around the wood using a marker.
Draw another circle about 2 inches outside of the first round circle.

Place small wood round in center and draw a circle about 1 inch larger.

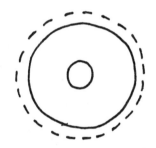

4 Using the electric knife, shape the foam into a doughnut by angling the knife from the outer circle into the inner circle. This will round and soften the edges and give the foam a doughnut shape. Cut the center of the doughnut in a cone shape with the large part of the cone being on top. Cut all the way through the foam doughnut in the center.

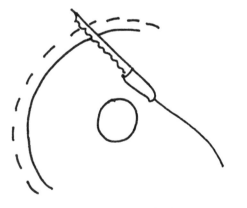

Continued . . .

5 Lay batting on top of foam. Cut a hole in the center of the batting and trim to fit all around the doughnut. Cut a strip of fabric the circumference of the wood round base and add an extra 2 inches. It's better to make this measurement too big than too small!.

Measure the width of the fabric by going inside the center hole to the wood round base and over the doughnut to the outside edge. Add an extra 6 inches. Use sheets, skirts, dresses, old drapes or purchase fabric.

Staple gun the length of the fabric to the outside edge of the second small plain wood round making small gathers. Turn under at fabric edge and overlap so there is no raw fabric edge.

Push the fabric attached small wood round down in the center hole of the doughnut. It doesn't have to go all the way down. Arrange the fabric around the doughnut, pulling down and around to the bottom edge of the tuffet base.

6 String a 36" length of sisal cord through the two holes in the smaller wood round, which is your center button. Glue gun a smaller circle of batting and fabric over and around the underside of the smaller wood round. Remember to leave the cord hanging from the bottom of your fabric covered "button".

Place fabric covered center button over the fabric covered doughnut hole and pull sisal cord down tightly through center hole of large wood round base. Staple tightly to the underside of wood round base. This will hold your fabric in place.

7 Pull fabric tightly all around the doughnut and staple gun to the edge of the large wood round base. Trim excess fabric and glue gun desired fringe around the stapled edge.

"How To"

CINDERELLA TUFFET

Materials needed:
4 small French legs
15" square piece of wood 1 inch thick
15" square of 2" foam
Center button
Sisal or strong household string
15" square pillow**
Fabric
4 Tassels
Non-fray product*
Electric knife

**If you don't have a 15" square pillow, see the pillows section in the Accessories chapter and make one. If you have a different size pillow--16", 17" or 18" square--use it and change the wood measurement to match the size of the pillow that you do have. The pillow should be very full and thick.

* See glossary

1 Using an electric knife, slice off the top edge of the foam square for a rounded edge.

Drill a center hole in the square piece of wood. Cut a small hole in the center of the foam and attach it to the wood with tacky glue or spray adhesive. Let dry.

2 Lay out a square piece of fabric, approximately 20" square, good side down. Lay out a square of batting on top of the fabric. Lay the foam-covered wood on top, pull the fabric over the sides and staple the fabric to the underside of the wooden square by stapling in the center section of each side. Make a fold at each corner and staple gun securely all the way around. Cut a small hole in center of fabric for center button. Squeeze a small ribbon of non-fray product around the small hole to prevent fraying.

Continued . . .

3 Cover the pillow with the same fabric. Do not put a zipper in the pillow casing. Stitch a silk tassel in each corner of the pillow. After completely finishing the pillow, cut a small hole through the exact center of the pillow. Put a ribbon of a non-fray product around the hole on both sides of the pillow. Use it if you are afraid the pillow fabric will tear or fray.

4 Cover the center button with fabric using a hot glue gun and thread sisal through the button. Using a strong piece of wire pull the sisal with the button through the pillow holes and the foam-covered base. Pull tightly and attach to the bottom piece of wood with a staple gun.

Put a liner on the wood bottom with a staple gun or glue.

5 Attach the small French legs with a screw driver to the bottom wood base.

NOTE: This is such an easy way to make the Cinderella tuffet and you have the exact same
        results as the complicated way!

MORE TUFFETS

CHAIR LEGS

I've found wonderful chairs that people were giving away FREE because a leg was missing or the family dog was teething!

It's easy to replace a bad leg or two. Measure the height of the leg and note how it is attached to the chair. Start shopping the sales for all kinds of damaged furniture until you find just the right fit and style.

Chair legs are often interchangeable. When you go to the furniture store and order dining room chairs, sometimes you have the option of picking out the style of leg. A Cabriole French style, Chippendale, Italian, ball and claw, straight leg, or upholstered leg.

It's easy to change the look of furniture just by changing the legs. When you see chairs at garage sales, look at the pieces of each chair instead of the whole chair. Look at the legs. How are they attached? What do they look like. If Fido chewed to bits a wonderful leg and you thought your chair was ruined, go ahead and sell it in your garage sale for a couple of dollars. I will buy the chair, replace the leg and have a beautiful new chair. Start thinking small . . . piece by piece.

UPHOLSTERED LEGS

Upholstered legs are another "no-brainer"! You usually find this technique used on a square box leg.

Measure the length and width of leg and cut fabric with an extra 1/2" or 3/4" of fabric for the top, bottom and side seam. If the legs are removable, remove them and cover with fabric using a spray adhesive and tacky glue for the edges. If they are not removable, use an iron and press the fabric edge under an extra 1/2" or 3/4" for a nice finished edge

and use tacky glue, rubber cement or spray adhesive to attach the fabric to the leg. If the leg has grooves in it, press the fabric down into the grooves using your fingers, a pencil or a heavy piece of cardboard.

You can use this same technique on any size square leg table. Cover them all over with fabric. Cover the table top, frame and legs. There is no sewing involved, just glue. Use a burlap or muslin fabric for a casual look, a wonderful decorator print or silk moiré and brocades for an elegant look. Cover the top with glass if desired.

HUTCHES and SIDEBOARDS

If you are lucky enough to have a big country kitchen I've got a wonderful project for you. Why don't you make a big country hutch to hold all of your garage sale collectibles? Make the kind of hutch that costs several thousand dollars in the store. It should cost only $50 to $75! I'll show you how!

After spending several weekends sale~ing and seeing waterbed after waterbed that no one wanted, I realized I could have the hutch of my dreams!

There are so many things you can do with old waterbeds and you can find them for next to nothing. There are lots of good pieces of thick wood to use, drawers, and that wonderful big back piece with shelves, sometimes cabinets, sometimes a mirror, sometimes even a light in the top. Waterbeds have lots of good things to work with.

I used the large back portion of a bed for the back of a hutch. It had a light in the center top and small shelves coming down each side with one cabinet section on each side. It had the drawers that went under the bed which I used for the hutch drawers.

I had everything I needed for the hutch except legs. No problem. I found an old beat up table that had four good strong legs. They were a thick colonial spindle type leg that would be perfect! Don't worry about finding matching woods. You can paint over everything and antique it. Look at the drawings and see how easy it is to assemble. It's heavy--you'll need help, but basically it's very easy.

If you can find a sturdy sofa table, most of your work will be already done. The style of your hutch will change depending on the type leg you use. Dress it up by adding embossed wood motifs.

Let's put this hutch together and then I'll show you what else you can do with old waterbeds.

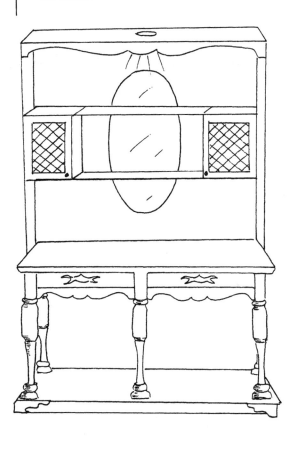

169

"How To"

"WATERBED HUTCH"

Materials needed:
Waterbed back
Waterbed drawers
Table top or 1" plywood or sofa table
Screwdriver
Nails
Small wood blocks or wood strips
Table frame if not using sofa table
4 large legs* (French or Colonial)
Trim molding (optional)
Embossed wood trim (optional)
Corner brackets (if making your own frame)

NOTE: If using a sofa table for a base you do not need legs or a table frame, nor will you use the waterbed drawers.

1 On top of the drawer assembly nail a large sheet of plywood or wooden planks, or--if you can find one large enough--an old rectangular coffee table top. If you use a sheet of plywood, trim the raw edges with molding.

2 Make a frame out of 1 x 3's or 1 x 4's or use a large table frame.

> NOTE: The local wood worker's shop recommended using 1½" x 3" oak for the frame to prevent bowing. This is usually a special order size of wood. You will need to decide how heavy the top portion will be.

Resize the frame to fit flush with the drawer assembly and sides of the hutch. Attach the frame to the bottom of the drawer assembly. Attach the legs to the corners of the frame with a screwdriver or wing nut. See "How To" Disassemble A Table in this chapter. It will help you assemble your frame and legs.

NOTE: If you make your own frame, buy the corner leg brackets at a wood working store.

Continued . . .

3 Take a look at the back portion of the waterbed. This will be the back and sides of the hutch. If it is too tall for your room, you may need to cut some of it off at the bottom. Remember to use a good quality blade. See the tools section at the beginning of this chapter.

4 Set the waterbed top on top of the base. Attach wood strips, wood blocks or molding to the inside bottom of the waterbed back and sides with finishing nails and wood glue. Let dry thoroughly. Screw the wood strips down onto the top of the wooden base. This is what secures the large back to the base.

5 Finish as desired. I like the "200-year-old pine" finish.

See the Finishes chapter.

OPTIONS

If there are cabinets on the waterbed back, you can remove the center insert portion of the cabinet door and replace with chicken wire. Staple gun the chicken wire to the back of the door.

Add shelving all the way across the back of the waterbed back for more shelf space.

If the waterbed has a mirrored back, leave the mirror or remove it--your choice.

Fill with all of your garage sale treasures--copper pots, dried flowers, pottery, ceramic dishes, cookbooks, silver, candleholders, oil lamps, tin ware, linens and tablecloths.

"How To"

WATERBED HALL TREES

Materials needed:
Tall waterbed back with mirror
Small coffee table
or
Table top
Frame
Legs
or
Bench
Flat decorative molding
1 x 3's
Wood glue

The same waterbed can also be cut down in size and used to make a hall tree.

You will want to find a waterbed back that has a mirror in it.

1 Make a cut on each side of the mirror, approximately 6" to 1 foot from the edge of the mirror. If the waterbed back has side shelves that you want to keep, make another lengthwise cut close to the shelving.

2 Nail the 1 x 3's to the back of the cut and join the two pieces together. Make sure the nails you use do not go all the way through to the front of the hall tree. To cover the seam in the front use a piece of flat decorative molding or fluted molding (casing) and attach with wood glue and finishing nails.

3 Make a bottom similar to the hutch bottom, but use shorter legs or attach to a bench. You want this to be a comfortable height to sit on.

> NOTE: Be careful when joining your two side pieces. This might affect the top back piece of the waterbed molding. If there is a wooden top piece across the back of the waterbed, you may want to remove this first, cut it down to size and then reattach.
>
> Finish as desired.

OPTIONS

Make a cushion to put on top of the wooden shelf, which is now a wooden bench.

Attach wood or brass hooks on the sides of the mirror to hang hats, coats and things.

"How To"

BOOKSHELF PLATE HOLDER

Materials needed:
Wood bookshelf
3/4" round wood dowels
Finishing nails
Wood edge molding

Optional:
Fabric
Wallpaper
Gimp*

*See glossary and the Upholstery chapter

1 Measure and cut the wood edge molding the same length as the inside shelves. Do this for each shelf. Apply wood glue to the bottom edge of the molding and place on each shelf halfway back. Let dry. Also, insert two small finishing nails into the molding to hold it in place.

Continued . . .

2 Measure and cut the wood dowels the length of the inside of the book shelves. Place them approximately 3 or 4 inches higher than a shelf, right over the edge molding. Nail them to the inside of the bookshelf from the outside using finishing nails. Cover the small nail marks with wood putty and sand smooth. Finish as desired and mount on wall or place on top of a table or cabinet.

OPTIONS

Apply crown molding to the top edge of the book shelf for a dressier look.

Apply casing molding and rosettes to the front side edges of the book shelf.

Cut the bottom sides of the book shelf into a curved shape. Add a round wooden dowel for towels or screw in cup hooks on the bottom of the shelf and hang cups.

3 Paint or refinish the entire shelf, inside and out.

Some popular painting techniques are:

TWO TONE:

Outside:	Dark hunter green
Inside:	Golden yellow
Distress:	Brown stain

Outside:	Slate blue
Inside:	Gray
Distress:	Black walnut stain

Outside:	Warm golden brown
Inside:	Warm golden brown
Molding:	Black
Distress:	Black walnut stain

OTHER TECHNIQUES:

Apply wall paper to the inside back and sides.

Apply fabric to the inside back and walls with spray adhesive or staple gun.

Cover the staples with gimp*

REPAIRING CANE FURNITURE

My friend, Michaela, found two beautiful French princess chairs at a sale. The seat and back were caned but unfortunately the cane had ripped out in the chair seats.

She took them to a furniture repairman and he said it would be around $180 to re-cane the chairs--$180 EACH! The seat was small and the amount to be re-caned was approximately a 12 inch square but it is hard to find people who can cane.

When Michaela told me about the chairs and how expensive it would be to have them recaned, I asked her, "Why not recane them yourself? I know a way to recane the chairs that will be very inexpensive."

How many lovely pieces of furniture have you passed up or even sold at your own garage sale where the cane was torn or ripped out and you couldn't afford to have it fixed? I've found beautiful old rocking chairs and lovely French bedroom chairs for only $2.00 just because the cane was torn. If you see a treasure with sagging cane, go ahead and buy it. You can usually get the cane to tighten up by soaking it with a sponge of hot water and allowing it to dry thoroughly. Sponge the underside of the cane. Repeat this process until the cane is stretched tightly again.

You can purchase sheets of manufactured cane and spline (the thin reed with a rounded top that is used to edge and hold the cane in place) at your local craft shop.

Spline comes in many sizes, so before purchasing, measure the size of the groove surrounding the area to be caned. The spline should be a snug fit and just a tiny bit smaller than the groove size so it fits snugly into the groove.

The same cane that you purchase in sheets at craft stores is easily found at garage sales in old kitchen chairs. I know you've seen these chairs with the metal tubing frame and caned back and seat. You might even own a few of these chairs yourself!

I've even seen this type of chair on the sidewalk for the trash man to pick up just because the cane was torn. If it is the small back piece of cane that is torn, grab the chair. You want to use the larger bottom piece of cane.

Some of the cane pieces that you find require a different type of cane than the small manufactured cane. It's a little harder to find a match but you can if you keep looking.

Where do you look?

Check out old coffee tables, end tables or sofa tables. Some of them have cane inserts and are covered with glass. Look for the tables that are really beaten up and hope that the glass is broken. You will be able to purchase them very reasonably. Remember, right now all we're interested in is the cane. We don't really care about the rest of the table or what kind of shape it's in. Although there are plenty of things you can do with those tables once you've removed the cane.

See the Decorating Your Rooms chapter.

Look for high-backed dining room chairs with a cane backing that is pulling out or torn. Usually this is a very large piece of cane and quite useable. The important thing to remember about cane when shopping at sales is to match the cane that you have. Cane comes in different designs.

Make a small drawing of your particular type of cane and carry this with you.

"How To"

REMOVE OLD CANE

Materials needed:
X-ACTO knife or utility knife*
Chisel
Water

***See glossary**

1 Use a utility knife or X-ACTO knife and cut along the outside edge of the spline to separate it out of the groove. Remove all of the old spline with a chisel.

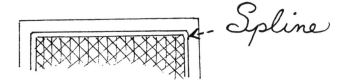

2 Soften the remaining old glue and any pieces of old cane with water and remove the old glue so you have a clean groove in which to place the new cane and spline.

50¢ Lampshades in 2 minutes!.......p. 114

Old feather dusters make great feathered lampshades

Miniature Lace Lamp shades p. 116

All with garage sale throwaways... skirts, blouses, stretch tights, vegetable bags, bracelets, feathers dusters, ponytail holders..

Half Crown Canopy...p. 44

Restored Picture Frame...p. 101

Bedroom Chest...p. 35

Fabric Half Canopy...p. 46

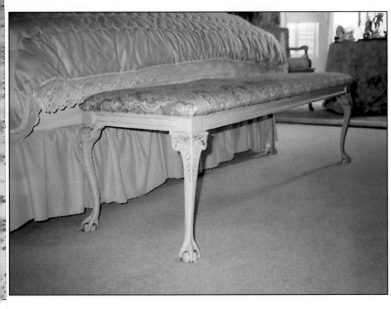

Candelabras....p. 118

Electric...$8.00!

Non-electric...$4.00!

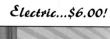

Non-electric...$1.50!

Electric...$6.00!

Shelley's Showcase Home
All Garage Sale Makeovers!

"How To"

INSTALL CANE

Materials needed:
Sheet of cane
Hot water
Thin wood pieces or wooden clothespins
White wood glue
X-ACTO knife or utility knife*

***See glossary**

1 Soak the sheet of cane in hot water to make it pliable. Soak for 1-2 hours.

2 Center the cane over the area to be caned.

3 Start at the front center section of area to be caned and push the cane into the groove with a small piece of wood. Half of a wooden clothes pin is what the professionals recommend. (I bought a whole bag of clothes pins at a sale for 10¢.) Keep tucking the cane down into the groove and securing with wood for a few inches. Make sure the piece of cane goes all the way down into the groove and curves up alongside the outer edges of the groove.

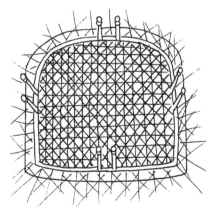

Pull the cane tight to the back portion, making sure the cane design is lying straight.

Secure the cane in place as above to the back portion with wood or clothes pins for a few inches. Let's do the sides.

Continued . . .

4 Tap the cane into the groove a couple of inches at a time, then push down a piece of wood to secure it. Do this in the center of each side for approximately 2 to 4 inches. Make sure you pull the cane snugly.

Start at the center portion of the front, back and sides and work the rest of the cane into the groove, moving from the center to each corner section.

5 Trim the cane using a utility knife, X-ACTO knife or a very sharp chisel. You want to trim the cane right below the outside edge of the groove. Do not push your utility knife or chisel down to the bottom of the groove. Your chisel or knife will be at an angle pressed toward the back edge of the groove, not pressed down.

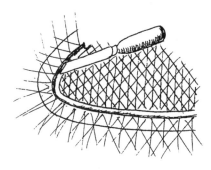

6 Gently remove some of your wood pieces and pour lots of white wood glue into the groove. Remember . . . the glue dries clear, wipe away any excess.

7 Cut a piece of spline to go all the way around your project plus an extra 6 inches.

Starting in the middle of the back section, use a small hammer and a small piece of wood to tap the spline down into the groove. Make sure the spline is down flush with the wood frame. Do this all the way around until you are back at your starting point. Cut off the excess spline with very sharp scissors or your X-ACTO knife.

Let dry for 24 hours. The cane should become tighter and tighter as it dries thoroughly.

CHAPTER FIVE

UPHOLSTERING

CHAIR SEATS

CHAIR WEBBING

SEATS, BACKS, ARM PADS

REMOVE OLD FABRIC

CLUB CHAIRS

Upholstering is something I have always wanted to learn. If you've ever priced what it costs to have a chair re-upholstered, you would know how expensive it can be. Having your favorite chair recovered every few years can really add up, so I decided it was something I needed to learn how to do.

Much to my surprise my husband had always wanted to learn how to re-upholster too, so we decided to buy a book on upholstering and give it a try.

We read the book . . . we read the book again . . . we read the book some more. We learned a lot of new terms, and ended up reading some more! Upholstering seemed to be an overwhelming and very difficult thing to learn. I had a lot of doubts after reading everything you've ever wanted to know about "tying springs," "railroading" and "webbing," etc. It was just much more than I thought I could do and believe me it was, and is much more than you will ever HAVE to do!

Luckily the chair that was to be our first attempt cost only $1.00, so I thought, "What have I got to lose?" I was determined to give it a try.

Upholstering is a lot easier than you think, and it is a lot easier than picking up an entire encyclopedia on re-upholstering as I did. Upholstering is definitely easier than making a slipcover, which requires a lot of intricate measuring, fitting, refitting, and stitching. Upholstering is mostly stapling and gluing and it requires only straight stitching. There is nothing fancy or difficult to do. If you can sew a straight line and handle a staple gun, you can upholster. Once you have mastered the instructions in this book for upholstering club chairs, you can apply the exact same techniques to upholster any chair, love seat, sofa, or just about any type of fabric furniture.

Start looking for chairs that have the dirtiest, most ripped and torn fabric that you can find. You'll be able to get this kind of chair really cheap, maybe even FREE. This will be perfect for your first attempt. Sit in the chair and make sure it's not lumpy. Make sure the springs are not popping out of the top or bottom. Make sure it's comfortable, and it's the size and style you want. Remember . . . you're going to recover the chair and it will be beautiful again.

The chair that I found for $1.00 was a terrific club chair. It was the right size and style, but the fabric was just awful. That's why I got it for such a good price. Except for the fabric, it was in really good shape and I didn't have to worry about hand tying springs and re-webbing. If I find upholstered furniture where the springs are sticking out, either on top, or falling out of the bottom, I don't bother with it. There are plenty of other furnishings out there that simply need new fabric--sometimes new foam padding. This is the project for me and probably for you too!

If you don't want to invest in fabric for your first attempt, I don't blame you. Neither did I, and, I still don't pay a lot for gorgeous fabric. I find all the fabric I need for upholstering in garage sale drapes. There is a lot of fabric in drapes. Plenty of fabric to easily cover a chair. Drapery fabrics are usually the same heavy weight chintz or damask that you would normally buy at the store to recover your furnishings. Simply rip out the sewn-in pleated portion at the top of the drapes and remove the lining. Save the lining--you'll use it later for all kinds of projects in this book! Take the large piece of drapery fabric to a bulk dry cleaner. The drapes will be very inexpensive to clean since they are now a plain, flat piece of fabric. You will be charged only for the weight of the fabric--not per pleat.

> NOTE: Be sure and smell the drapes. If you are a non-smoker like I am, you don't want to buy the drapes if they smell like smoke. The smoke will not come out. Keep looking--you will find what you need!

For smaller projects like seat covers, you can use drapes or take a look at the clothes racks at garage sales. There will be all kinds of fun things to choose from and don't forget to use garage sale sheets or the drapery linings for chair linings. There is no need to go out to the store to buy anything. You will find everything at garage sales. Let's start with something very easy. How about recovering your dining room chair seats? This is so easy you may want to change them twice a year. Have a different look for summer and winter. The black hand-painted empire chair in my living room had this kind of a seat and just by replacing the old ripped blue vinyl seat to a deep red silk moiré turned a $15.00 chair into a $300.00 chair.

See the Decorating Your Rooms chapter for more information on this chair.

"How To"

RECOVER CHAIR SEATS

Materials needed:
Screwdriver
Fabric
Cording/welt or gimp* (optional)
Claw tool (optional tool)
Staple gun

*See glossary

1 Turn the chair upside down and notice the screws in the corners of the chair frame. Unscrew the screws and the chair seat will come right off. Remove the old fabric that is attached with staples by using a flathead screw driver or a claw tool.

2 Measure and cut a square of fabric the same size as the fabric piece you removed, or measure the chair seat and add approximately 5 extra inches all the way around.

3 Staple gun the new fabric to the center back of the chair seat edge. Pull the fabric snugly and staple the center front edge of the chair seat making sure to align the fabric pattern if necessary. Repeat this for the center sides of the chair seat. Staple all the way around, keeping the fabric stretched smooth. Make a small fold over at the corners if you have excess fabric.

4 Attach optional cording/welt either to the chair frame or to the underside of the removable chair seat by using a staple gun. Cut the cording, and tuck under in an inconspicuous place. Usually the center back or one of the back corners. Secure ends with a staple gun.

5 Reattach the chair seat with the screws and screwdriver.

"How To"

CHAIR WEBBING

Materials needed:
Jute webbing
Staple gun

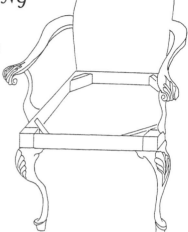

NOTE: Jute webbing can be found in fabric stores. It is usually 3.5 to 4 inches wide. Some of the chair bargains I find at garage sales do not have a seat in them so it is necessary to replace the webbing. I've found that placing a very thick piece of heavy duty upholstery foam on top of the webbing gives me the same results as springs and it's much easier to do.

1 Remove any nails or screws or staples from the wood chair frame so you have a clean surface to work with.

2 Cut a strip of webbing the width of the chair seat with an extra 2 inches on each side.

3 Fold the extra webbing over at each end and staple securely to the seat frame. Repeat this step until you have covered the entire seat area with webbing. Make sure that each webbing strip is placed snugly against the previous strip.

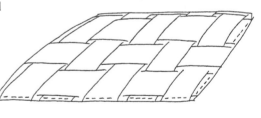

4 Repeat the same process going lengthwise. Fold and staple the end of a strip of webbing and interlace the webbing over and under the existing strips of webbing. Pull tightly, fold and staple the ends to the chair frame. Cover the entire chair seat in this fashion.

5 Lay a piece of thick foam on the webbing and cut the foam to match the shape of the chair. Use an electric knife to cut and carve the foam. Cut the sharp edge of foam off to give the chair foam a nice rounded edge. Cover with batting and fabric of your choice.

"How To"

UPHOLSTER SEATS, BACKS, ARM PADS

Materials needed:
Fabric
Screwdriver
Cording/welt or gimp*
Glue gun
Scissors
Staple puller* (optional)
Staple gun
Utility knife or X-ACTO knife*

***See glossary**

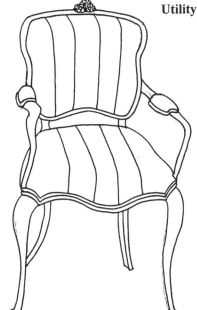

1 Remove the cording/gimp by inserting a mat knife or X-ACTO knife in between the cording and fabric. The cording/gimp has either been stitched on or glued on. Once you determine how it was attached, it's easy to remove. Do not cut the cording/gimp as you will want to use the same pieces again. When one piece of cording is removed, take the old fabric off of it and label it with a piece of paper. If you are working with gimp, label it if you plan to reuse it.

E.g.,   Chair cording/gimp, back cording/gimp, right arm or left arm.
Label all pieces as soon as they are removed.

Continued . . .

2 Remove the chair seat and back fabric with a screwdriver or staple puller. Label each piece of removed fabric. Remove the arm pads (if applicable) with a screwdriver or staple puller and label them.

3 Lay the old fabric pieces out on your new fabric. The old fabric pieces will be your pattern. Notice how much excess fabric there is between the raw edge and the stapled line. Follow this exactly. Replace the old foam and batting, if necessary, with the same size foam and same thickness of batting. Usually this isn't necessary. It's up to you.

4 Staple the new fabric on the seat over the foam and batting. Pull tightly. Trim off excess fabric, if necessary.

5 Lay cording strips on new fabric and cut a strip of fabric approximately 1" wider than cording. Keep the cording labeled. Stitch all of the strips of cording. I stitch the cording twice. You want this seam to be extra strong. Cut off the excess fabric right next to the stitched seam. If you are using gimp, you can skip this instruction.

The arm pad cording needs to be one continuous circle with no ends. Turn under one edge of the cording fabric so there is no raw edge. Insert the piece of cording in this finished end and squeeze a small amount of tacky glue on the sewn seam inside the casing to hold the cording in place.

If you are using gimp, just turn under the raw edges and glue.

Gently lay out the arm pad cording around the pad and in the grooves of the chair arm. Attach with a hot glue gun. Use a very small amount of hot glue, as you will be able to see the glue if you use too much.

GIMP

6 With a hot glue gun, glue the cording/gimp back to the chair edges at the same location you removed it. The seam side is the glue side.

"How To"

REMOVE UPHOLSTERY FABRIC

Materials needed:
Screwdriver (flathead) large & small
Claw tool* (optional)
Utility knife or X-ACTO knife*
Pliers

*See glossary

When you remove the fabric pieces, make a note on a pad of paper the order in which the fabric pieces were removed. You will probably remove them in the order described below-- however, some chairs could be assembled a little differently. They will all be basically just about the same. Just make sure to write down the order and what piece you removed. Label each piece. When you put the new fabric on, you will follow this same order in reverse.

E.g.,　　Skirting front 1
　　　　　Skirting back 2
　　　　　Right skirting side 3
　　　　　Left skirting side 4
　　　　　Skirting cording 5
　　　　　Outside back 6
　　　　　and so on . . .

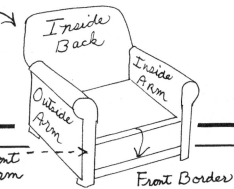

1 CHAIR CUSHION:

The cushions are easy. Just unzip the zipper and remove. Using the utility knife or X-ACTO knife, make a cut of the sewn threads so you can start ripping the fabric. Rip the seams out. As each piece is separated, label it with a piece of paper and pin the paper to the appropriate piece. Watch carefully when you rip apart, making sure you notice how each piece was sewn together. If the seams won't rip without tearing the fabric, use your razor knife or scissors to cut the seam threads. You want to leave the fabric pieces intact as this is your pattern.

Label the fabric for each cushion part:　　Cushion top
　　　　　　　　　　　　　　　　　　　Cushion bottom
　　　　　　　　　　　　　　　　　　　Front boxing* see glossary
　　　　　　　　　　　　　　　　　　　Back zippered boxing
　　　　　　　　　　　　　　　　　　　Cushion cording
　　　　　　　　　　　　　　　　　　　Fabric strips for cushion cording
　　　　　　　　　　　　　　　　　　　Zipper

Continued . . .

185

1 SKIRTING:

Lift the skirt up and right below the cording you will notice that the skirt has been stapled to the chair from the underside. Using your screwdriver/ claw tool and pliers, remove the staples.

Sometimes after a few staples are removed, you can pull the rest of the skirt off.

There may be a cardboard tacking strip. Remove this also and be careful not to tear it as you will reuse the tacking strip. Label the tacking strip (such as "front skirt strip") and also label in what order it was removed.

2 Separate the cording from the skirt pieces and remove the fabric on the cording. Label each skirt piece, the corner squares and the cording. The skirt pieces will usually be lined with a piece of muslin and a heavier piece of fabric inserted in the pocket. Save and label all pieces.

Skirting:
- Front skirt
- Back skirt
- Side skirts
- Skirt cording
- Corner squares
- Tacking strip

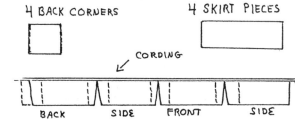

1 BACK:

At the top back of the chair use the screwdriver to pull away the fabric and the metal strip from the back wooden frame of the chair. Be very careful! The metal strip has very sharp tacks on it. Work the screwdriver completely down the sides, being careful not to tear the cardboard strip, if there is one. Save the strip and reuse it. If the cardboard strip becomes ripped and torn, you can purchase another at any fabric store. They are inexpensive. Remove the staples from the bottom of the chair back and label this piece. Save the metal strip. In fact, leave the metal and the cardboard strips attached to the old pieces of fabric if you can. If not, make sure you label and number the order in which it was removed.

Remove cording and label, if applicable.

Back labels:
- Back
- Back cording
- Top back metal strip
- Back side strips,
- Metal or cardboard

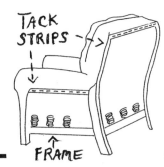

1 OUTER SIDES:

Repeat the steps for the back to remove the side fabric with a screwdriver, claw tool and pliers. Remember to save any metal and cardboard strips. Leave the strips attached to the fabric piece if you can. Label each piece with right outside and left outside. Remove the front arm piece and label right or left front arm. This will either be a piece of fabric or a separate board with fabric that is nailed to the front of the arm.

Place a pin at the end of the curved front arm piece and at the end where the cording is no longer sewn to the outer side piece of fabric. Place a pin in the cording at both ends where it is no longer sewn to the front arm piece.

Label: Right outside
         Left outside
         Cording, if any
         Right front arm
         Left front arm

1 INNER SIDES:

Remove inner side fabric with screwdriver, claw tool and pliers. This should be attached by staples to the underside of the outer arm and pulled down through the chair frame and stapled to the outside bottom chair frame. Label the pieces.

Label: Right inner arm
                Left inner arm

1 INNER BACK:

Remove inner back fabric with screwdriver, claw tool and pliers. It should be attached to the back of the chair frame and pulled through the seat portion and stapled to the bottom back frame. Label this piece of fabric.

Label: Inside back

1 BOTTOM CHAIR FRONT:

Remove bottom front piece of upholstery fabric that is attached to the white muslin chair bottom.

Keep both pieces (front fabric and white muslin) stitched together at this time.

The chair should now be free of fabric.

Remove any excess staples.

"How To"

RE-UPHOLSTER CLUB CHAIR

Materials needed:
Screwdriver (large & small flathead)
Electric staple gun
Pliers
Needle (large upholstery needle*)
Sewing machine
Scissors
Tape measure
Fabric tracing paper
Tracing wheel
Small hammer

NOTE: ALL CHAIRS AND SOFAS ARE ASSEMBLED AND UPHOLSTERED IN A SIMILAR FASHION. THERE MAY BE SOME SLIGHT DIFFERENCES. ALWAYS PAY PARTICULAR ATTENTION WHEN REMOVING THE OLD FABRIC FROM YOUR FURNITURE PIECES. I LEARNED MUCH MORE BY TAKING THE FABRIC PIECES APART AND SEEING HOW THEY WERE ASSEMBLED THAN READING ANY "HOW TO" BOOK.

SAVING THE OLD FABRIC PIECES, LABELING THE PIECES AND NUMBERING THEM IN THE ORDER REMOVED IS THE MOST IMPORTANT INSTRUCTION.

THE MORE YOU DO, THE EASIER IT WILL BECOME. YOU WILL PROBABLY EVEN FIND A WAY THAT YOU LIKE BETTER.

UPHOLSTERING IS NOT ROCKET SCIENCE. IT IS VERY EASY . . . IT JUST TAKES TIME.

Now that all the fabric is removed, you can easily measure to see exactly how much fabric you will need to recover your chair. Lay out the entire piece of new fabric on the floor. Lay each pattern piece out on top of the fabric. Pin each pattern piece to the fabric. If the fabric has a pattern in it, make sure you line up the pattern design to match. Pin down the pieces before cutting.

NOTE: For your first attempt, I strongly recommend you choose a fabric
            without a pattern or stripes.

Continued . . .

The long cording strips can run down the bottom or the sides. Some books tell you to run the cording on a diagonal (bias). I've seen it done both ways. If you have the extra fabric you may want to cut the cording fabric on the diagonal.

NOTE: You may prefer to use a decorative type cording or the very popular heavy cotton fringe. This will eliminate using the old cording and fabric. You will still need to save your cording pieces and cut and label the store bought cording or fringe to match.

MAKE SURE YOU CAN SEE THE OLD STITCHING LINE ON THE PIECES TO BE SEWN. YOUR OLD PIECES OF FABRIC SHOULD HAVE A ONE-INCH SEAM ALLOWANCE OUTSIDE OF THE STITCHING LINE. YOU MAY WANT TO ADD ANOTHER INCH OR SO OF FABRIC ALL THE WAY AROUND. YOU CAN ALWAYS TRIM LATER.

WHEN YOU CUT YOUR NEW FABRIC FROM YOUR OLD PATTERN PIECE MAKE SURE THEY ARE PINNED TOGETHER SECURELY AND WELL MARKED.

LAY THE NEWLY CUT PIECE OF FABRIC THAT IS STILL PINNED TO THE OLD FABRIC ON A TABLE. INSERT FABRIC TRACING PAPER IN BETWEEN THE OLD FABRIC AND THE NEW FABRIC. MARK WITH A TRACING WHEEL OVER THE OLD STITCH LINE. MARK ALL THE WAY AROUND YOUR PIECE OF FABRIC. THIS IS WHERE YOU WILL STITCH, RIGHT OVER THE TRACED LINE.

1 Begin with the bottom muslin piece of fabric. Remember it was the last piece removed, so it's the first piece back on. Place a straight pin at the front corners of the bottom front section. Place two straight pins at each edge of the seam where attached to the white muslin.

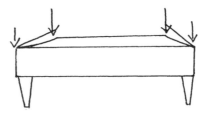

Continued . . .

2 Remove the old stitching. You now have two separate pieces. A muslin piece, and a fabric piece. Lay the fabric portion out on the new fabric and cut this out.   Stitch the large corner Vs together stopping at the straight pin. This will be the point of your V. This is very similar to sewing a dart*.

3 Lay the white muslin out on a piece of garage sale sheet or old drapery lining. Cut to match the piece of muslin. Stitch the fabric piece to the muslin seat bottom. Lay the muslin down on the seat and pull the back and sides through the wooden frame. Make sure the front fabric piece smoothly fits the chair frame. Staple the muslin fabric and front fabric to the chair frame just as you removed it.

NOTE:　　　　I find if you do these two pieces first, right after you remove them, you won't forget how to do it.

4 Take the large needle and with heavy cording type thread stitch the muslin fabric down to the bottom of the chair seat in the same area where you removed the old cord.

Continued . . .

5 Using a staple gun, replace the rest of the fabric pieces, metal and cardboard tacking strips in the reverse order that you removed them. The metal tacking strips require a small hammer to tap them in tightly. Sew each piece of cording when it is needed and attach to the chair when needed. Don't sew all of the cording strips at one time. It's too easy to get them mixed up. Notice most of the cording is attached with a staple gun. Make sure each piece of fabric is smooth and if there is a pattern in the fabric, make sure the pattern lines up.

6 SKIRT ASSEMBLY:

If the stiff muslin backing for the skirt pieces are not reusable, cut pieces of garage sale sheet for the skirt backing. Follow your tracing lines and insert the heavy liner piece back inside the skirt pocket. Sew the four corner squares and attach cording strip to the entire skirt. You will have one continuous piece, just like it was when you removed the old skirt.

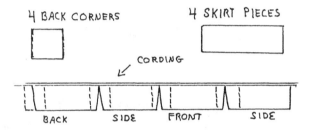

REMEMBER YOU CAN USE DECORATIVE CORDING OR THICK FRINGE IN PLACE OF YOUR SEWN FABRIC CORDING. THIS IS EASIER AND QUICKER BUT A BIT MORE EXPENSIVE.

YOU CAN ALSO MAKE DIFFERENT STYLE SKIRTS FOR YOUR FURNITURE OR BULLION FRINGE.

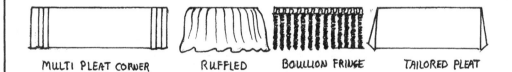

MULTI PLEAT CORNER   RUFFLED   BOULLION FRINGE   TAILORED PLEAT

Continued . . .

7 CUSHIONS:

Sew the old zipper into the new fabric. Stitch a separate small square of heavy fabric at each end of the zipper so the zipper tab will not come off of its tracks. Stitch each side.

Work the machine by hand to sew across each end when you stitch over the zipper teeth. You don't want to break your needle.

8 Sew two long cording strips. The strips should go completely around the cushion top plus an extra 3 inches on each end.

NOTE: I sew these two cording strips very loosely. Do not sew the stitching right up against the cording as you have done previously. Attach the sewn cording to the fabric for the cushion tops and bottoms, sewing right over the existing stitching line.

Start stitching at the center back of the top and bottom fabric. The cording will be joined at the center back. Leave an extra 3 inches hanging free.

Sew all the way around the cushion top fabric. Both ends of the cording will be left hanging. Trim both ends of cording to be joined at an angle. Do not cut the cording fabric yet.

TRIM CORDING

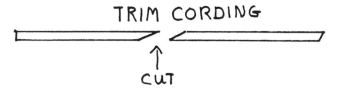

CUT

Continued . . .

Trim one end of the fabric so that it can be inserted in the other piece of cording fabric. Fold the longer piece of fabric over the joined cording section and stitch the fabric to the top and bottom cushion fabric.

THE CORDING SHOULD NOW BE JOINED TOGETHER IN ONE CONTINUOUS PIECE AND IT SHOULD BE STITCHED TO THE TOP AND BOTTOM CUSHION FABRIC.

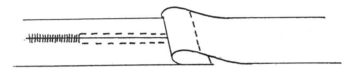

NOW IS WHEN THE BOXING SECTION OF FABRIC IS JOINED TO THE CUSHION TOP AND BOTTOM.

THIS IS WHEN YOU STITCH RIGHT UP AGAINST THE CORDING.

Believe me, this is much easier. You will get a nicer look if you take this extra step.

9 Sew boxing strips together. They are usually joined at the sides of the cushion or toward the back zipper boxing piece.

Do not sew one end of zippered boxing piece. Pin boxing to top cushion fabric by centering the boxing fabric so the zippered portion is in the back of the cushion. Place a pin in each of the four corners of the cushion fabric. Sew cushion top and bottom to boxing fabric starting at one end. When you come to a corner pin, leave the sewing needle in the fabric, lift the foot and turn the fabric 45 degrees for a nice straight corner. Do this at each corner.

Overlap the excess boxing at the seam near the zipper to make a pocket.

Stitch over this pocket all the way across the boxing.

Turn the cushion fabric inside out and repeat for the other edge of boxing.

Trim excess fabric and trim corners.

CHAPTER SIX

FINISHES

As you've read over and over in almost every chapter in this book: You can paint or refinish just about any surface--wood, metals, glass, pottery, even fabric.

There are so many new wonderful products on the market and so many of the old standard finishes are becoming popular again with imitation style products that make them inexpensive and very easy to do--such as gold leaf and the patina finishes.

Most of the paints, stains and refinishing products can be found at garage sales. In fact, I recently found an entire collection (20 bottles) of the 4 oz. bottles of craft paint in just about every color. The collection came with seven different size brushes and four brand new sponge brushes. The entire set was only $3.00. Just one bottle of craft paint sells for 89¢ at the store!

Moving sales are a good place to find paints, stains, varnishes, spray paints, polyurethane, turpentine and linseed oil. Most of these materials are considered flammable, so professional movers will not haul them and they need to be disposed of. I can't begin to tell you how many of these types of materials I've gotten for FREE just because people needed to get rid of them. I've found brand new marbleizing kits, stone kits, feathers, sponges--just about everything you need to accomplish all of the exciting, new finishing techniques.

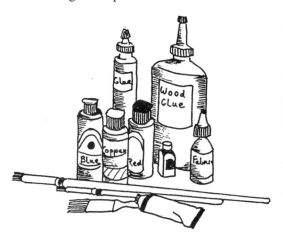

It is a rare day when I strip down a piece of furniture to the bare wood. However, if you have a piece of furniture with gobs of old paint on it, most of the stripping materials can be found at garage sales too. If I find a wonderful antique piece I will restore it to its original finish. Otherwise I feel it's just as easy to use paint and make a piece of furniture look like wood. In my opinion, this is easier, quicker and not nearly as messy. If you do plan to strip away the old finish, make sure with any stripper, paint or stain, that you work in a well ventilated area. A lot of these products are toxic, so please follow all of the package directions very carefully.

PREPARATION

Most of the furnishings that I purchase at garage sales are not painted. They are usually wood products that have been stained and finished with varnish or some kind of protective finish. Since I prefer to paint furniture and not to strip, it is necessary to wipe the furniture piece

thoroughly with deglosser. A deglosser removes the slick surface of the finish and allows the piece of wood to accept the primer and paint. You can still sand if you think your piece needs it. Usually just wiping down thoroughly with the deglosser will work. Sometimes I do both. If you choose to sand, make sure to wipe the piece afterwards with a soft cloth to remove any grit and dust.

Priming the pieces is also very important. A primed piece of wood, metal or glass accepts the paint much easier and makes applying it easier too! One of the best primer/bonders I've used is called BIN. This product claims that it will prime most any surface, allowing you to paint or finish surfaces such as glass, glossy finishes and metals. I've even primed fabric with this product and painted over it! So far I have not been disappointed with this product. You might want to buy a can. It is very easy clean up to! You will definitely use it for many of the projects in this book.

STAINING

There are two kinds of stain--oil based and acrylic based. They both do about the same thing. Acrylic cleans up easier, requiring just water. An oil base stain requires turpentine to clean the brushes. Stain is used on a raw wood surface. You cannot use stain on a painted surface unless you are using it as a glaze. *See the antiqueing section.*

Stain can be applied with a brush or wiped on with a soft cloth. If using a brush you will still want to wipe the stain out using a cloth for a smooth finish. Stain is very thin and you can see the wood grain coming through it. For a deeper, richer finish, apply another coat and wipe with a soft cloth. After the stain has dried, seal it with a coat of varnish, or polyurethane. You can also use a fabric dye on raw wood in place of a stain. Mix it following the directions on the package. This is a great way to use special colors, either for the entire piece or just decorative trim. The wood grain will show through just like stain. You can mix dyes together to achieve your own unique color. Just as you do with stain, apply more coats of dye for a deeper, richer look. Finish with varnish, lacquer or polyurethane.

PAINTING

Paint is also available in both oil based and acrylic based. Again, the acrylic is easier to work with because of the water cleanup. You will see brush strokes when using acrylic paints. To avoid this use a foam brush. A good rule of thumb is to stick with one type of product. If you are using an oil based product, use it all the way through--oil based primer, stain or paint. If you are using acrylics, use an acrylic primer, paint and finish. BIN primer-bonder-sealer can be used with anything. I can't stress enough just how important it is to use a good product for priming. After all of your hard work--hand painting and creating just the look you want, you most definitely want it to last. You want the best results possible for your efforts. I've always believed rules are made to be broken! I have successfully used BIN primer and have never had a problem. However, the experts will tell you the general rule of thumb above. Remember to prepare your surface either by sanding or using a deglosser, or both. When painting you will probably need two coats of paint, perhaps more, to cover thoroughly.

If you are trying to match a piece of painted furniture, remove a small drawer or a door of the piece and take it to the paint store to match the color. If you can't take a part of your furniture, go to the paint store and bring paint chip samples home for matching. Look on the inside of a drawer or door or perhaps underneath the piece to see a sample of the base color without antiqueing or distressing. It's much easier to match the base color. I've had good luck turning a wooden piece of furniture upside down or inside out if necessary to see just the wood color without its distressing or antiqueing. Today, my favorite finish is "200-year-old pine." It's a mixture of yellow, orange, and brown colors with distressing. I've used this finish on many garage sale pieces throughout our home. It's a very popular finish right now and of course, if you were to buy a piece of furniture with the real "200-year-old pine," you can imagine how very expensive it is! It's so easy to duplicate the look of "200-year-old pine." This chapter shows you how.

FINISHES & SEALERS

There are many of these products available in paint stores, craft and hobby shops and at garage sales. They all have different names: varnish, polyurethane, sealers and finishers. These products are all made to protect the surface. They are available in different types of finishes. High gloss is extremely shiny, gloss is shiny, yet not as shiny as high gloss. Satin has a medium sheen and matte has very little sheen. Whatever finish you choose to use, always apply several light coats for the best effect. Lightly sand and wipe away the sanded residue with a soft cloth between coats. Most projects usually require two coats of a finishing product. You may want to use more, perhaps three or four coats for furniture. An optional finish for very fine furnishings is to polish the final coat of finish with #0000 steel wool, wipe with a soft cloth and apply two coats of paste wax. This will give your project a finish as smooth as glass. When you see furniture on display at the showrooms and one set is priced so much higher than another almost identical set--it's probably a hand-rubbed finish.

HAND PAINTING TECHNIQUES

It's not necessary to be a trained artist to accomplish the decorative hand painting techniques used in this book. Let your brush do the work for you and start painting something you know like geometric shapes. The painting techniques used for the Florentine pots on page 238 were simply different sized circles for the grapes and pears, a few curved lines for the stems and rows of "X's" around the top and bottom. The clover design is three small round circles.

If you can hand write letters then you can paint decorative borders and designs. Don't worry about perfection. Hand painted furniture and accessories are never perfect-- just uniform in design.

"How To"

HAND PAINTING TECHNIQUES

Materials needed:
Pencil
Ruler
Masking tape
Paint marker or paint
Paint brushes or sponge brushes

DECORATIVE BORDERS AND DESIGNS
Use a ruler and draw two straight lines for the top and bottom borders. Use a letter or a number that you're good at writing. Repeat this letter or number for your pattern .

eeeee SSSS eeee

88888 6666 3333

CLOVERLEAF PATTERN
Draw two straight lines for the borders. Draw a "V" shape and three overlapping circles.

CHECKERBOARD PATTERN
Decide the width of your checkerboard pattern and choose that size brush. Draw the top and bottom borders, fill the brush with paint and place on the top border line. Pull down to the bottom border line.

BORDERS
Draw a line or two wavy lines and long "0's" on each side.

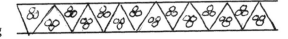

ANTIQUEING OR DISTRESSING

Just applying paint to wood furnishings or accessories makes them look very flat. Wiping a glaze (stain) over the painted surface gives the piece depth and richness. If you plan to antique or distress a painted piece, make sure the paint you use is an eggshell paint. This is not a color, it is a type of paint. The paint store can mix any color paint in an eggshell finish. The eggshell finish provides a harder finish so the stain will not soak down into the paint.

Distressing and antiqueing are basically the same thing. These techniques make the piece look old. After applying the paint and wiping with a glaze (stain) you can add fly-specks* (the small dots of dark stain). You can also use a hammer to pound dents into the furniture and smack the furniture with a piece of chain. This is exactly what the professional refinishers do to get a piece of wood furniture to look old! Some of them use an ice pick to put small gouges into the furniture. I prefer not to do this, as it tears the fibers of the wood. Go to the showrooms and examine the very expensive furnishings. Notice the dark flyspecks. Notice the tiny gouges and the dents and scratches. This book shows you exactly how to do these techniques and at what stage to get out the hammer, chain and ice pick. What . . . no whips? No whips!

You might want to start with a small item like a wooden shelf and try out all the different techniques so you can see what look and techniques you like. If you have an old piece of wood lying around, try your first attempt at antiqueing or distressing on it. Also experiment with different shades of stain. Paint the piece first with your desired color of paint. After the paint has dried thoroughly, tape off three or four different sections and apply a different shade of stain to each section. Your finished product will look different if you use a black walnut stain versus a mahogany stain or an oak stain. Try it out first until you achieve the desired result. After awhile, you will know how your pieces will turn out just by seeing the stain in the can.

SPECIAL EFFECTS

ANTIQUE WHITE

ANTIQUE WOOD

TRIM

VERDIGRIS

GOLD LEAF

ANTIQUE GOLD

CRACKLE

MARBLEIZE

PAINTED INLAY

STIPPLE/SPONGE

COMB FINISH

RUSTIC FINISH

SHELLEY'S RECIPE

"How To"

ANTIQUE WHITE FINISH

Materials needed:
Deglosser*
Sandpaper
White or cream paint (eggshell finish)*
Brown stain
Soft cloth
Toothbrush
Chain, hammer & ice pick (optional)
Trim color
Paint brush
Varnish or polyurethane finish

*See glossary

1 Sand the piece or wipe thoroughly with a deglosser. Use a special primer (like BIN) if you are working with a surface other than wood.

2 Apply a coat of white or cream paint and let dry. Apply another coat of paint and let dry thoroughly. If painting over a very dark surface you may need a third coat of paint. Lightly sand with fine grained paper and wipe down with a soft cloth between coats of paint.

3 Apply trim color if desired. You may draw a line with a pencil or use masking tape and tape off the area that will not be trimmed. Some suggestions for trim are a different color eggshell paint, gold paint or gold leaf.

Do step 6 now if you want dents and gouges.

4 Apply well stirred stain with a soft cloth over the entire piece. Keep wiping the stain out for an even look. See how much better your pieces look with the stain glaze on top. Allow the stain to dry thoroughly. If you want a deeper look, apply another very light coat of stain--not too much! Remember your test piece!

Continued . . .

5 After the stain has dried thoroughly, take an old toothbrush and dip the bristle end into the stain. Using your thumb, pull over the bristles of the brush to spray small dots of stain on the piece of furniture.

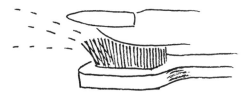

Practice this technique on your test piece until you have control of this motion and can achieve the right consistency of dots. These dots are called "flyspecks." Applying flyspecks to the piece will make it look darker.

6 If you want a heavily antiqued look with small dents in your piece, after you've applied all coats of paint and before you apply the stain, take a piece of chain and strike the piece of furniture in various parts with the end of the chain. When you apply the stain, the dents will pick up the darker stain. When you wipe down the stain, wipe these dents free of any puddles of stain. The stain will smudge outside of the dent leaving a real antique, worn look.

7 Seal with varnish or polyurethane.

NOTE: THE ONLY STEP THAT IS NOT REVERSIBLE IS APPLYING DENTS AND GOUGES. ALWAYS TEST THIS LOOK ON A PIECE OF WOOD FIRST. FINISH THE WOOD AS DESIRED.

I USUALLY TEST A PIECE FIRST, ESPECIALLY IF I'M TRYING TO MATCH FURNITURE THAT I ALREADY HAVE, BE IT WOOD OR A PAINTED COLOR. THERE ARE SO MANY VARIANCES IN COLORS AND YOU NEED TO KNOW JUST HOW MUCH STAIN TO WIPE ON, HOW MUCH FLY SPECKING TO DO, ETC. IF YOU'RE TRYING SOMETHING FOR THE FIRST TIME, ALWAYS TRY A SMALL WOOD SAMPLE FIRST.

"How To"

ANTIQUE WOOD FINISH (PAINTED)

Materials needed:
Eggshell* paint (color of wood)
Varnish or polyurethane finish
Sandpaper
Toothbrush
Stain (brown color)
Chain, hammer & ice pick (optional)

*See glossary

1 Once you've determined the exact color of paint to use, degloss, sand or do both to the piece. Let dry. Wipe with a soft cloth. Paint at least two coats of the new paint on the piece. Lightly sand with a fine grain paper and wipe with a soft cloth between coats. You might need a third coat of paint.

2 If you require dents, hit the piece with the end of a piece of chain now. Do optional hammer and ice pick gouges.

3 Apply the trim color now, if necessary. *See Trim on the next page.*

4 Take a soft cloth and wipe the piece down with a thin coat of brown (your shade) stain. You will have a lot of control over this color by using a soft cloth. You can put it on heavy or wipe it down to soften the color. You are in control here! Let dry thoroughly. You may desire another thin coat of stain.

5 Take a toothbrush and dip in the stain. Rub your thumb over the toothbrush creating small dots on the furniture piece (flyspecks).

See option 5 on the previous page.

6 Seal with varnish or polyurethane. I like the spray and usually use several light coats. Choose satin or gloss depending on your style. I prefer satin.

"How To"

TRIM

Materials needed:
Trim color paint (eggshell*)
Masking tape (optional)
Pencil (optional)
Stencil (optional)

*See glossary

Choose a trim color and trim your furnishing or accessories with a small brush in the desired trim color.

1 Choose a brush the size of the trim you desire, if you can. This allows the brush to do all the work. If the trim area is 1/4 inch wide, choose a 1/4 inch brush. Draw the brush around the trim area without lifting. This will give you a straighter line.

or

2 Draw a line with a pencil or tape off the trim area with masking tape. Don't worry if you can see your pencil line. I've seen it on the most expensive pieces of furniture.

Usually the trim color is around a routed* table edge, a dowel/spindle edge or on finials.*

You can very easily make a piece of furniture unique with a decorative trim color. Decide on the design you want and the trim color. Tape off the trim area with masking tape or use a straight edge and a pencil to mark it off.

I've seen a lot of hand-painted furniture with ribbons and flowers all outlined with a black pencil and colored in with paint. It's a beautiful look and very expensive to buy. If you are talented enough to be able to paint these designs or copy them from a magazine you'll have a beautiful piece of custom furniture to use for your own enjoyment or to sell for someone else's!

After applying the trim color/colors, wipe down with stain, flyspeck (optional), distress (optional) and seal.

"How To"

VERDIGRIS

Materials needed:
Primer (if necessary)
Black paint
Copper paint
Green paint (light & dark)
Sealer

Verdigris is a very popular finishing technique right now. I use it on concrete and plastic outdoor flower containers. I've used it on candlesticks and baskets as detailed in the Accessories chapter. Spray paint makes this type of finish very easy, but use whatever you have on hand. Either one works very well.

1 Prime if necessary.

2 Paint the entire surface with black paint.

3 Before the black paint is dry, paint over the black with a copper paint and smear the colors together using either a brush or a rag.

4 Before the other paint is dry, brush over the surface very lightly with a dark and light green paint. You may want to wipe over the wet paints with a cloth. This should meld all the colors together for a distressed, aged copper metal look. If it is too dark, add more green or copper. If it is too light, add more dark green, black or copper. You can't mess this up. Keep on adding and rubbing until you get the desired effect.

Experiment first if you want. This is a real easy technique. There are lots of verdigris pre-packaged kits on the market. You may want to try one of these.

"How To"

GOLD LEAF (GILDED FINISH)

Materials needed:
Gold size (adhesive)*
Burnt umber paint (undercoating)
Gold leaf sheets*
Soft brush
Sealer
Velvet (optional)

1 You can gild just about any surface. I've gilded glass, metal, wood, fabric--everything! Start with a clean surface that is free of wax and grease. You might need to use a deglosser if you are using a piece of wood that has been varnished. Prime with a good primer if necessary.

2 Paint the surface with a burnt umber or reddish brown color. This color will appear through the tiny cracks of the gold leaf just like you see on gold leaf picture frames or furnishings.

THIS IS A GOOD WAY TO TELL IF A GARAGE SALE PIECE IS LEAFED OR JUST PAINTED GOLD. YOU WILL SEE CRACKS IN THE GOLD WITH A REDDISH BROWN COLOR SHOWING THROUGH THE CRACKS.

3 Apply gold size, which is a very sticky tacky substance. Follow manufacturer's instructions. It should set for 30 minutes to an hour. It will be very sticky.

4 When the gold size is sticky and clear, lay the gold sheets over the surface and smooth down with a soft brush. Keep reapplying the pieces of gold sheets until your entire piece or area is covered with the gold. Use the excess gold sheets that dust off to reapply over bare areas. Smooth out with a soft cloth (preferably velvet) and wipe away excess gold clumps with your soft brush.

5 Finish with a sealer. To tone down the bright gold, apply a coat of brown stain with a soft cloth over all, then seal again. Save excess gold pieces for your next project.

Just as you can use gold on your projects you can also use silver paper for a pewter look. You will need silver paper and black colored paint for the undercoating. Follow the directions just as you do for gold leaf--only use black paint, size (glue) and silver paper!

NOTE: For intricate work--use a spray adhesive.

"How To"

ANTIQUE or BURNISHED GOLD

Materials needed:
Gold paint
Stain (brown)
Soft cloth
Toothbrush (optional)
Sealer

If you want a darker antique gold look, it's more economical to use gold paint. However, you can use gold leaf.

1 Treat your furniture or accessory piece first by sanding or using a deglosser, if necessary. Prime the piece if necessary. Paint the piece with gold paint and let dry thoroughly.

2 Antique/distress the gold by applying brown colored stain. Use a soft cloth to wipe on the stain. Apply more stain if you want a deeper, richer color.

3 Flyspeck with a toothbrush if desired.

NOTE: See step 5 of antique white finish.

4 Seal with varnish or polyurethane

"How To"

CRACKLE* FINISH

Materials needed:
Crackle medium*
Sponge brush
Wide bristle brush
Acrylic paint
Spray sealer (varnish or polyurethane)

***See glossary**

This is so much fun to do and very easy. This type of finish is very popular on furniture and accessories. It's hard to make a mistake using this crackle technique.

You can crackle right over wood or over another color of paint. The top coat of paint that you apply will crack showing the color that is underneath. I've done a lot of crackle finishes on cherry or walnut pieces. I usually use a cream color paint. When the cream paint crackles it allows the dark cherry or walnut to show through the cracks.

For an elegant accessory use a base coat of gold with an ivory crackled paint on top. The gold will show through the cracks. I've used this on old lamps that I've turned into large candleholders

Try crackle on your clay flowerpots, picture frames, or anything you can think of.

1 Sand your wooden pieces and wipe with a clean soft cloth. Apply crackle medium (available in craft stores) with a sponge brush. Follow manufacturer's instructions. Let the crackle medium dry for approximately 20 to 60 minutes. It will become very tacky.

2 Apply the top coat of paint using a bristle brush. <u>Apply in one stroke. Do not go over your painted strokes</u>. You will start to see cracks appearing.

NOTE: Apply a heavy coat of paint for wider cracks.

        Apply a thinner coat of paint for smaller cracks.

3 Let dry and seal with a spray varnish. Apply several light coats of the spray, letting dry thoroughly between each coat.

"How To"

MARBLEIZE

Materials needed:
Base color paint (black, white, tan or rose)
Two or three shades of marble color
E.g., two greens, dark and medium for green marble
E.g., light brown and cream for ivory marble
White paint
Feather or fine tipped brush
Sponge
Spray sealer
Styrofoam plate
or
Purchase a marble kit

1 Paint the object to marbleize with base color and let dry. Use a sponge brush to avoid brush strokes.

2 Tear bits and pieces out of the sponge and especially on the sides of the sponge.

3 On the Styrofoam plate squeeze out the marble colors in two or three large circles.

4 Dip the sponge in the paint and press down on your object and lift the sponge straight up. Don't rub the sponge across the object. Repeat this motion over the entire piece until you have the desired effect.

5 Dip the feather in water and pull it through a puddle of white paint. Pull the feather over your object in a diagonal while you flicker the feather gently. This technique will add the marble veins. You can also use a small, fine tip brush instead of a feather.

6 Let dry thoroughly and seal with a spray sealer.

> NOTE: There are several wonderful marble kits on the market. You may want to purchase one of these for your first attempt. They have all the tools you will need.

"How To"

PAINTED INLAY

Materials needed:
Masking tape
Gel stain* (different shades)
Wood stain marker

*See glossary

Inlaid wood is very expensive. Each piece of wood is cut and placed in an intricate design. It's easy to reproduce this look with several colors of stain.

1 Draw the inlay design on a piece of paper. Assign each different colored section a letter.

      Example: A: Black walnut
                       B: Cherry
                       C: Colonial brown

Make a copy of the outline so that you have two separate identical diagrams.

2 Tape the paper diagram on top of the wooden piece that you plan to inlay.

3 This step is optional. If you think you might redo the table at a later date--do not make the cuts. Cut through the paper into the wood with an X-ACTO knife around the diagram. This small cut will help keep the stain in place so it will not run over into the other areas. Remove the paper diagram.

4 Tape off the areas of wood for each section of your design. For instance, tape around all areas marked A.

5 Stain all of the A areas with chosen color of stain using a small rag, swab or stain marker. Let dry. Repeat steps 4 and 5 for each stain color, B, C, etc.

6 After all stain colors have been applied in your design, seal with varnish.

"How To"

STIPPLE or SPONGE

Materials needed:
Sea sponge or household sponge
Base coat paint
Styrofoam plate
Top color paint or paints

NOTE: If using a household sponge, tear bits and pieces out of it, especially along the edges so you have an uneven effect.

1 Prepare surface of item to be painted.

   NOTE: A piece of furniture might need to be sanded or wiped down with a deglosser.

2 Apply base coat. You may need two or more coats of paint depending on surface. Allow to dry.

3 Pour top color paint or paints onto a Styrofoam plate. Dip a damp sponge into the paint on the plate and press sponge down onto base coated surface. Lift up . . . do not wipe the sponge. Repeat this process over entire area of base coat until you have the effect you want.

4 Finish with a varnish or polyurethane.

"How To"

COMB FINISH

Materials needed:
Hair comb (wide tooth plastic)
or
Hair pick (plastic)
or
Commercial comb
Base coat of paint
Top coat of paint or gel stain
Finishing product

NOTE: I like to use this technique for a fancy design on the plywood insert of a double framed mirror.

See the Accessories chapter.

1 Apply base coat to your project and let dry thoroughly. You may need more than one coat.

2 Apply the top coat of paint or a thick gel stain. While this coat is still wet, drag the comb through, making patterns, straight lines or wavy lines.

Apply finishing product when dry.

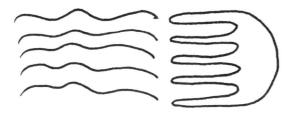

This is a fun technique. You may want to try this on a piece of plywood first to experiment with all the different designs you can get with a comb.

"How To"

RUSTIC FINISHES

Materials needed:
Wood project
Primer
Paint or stain
Sponge or brush
Paper towels
Sand paper

1 Prime the piece to be finished. Apply the primer roughly, letting some of the wood to show through. Let dry.

2 Paint or stain. The paint or stain will look different over the various areas. It will have one look over the primed surface and look entirely different over the raw wood surfaces.

3 Wipe all over with a paper towel or rough cloth.

4 Paint designs on the surface or stencil designs. Rough up with a little sand paper and wipe all over with a soft cloth.

5 You can either seal the project now or wipe all over with a dark stain. The amount of stain you wipe on and off depends on how light or dark you want the top distressing to be.

6 Finish with a sealer.

SHELLEY'S RECIPE

Many of the wood furnishings that you find just need a little touch up. They may have some scratches or small nicks. I came up with this special formula years ago when I moved into a "fixer upper" house. This house had been badly abused, especially the woodwork. There was a lovely curved wood handrail going up the center staircase that had completely lost its luster. The wooden kitchen cabinets were in such bad condition that I thought I might have to replace them. I tried a lot of store bought products that just didn't do the job so I put my chemist hat on and started making my own special brew. It works wonders for any wood product. Old kitchen cabinets come back to life. Stair railings and wood trim start to glow again and it's perfect for all the wood pieces of furniture that you find at garage sales. Dried out, old wooden pieces will love this recipe. If there is a bad spot on the wood just wipe it down with a few coats of Shelley's recipe. I've even used it on wooden desks and tables that have a leather embossed top. Saddle soap works well to cleanse the leather, then apply a coat of Shelley's recipe over the entire piece of furniture. Furnishings that you thought would have to be completely stripped down and done over can be brought back to life with this recipe. Mix up a batch and try it here and there. I think you will like it.

"How To"

SHELLEY'S RECIPE

Materials needed:
8 parts boiled linseed oil*
2 parts paint thinner
1 part deglosser (liquid sandpaper)

***See glossary**

1 Measure and pour all ingredients into a large covered glass jar. Stir the ingredients gently.

2 Pour a small amount on a soft cotton cloth and wipe over wood area. If necessary, let the wood absorb the liquid and apply as many coats as needed.

CHAPTER SEVEN

TVs & ELECTRONICS

TELEVISIONS

VCRs

STEREOS

RADIOS

SECURITY SYSTEMS

"Why do you have 14 televisions?," my friends ask. "Well, why not?," is the only response I can think of!

Yes, we really do have 14 televisions. There is a television in every room of the house. Three of them are in the basement and one is in the garage. Doesn't everyone need a television in the garage? I know we do! When I'm out in the garage working on projects, it's great to have a television turned on. This way, I don't have to miss my favorite soap opera! Plus, I get a lot more work out of my husband when he's working in the garage because he can watch his favorite weekend sports shows instead of lying on the couch munching chips all weekend!

The children all have their own televisions and in the fall when it's time to go back to college, it's simply a matter of going downstairs and picking out the television each wants to take.

All of the televisions are color. They all have a great picture and good sound and not one of the garage sale televisions cost over $20. A wonderful little 15" Sony color TV was only $15. A 15" GE color television was just $5.00! We use the GE television in the guest bedroom and the Sony was just the right size for my son's college dorm room.

See Outfitting the College Dorm Room in the Decorating Your Rooms chapter.

We especially enjoy the little 3.5" Casio pocket size color TV that I purchased brand new in its original wrapping for only $15. It was complete with brand new batteries! It's great to take on car trips or to use on vacation while lazing at the pool.

Altogether our 14 televisions didn't even total $280. That's what you would pay for just one brand new television!

ALL OF OUR TELEVISIONS ARE 115 CHANNEL CABLE READY WITH RE-MOTE CONTROL.

No . . . they didn't come that way. Not for $5.00! They were just ordinary color tele-visions. There was no remote control and they were not cable ready. Some of them had a digital panel while others were the older style rotary dial tuner television. My husband and I turned them into cable televi-sions with remote control for FREE just by shopping at garage sales.

HOW? . . . READ ON.

Most older televisions receive the standard channels:

2 through 13   (*VHF*)--*very high fre-quency.*

Some televisions may receive other chan-nels:

14 through 82   *(UHF)--ultra high fre-quency.*

Both of these sets of frequencies are called broadcast frequencies, meaning that televi-sion companies broadcast these frequencies over the air. You receive these stations through your antenna.

CABLE CHANNELS USE DIFFERENT FREQUENCIES.

To receive the cable frequencies you need a cable ready receiver. These receivers are typically the cable boxes that are provided by the cable company for a monthly cost.

The cable box from your cable company receives all the channels from the different cable companies and changes the frequency of the **"receive"** channel to match channel **"3"** on your television, much the same as a VCR does.

You must have cable run into your home from the local cable company to receive these cable channels.

The older style televisions that aren't cable ready cannot receive the signals from the cable that is run into your home from the cable company because it doesn't understand the frequencies.

Remember . . . it only understands:

channels 2 through 13   (VHF)

and

channels 14 through 82   (UHF)

However, it is easy to make the older style televisions understand the new cable fre-quencies.

HERE'S HOW . . .

You can either have a box from the cable company that will convert the cable signals into a signal your TV will understand for a monthly charge . . .

or

Use a VCR that is capable of understanding the new cable frequencies.

VCRs

The easiest way to get cable for your perfectly good older television is to start garage sale~ing and find a VCR where the tape mechanism is no longer working.

Why do most people buy a VCR? They want to tape television shows and play movies. When the tape portion of their VCR no longer works and they find out just how expensive it is to fix the tape mechanism, the VCR usually ends up in the trash or in the FREE box at garage sales.

These VCRs usually have their own remote control, which will now operate on your television!

Look for the front loading VCRs. Do not get the older style top loading VCRs.

ALL VCRs ARE TV SETS IN THEIR OWN RIGHT. THEY CAN RECEIVE A TELEVISION SIGNAL AND CONVERT IT TO A PICTURE.

THE ONLY THING MISSING FROM THE VCR IS THE TELEVISION TUBE.

THIS IS HOW YOUR VCR CAN RECORD ONE CHANNEL WHILE YOU WATCH ANOTHER.

REMEMBER . . . VCRs ARE REALLY TELEVISIONS WITHOUT THE SCREEN AND IF THEY ARE CABLE READY, THEY HAVE THE ABILITY TO RECEIVE TELEVISION PROGRAMS ON THE CABLE TYPE FREQUENCIES. THE VCR IS NOW YOUR TELEVISION AND IT IS DOING ALL THE WORK. YOUR OLD TELEVISION IS NOW JUST A DISPLAY DEVICE.

"How To"

ATTACH GARAGE SALE VCR TO TV

Materials needed:
Working TV
VCR (tape does not need to work)
"F" type connector (optional)*
Screwdriver
Coaxial cable*
Coax adapter (optional)*

*See glossary

1 Attach the cable from the cable company to the INPUT connector on the VCR. On the back of the VCR, the input connector is typically located by the output connector that goes to your TV.

NOTE: If your TV has a coax type connector ("F" type connector) on the back, simply connect it to the OUT connector with coax cable.

"F" CONNECTOR:

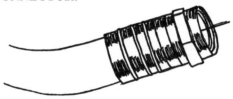

If the TV doesn't have a coax connector, you will need a coax adapter. Check your local electronics store for this adapter.

All older TVs have a twin lead, which is 2 wires connected to the antenna (newer ones have coaxial cable).

THE TWO TYPES OF VCRs

Make sure you shop for the front-loading VCRs. The old top-loading VCRs are not recommended. The following instructions are for the top-loading VCRs.

1 The first type of VCR has a digital readout for channels 2 through 115 and an up and down channel selector. The VCR with the up and down channel button is the more desirable. It indicates that you don't have to manually pre-select a button and associate it with a channel. You'll be able to up and down channel to all the cable channels on the remote control.

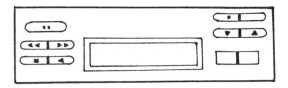

2 The other type of VCR will have separate push buttons for each channel. Usually the buttons are pre-labeled 2 through 13 or "A" through "L."

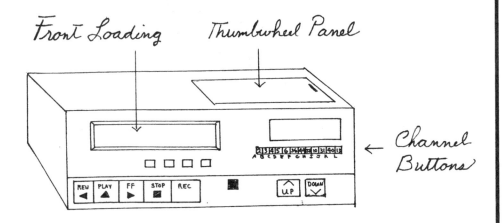

The difference between a VCR with 12 or 15 buttons and one that doesn't have buttons is that a button VCR limits you to viewing pre-selected channels. You must pre-select and tune in those particular channels. This is the only limitation with this type VCR. You can still receive all the cable channels that you wish, but you must have a button assigned to each channel.

They both work well and both will give you all cable channels on your existing TV. You will also have remote control for your TV . . . SUCH A GOOD DEAL!

"How To"

TUNE IN THE BUTTON STYLE VCR

NOTE: If your VCR has an AFT switch (automatic fine tune), turn it off while tuning in the thumb wheels. Turn back on after tuning in.

1 The button-style VCRs will have some kind of access panel--a pull down door, or a plate that snaps out--something that allows you to get to the multiple rows of thumbwheels.

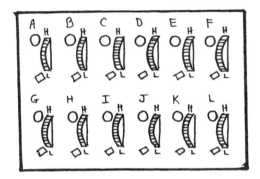

The thumbwheels are individual and are on a one-to-one basis to the buttons on the front of the VCR.

Each thumbwheel has associated with it some type of switch or three different bands of frequencies.

The frequency band widths are ranges:

Channels 2 through 6   VLOW

Channels 7 through 13   VHIGH

Channels 14 through 83   UHF

Continued. . .

2 Set the TV to channel "3." ALWAYS LEAVE THE TV SET TUNED TO CHANNEL 3. This is the universal output channel for most cable boxes and VCRs. Some VCRs (very few) have channel "4" as an alternative. Try it first on channel "3."

3 Select which range of channels you want to tune in and manually turn the thumbwheel until the channel is tuned in and visible on the television set.

Make sure the tuner on the VCR indicates the channel you are trying to thumbwheel in or else you won't see any picture change.

Each number button on the front of the VCR is associated with the corresponding thumbwheel.

Button "A" on the front of the VCR is thumbwheel "A."

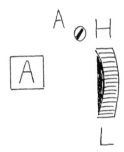

If you want to tune the thumbwheel, you need to push the button that you want this channel to be associated with.

EXAMPLE: IF YOU PUSH BUTTON 1 AND WANT TO RECEIVE CHANNEL 23 ON THIS BUTTON . . . TURN THE THUMBWHEEL UNTIL YOU SEE CHANNEL 23 IN FOCUS AND HEAR THE SOUND.

STOP. IT IS NOW LOCKED IN.

BUTTON 1 HAS BECOME CHANNEL 23.

You have to tune in and assign a button to your regular channels also.

Remember . . . the TV is always set to channel "3." Your television has now become what you call a "DUMB TUBE."

The VCR now has all the smarts and is in charge of receiving and changing channels.

STEREOS

We found a wonderful Sony 6 CD changer for only $10 at a garage sale. The changer portion did not work. Even though you could load several CDs at a time, the changer would only play what was on disc one so it was simply a CD player and not a CD changer. You had to manually load the CDs and play them one at a time. For only $10 this CD changer would please my son perfectly. He was quite willing to change the CDs when he was ready to listen to something different.

Years ago I bought a stereo cassette recorder at a store for $89. It was on sale and a really good deal, however, a few months later I wish I had bought a dual cassette recorder so I could make recordings. So, I really considered myself lucky to find a complete stereo system at a garage sale with turntable, dual cassette recorder, equalizer and amplifier for just $10. The fact that it didn't have speakers was not a problem since I have a collection of garage sale speakers in the basement just waiting to SPEAK! The new turntable was considerably better than the one I purchased at a store for $189 and the amplifier had much more power and watts per channel than my original amplifier. I ended up selling the old stereo equipment at my garage sale, which made the new stereo system FREE.

The boom boxes, cassette players, headphones and portable CD players for the children were all purchased at garage sales--as were the small wallet-sized speakers, desk-sized speakers and those great big speakers that the kids like to kill your eardrums with! The speakers range anywhere from 25¢ to $8.00 a set.

See the Computer chapter for more ways to use garage sale speakers.

RADIOS

Clock radios, digital radios, multi-band radios, scanners, car radios and speakers, and answering machines are just a sampling of the different kinds of electronic equipment that you can find at garage sales. A lot of these items are brand new and in their original carton. Some of these items I wouldn't buy unless they were new in the box!

SECURITY SYSTEMS

Intercom systems and even full house security systems with brand new digital access panels, sirens, and motion detectors can be bought at garage sales.

We just had a brand new security system installed and paid retail, yes, retail! I really didn't think there was a chance of finding a whole house security system at a garage sale. A few months later I found three brand new digital access panels. They were the same brand that we had installed earlier, only they were the more expensive deluxe model--the model with full digital readout for every room. I bought them for just $1.00 apiece! Mine cost $120 apiece just for the economy model. I took the new digital access panels to the security company that sold and installed our system to see if they could change out the inexpensive models for the more deluxe models. Unfortunately, they couldn't use them unless they changed the entire monitoring unit. What they did do for me however, was give me credit towards the monthly security monitoring service in exchange for the panels I traded. For two years I didn't have to pay the monitoring service bill, which resulted in a savings of $240! A pretty good deal for a $3.00 garage sale purchase!

CHAPTER EIGHT

GARAGE SALE COMPUTERS

HARDWARE
CPU
MONITORS
PRINTERS
JOYSTICKS
MOUSE

SOFTWARE
DOS
WINDOWS
GAMES

INTERNET
MODEMS

SPEAKERS &
SOUND

This chapter should save you thousands of dollars and keep you from buying garage sale "dinosaurs!"

I can't begin to tell you how many times I've seen people buying computers at garage sales that are so old and outdated that they are totally unusable.

They think they will buy a computer so their children can play games.

WRONG!

Sometimes they'll want it just for typing letters and maybe balancing their checkbook with the latest software.

WRONG!

Most of the people at garage sales don't even know what type of computer they are selling and it's for sure, most people don't know what they are buying! There are a few simple facts outlined in this chapter that will help avoid making these mistakes and allow you to make the right decision.

223

Ask the seller, "Is this a '386' or a '486' ?"
"How much memory does it have?"
"How much disk space does it have?"

It will be a rare day when you can get all of your questions answered.

A lot of the computers that you buy at garage sales are so old it's like buying an old car with no wheels, no engine, no interior and guess what? Parts are no longer available! You've got absolutely nothing--a real "dinosaur!"

I've had friends call to tell me about their wonderful computer buys and I ended up having to help them carry their "bargains" out to the trash! I see a lot of money changing hands at garage sales for computer equipment and this chapter will help you avoid making some costly mistakes.

My husband and I have worked in computer engineering for over 36 years between us! He is still a certified network engineer. I am now a certified garage sale~er! We hope this chapter will help you avoid making a lot of wrong decisions when you buy your computer equipment at garage sales.

There are great bargains to be found out there. We've bought several computers and computer peripherals for our children, ourselves and friends at garage sales. We've helped them save thousands of dollars!

Last week we found a "386" computer with a keyboard and Super VGA color monitor for $50! We also found a "486" with Super VGA monitor, keyboard, a mouse, internal modem, soundcard and another brand new mouse still in the wrapped box for $100. The monitor alone cost over $200 retail.

We found a "386" with keyboard and VGA color monitor for $5! It can be upgraded very easily.

You too can find these bargains! All you need is a little basic information to know what to look for and why. GO FOR IT!!!

Please note . . . this chapter is written for the complete novice. It is not intended to teach you everything you've always wanted to know about computers. That's a whole book in itself! This chapter deals only with IBM or IBM-compatible personal computers (PCs).

THE BEST WAY TO PURCHASE COMPUTER EQUIPMENT IS TO TURN IT ON AND TEST IT OUT. IF YOU CAN DO THIS, MOST OF YOUR QUESTIONS AND CONCERNS ARE EASILY ANSWERED.

Most sellers have electric outlets in their garages and extension cords, so this is usually not a problem. The only place that you would not be able to plug a PC in and test it is at a large church sale or flea market type sale.

This chapter will give you the guidelines you need to help you make a good decision in both cases.

WILL THE COMPUTER WORK?

WILL IT DO WHAT I WANT?

HOW LONG WILL IT LAST?

There are two areas you need to be concerned with when buying computer equipment. They are computer hardware and software.

HARDWARE

THE FOUR PARTS THAT MAKE UP COMPUTER HARDWARE ARE:

1.   MONITOR

> This is the screen that displays your information.

2.   CPU/CASE
     Central Processing Unit

> This is the square box that either sits under the monitor or stands up by the side.

3.   KEYBOARD

> A typewriter style keyboard with extra keys.

4.   MOUSE

> This hand-held device allows you to move around the screen. It acts as a pointer.

CASE OR CPU

ALWAYS ASK TO SEE THE PAPERWORK AND ASK FOR THE ACCOMPANYING BOOKLET FOR THE CPU.

If the paperwork is missing, there are ways to tell what kind of a CPU/case it is.

The different size CPUs to look for are "286," "386," "486," and "586-Pentium."

The only reason I list a "286" is that you will see a lot of them out there.

It is very doubtful you will want a "286" because of its limitations, but depending on what you want to do with your PC--this might work for you.

See the matrix at the end of this chapter to help make your determination.

It is very doubtful you will find a "586" (Pentium) as this is the latest technology. A "386" or "486" will probably be your best bet.

CPUs come in basically two styles:

TOWER

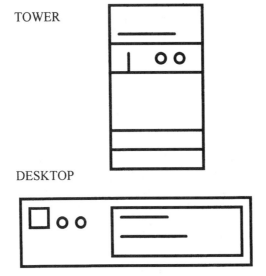

DESKTOP

Either of these two styles is acceptable.

HOW TO TELL THE DIFFERENCE BETWEEN THE CPUs.

"286" - "386" - "486" - "586"

Look for a button on the front of the CPU case that says TURBO.

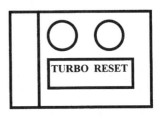

Plug in the CPU and see the red indicator light for TURBO.

IF THERE IS NOT A <u>TURBO</u> <u>BUTTON</u> <u>AND LIGHT</u>, IT IS <u>NOT</u> A "386" OR HIGHER.

Typically a "286" does not have a turbo button & light.

Remember . . . the TURBO button and light are different from the power indicator light.

If the CPU has a digital LED readout with numbers such as 16, 20, 25, 33, 40, 50, 66 or higher, this is a sign of a later model CPU such as a "386" or "486." <u>THIS IS GOOD!</u>

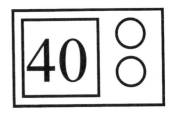

Turn the case around to see the back.

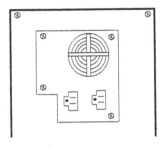

Look for the power supply. (You'll see a fan and vent area.)

Turn on the power supply. Make sure the fan blows air from the power supply.

This means the power is good because the fan runs at 12 volts DC and converts 110 AC to 5 & 12 volt DC. Don't really worry about this last statement. Just make sure the fan runs OK.

MONITORS

ALWAYS TRY TO SEE THE MONITOR UP & RUNNING.

Some monitors have green, yellow, orange or white text. You do not want these. They indicate an old style, low quality monitor.

YOU WANT A FULL COLOR MONITOR.

If it's not possible to see the monitor up and running, here's what you need to do:

On the back of the monitor you should see two cables. One is the power cord that you plug into the wall. The other cable is a "D" shaped plug with pins in it.

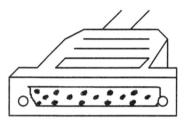

The "D" shaped plug should match the "D" shaped receptacle on the back of the CPU.

THE "D" SHAPED CONNECTOR IS HOW YOU DETERMINE IF THE MONITOR IS COLOR.

The "D" plug should have three rows of pins. The holes for the pins will total 15. The pins on the cable plug can be 15 or fewer.

IF THE MONITOR HAS THE "D" SHAPED CONNECTOR WITH THREE ROWS OF PINS, IT IS A COLOR MONITOR.

The cable connector on the back of the CPU should receive the "D" shaped connector plug from the monitor, meaning that the receptacle is a "D" shape and has three rows of holes that will receive the three rows of pins on the monitor cable.

The important thing to remember about connectors & cables is that they must "FIT" together.

If the back of a CPU has a "D" shaped connector with only two rows of holes, it will not accept the monitor with three rows of pins.

Also, check for dust and dirt in the slat openings on top of the monitor. If it is very dusty and dirty, you might want to pass. The very nature of electronics is that they attract dust. Hardware that is very dusty indicates long hours of use. Try to avoid these.

It's OK to pass--you'll find many more.

PRINTERS

On the computer case there should be a connector that takes 25 pins. The cable that is attached to the printer will have a 25-pin connector plug that will fit into the 25-pin connector receptacle on the computer case. Remember . . . one connector has pins, the other small holes. All printers, either an impact or laser printer, require a 25-pin or IBM-compatible pin connector.

25-PIN CONNECTOR "CENTRONICS"

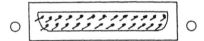

Considering that printers have a large number of movable parts, try to test out the printer before you buy. There are lots of dot matrix type printers at garage sales for $20 or less. These are OK for text and they will print out some graphics, but they will be rudimentary. The' output is not the same quality as an ink jet or laser printed product.

Laser printers can be found at garage sales too, but again, test them out. With any printer you buy, make sure you have the documentation that goes with the printer.

You will definitely need the documentation to learn how to change cartridges, insert paper, use the tractor feeder, etc. All of these computer supplies are readily available at the sales too. Stock up on paper, tractor feed paper, forms and printer labels.

JOYSTICKS & MOUSE

A mouse is a necessity when running Windows software. We've found them for 50¢ apiece at several sales. The last complete "386" system we bought for $5.00 had a brand new $59.00 mouse attached!

Joysticks are highly recommended for games. The majority of joysticks have a common plug (interface). Joysticks vary in size, for everyone from a 5-year-old to a 300-pound lumberjack! The plug is standard. They are all the same.

What you need to consider in purchasing a joystick is the hand size and the durability of the joystick.

Consult the game manufacturer's requirements. The game will tell you if you need a joystick.

HARDWARE CHECKLIST

✓ **Check CPU for Turbo button and Turbo light or numbers.**

✓ **Plug in the CPU to see if the fan works (power supply).**

✓ **Check monitor plug for "D" connector with three rows of pins.**

✓ **Check for dust in air vents.**

✓ **Check for 25-pin "Centronics" connector for the printer.**

SOFTWARE

Software refers to the internal smarts that make your computer do everything you tell it to do.

Software is purchased on disk, diskettes or CD-ROM.

All software has a version number associated with it and the version number is important for you to know--for example "3.0" or "3.1."

You will see all kinds of software at sales, software that you've heard of and probably have been wanting to buy, but . . . BUYER BEWARE!

IT IS EXTREMELY IMPORTANT TO KNOW THE VERSION NUMBER OF THE SOFTWARE.

THIS IS WHY . . .

Some versions of software are made to run on older machines such as a "286" and will absolutely not work on the newer model computers. You might have a brand new "586" Pentium at home and see software at sales that you've been wanting. Don't assume because you have the latest and greatest hardware that anything and everything will run on it. It won't!

We've seen so much money thrown away at garage sales by people buying packages of software that they have seen selling in the stores for hundreds of dollars. They will gladly pay $10 to $20 at sales instead of hundreds of dollars at the store, only to find that the software will not run on their computers.

Let's talk about two very important software packages.

DOS   (MS-DOS) (PC-DOS)

and

WINDOWS . . . WINDOWS95

DOS SOFTWARE

All of the computers that we have talked about in this chapter run DOS of some kind.

All kinds of DOS will have a version number.

THE LATEST VERSION OF MS-DOS IS 6.22.

DOS VERSION 3.3 (an older version) WILL RUN TODAY'S DOS BASED SOFTWARE.

DOS VERSION 3.3 IS THE OLDEST VERSION OF DOS THAT YOU WOULD WANT TO HAVE.

Any DOS from version 3.3 upward will run most of today's software.

DO NOT BUY ANY DOS THAT IS AN EARLIER VERSION SUCH AS 3.1 OR 3.2.

To see what version DOS the PC is running, do the following:

TURN THE CASE AND THE MONITOR ON.

THE MONITOR WILL DISPLAY SEVERAL SCREENS FULL OF TEXT.

WHEN THE MONITOR SCREEN STOPS SCROLLING, IT WILL STOP AT THE C:> PROMPT.

At the **C:> PROMPT**

TYPE   VER

PRESS THE ENTER KEY.

This is what will appear on the screen:

C:>\VER

MS-DOS Version 6.20

C:\>

This screen tells you that version 6.20 is loaded on the computer.

Do not buy a PC if the version number is lower than 3.3.

WINDOWS SOFTWARE

YOU WILL DEFINITELY WANT TO HAVE WINDOWS SOFTWARE!

Windows software eliminates the need to type in commands. You simply click your mouse pointer on a small drawing (icon) to issue commands to the computer.

Windows makes working with computers fun!

The very popular Windows software runs on top of DOS software. Version 3.3 DOS is the oldest version that you can run with Windows software.

This, however, is not what version I would recommend.

THE LATEST VERSIONS OF WINDOWS SOFTWARE ARE 3.11 AND WINDOWS 95.

THE OLDEST VERSION OF WINDOWS THAT I WOULD RECOMMEND IS 3.1.

REMEMBER YOU NEED AT LEAST VERSION 5.0 DOS TO RUN WINDOWS 3.1

You will always want a mouse with Windows software.

GAME SOFTWARE

Everyone--well, almost everyone--likes to play computer games and it is very important when you are buying games at garage sales to buy them in the original packaging with their instructions. If not, you will be wasting your time and money.

Games are peculiar to hardware and software systems.

Make sure you know what hardware you have, and what software you are running such as what version of DOS and what version of Windows before you go shopping for games.

The game packaging will tell you what type of hardware is required to run them, such as "386" or "486," etc., and what version software (DOS and Windows) is needed.

You will most likely want a sound card in your PC to play the latest and greatest games.

See the Speakers & Sound section in this chapter.

RAM
(Random Access Memory)

You need to know how much RAM (memory) your computer has. Most, if not all, PCs when powered on will flash a series of numbers in the upper left hand corner, which indicates the memory.

Here's how to check the RAM (memory):

1. **Turn the PC and the monitor on.**

2. **Look in the upper left hand corner and notice the numbers flashing.**

3. **When the numbers stop, the final number shows the amount of RAM the PC has.**

If the PC has 4 MB (megabytes) of RAM, the number will read somewhere around 4000--give or take a few numbers.

This number displays in thousands (kilobytes.)

THE MINIMUM AMOUNT OF RAM NEEDED TO RUN:

WINDOWS 3.1   4 MB

WINDOWS 95   12 MB

THE MORE RAM--THE BETTER

It's important to know that most of the time you can increase the amount of memory your machine has in it. You will need to take it to a store and have them do this for you. If you purchase more memory they will usually install it for free.

There is also a command that you can type in to see how much memory the machine has.

At the **C:> PROMPT**   TYPE   **MEM**

```
C:\>mem

Memory Type        Total    =   Used   +   Free
----------------   -------      -------    -------
Conventional         636K        152K       484K
Upper                  0K          0K         0K
Reserved               0K          0K         0K
Extended (XMS)    19,456K      4,545K    14,911K
----------------   -------      -------    -------
Total memory      20,092K      4,697K    15,395K

Total under 1 MB     636K        152K       484K

Largest executable program size     483K  (494,672 bytes)
Largest free upper memory block       0K      (0 bytes)
MS-DOS is resident in the high memory area.

C:\>
```

See the Total column on the Total memory line. This display shows the PC has 20 MB of memory

DISK SIZE

There are two commands available that will tell you how many bytes are available on the disk.

The following command is for all versions of DOS:

At the **C:> PROMPT**   TYPE   **CHKDSK**

This command tells you the total amount of bytes on the disk

```
C:\>chkdsk
Volume Serial Number is 2359-18D6

   540,672,000 bytes total disk space
     8,617,984 bytes in 7 hidden files
     4,751,360 bytes in 289 directories
   349,765,632 bytes in 5,639 user files
   177,537,024 bytes available on disk

        16,384 bytes in each allocation unit
        33,000 total allocation units on disk
        10,836 available allocation units on disk

       651,264 total bytes memory
       494,672 bytes free

Instead of using CHKDSK, try using SCANDISK.  SCANDISK can reliably detect
and fix a much wider range of disk problems.  For more information,
type HELP SCANDISK from the command prompt.

C:\>




C:\>
```

The **SCANDISK** command is for all versions of DOS 6 or above.

THE INTERNET

Just about everyone wants to get on the Internet. It's easy as long as you have the right hardware and software. Take these facts into consideration when making your purchase!

Internet access has evolved as a product based on "486" and higher computers.

The latest software products (graphic interfaces) that make the Internet more user friendly are available only for "486" and higher computer products.

Yes, you can certainly get on the Internet with a "386" product. If you are familiar with computers and commands then this would be OK for you.

TO ACCESS THE INTERNET YOU WILL NEED 4 OR 8 MB OF RAM AND A HIGH SPEED MODEM.

Most "486" or higher computers will have an internal modem--one that is built into the CPU.

To see if the computer has an internal modem, look on the back of the CPU for a slot with a standard telephone jack. This is where you would plug your phone in and allows you to dial up the Internet. There are usually two jacks. One goes to the telephone company (the outlet in your wall) the other plugs into your telephone.

You will then need to find a service to connect you to the Internet or you may want to check the local universities. Some of them offer Internet access for FREE!

MODEMS

One of the many computer devices you may find at a garage sale is a modem. Modems are used to connect the PC to a phone line. By dialing a number, one can connect to other computers and share information. In the past, modems only needed to send and receive text. Characters, like "a," "b," "c," and so on. The modems were not especially fast. When the new graphical interfaces such as Windows became popular, the amount of data transmitted across the telephone lines via modems increased dramatically. This is why newer, faster modems have been developed making the older, slower modems obsolete. I have never seen a modem at garage sales that meets the demanding data requirements of today's PCs.

The reason you see older modems for sale is because the owners upgraded to a much faster modem. My advice is to pass on garage sale modems and buy a new fast speed modem that transmits at 14,400 bits per second. These modems are usually called "Fourteen Four." This is an acceptable modem speed for today's communication requirements and to download information from the Internet.

Yes, you can do data communications and get on the Internet with a slower modem. Just remember however, you are paying for time. The faster you can communicate and exchange information means less money spent in billing time.

SPEAKERS & SOUND

If you play computer games, you will definitely want sound.

After saving all this money by buying your computer equipment at garage sales you certainly don't want to go to the store and pay $50 for a tiny set of computer speakers!

Any speakers will do.

Here's how to have great output for only $5.00!

First you will need a sound card in the CPU.

A sound card is like a miniature amplifier and recording device. The output is to some external thing like speakers, a bigger amp or headphones.

HOW DO YOU KNOW IF THERE IS A SOUND CARD IN THE PC?

Look for a small mini-plug or standard RCA jack connection in the back of the CPU and a thumbwheel for volume control.

HOW CAN YOU HAVE GREAT SOUND FOR $5.00 OR LESS?

Look for an old 8-track stereo set at the sales. You will find hundreds! These make great amplifiers and speakers for your PC.

Remember . . . you're not buying it for the 8-track. All you need to have working is the amplifier and the speakers. It can be 15 years old and the 8-track could have died 10 years ago, but if the tuner and speakers work well, you're in business!

You can also use one of the several amplifiers you'll find either with speakers or without. If the amplifier is a good buy-- $3.00 or $5.00--go ahead and buy it. You'll find your speakers at another sale.

Buy your headphones at sales too! These will plug right into your sound card. You'll especially want headphones if you have children playing games all the time!

OVERVIEW

It's always a good idea to know what you are going to do with a computer before you make a purchasing decision. If you are just going to use it to type letters or do papers for school then a "386" will do nicely and you can easily find one with a color monitor for around $50 to $75 at garage sales. If you want to get on the Internet and are not an experienced computer user and familiar with UNIX commands then you would want a "486."

Take a good look at the matrix on the next page to decide what it is you want to do with your computer and it will give you some guidelines for your purchase.

Also, check the appendix in the back of this book for a complete price list of computers and their peripherals. I hope you will never again buy a "dinosaur" and will use these guidelines to help you save thousands of dollars!

Below is a diagram that shows the back of a fully loaded PC. This will help you know what you are looking for and determine if the PC you are looking at contains these items.

A FULLY LOADED PC

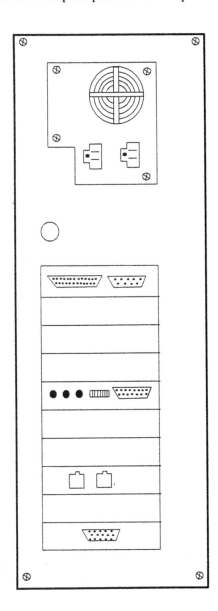

← POWER SUPPLY

← 25-PIN PRINTER CONNECTOR

←——————SOUNDCARD
JACKS AND VOLUME CONTROL

← INTERNAL MODEM
2 TELEPHONE JACKS

← VIDEO CARD
15-PIN THREE ROW CONNECTOR

CPU (CENTRAL PROCESSING UNIT)

CPU	TURBO LIGHT	RAM	DOS	WINDOWS	WIN95	MOUSE	GAMES	INTERNET ACCESS
XT	N	640K	Y	N	N	N	N	N
286	Y	1-2M	Y	N	N	N	N	N
386	Y	2-4M	Y	Y	N	Y	Y	Y
486	Y	4+M	Y	Y	Y	Y	Y	Y
586	N	8+M	Y	Y	Y	Y	Y	Y

GARAGE SALE PRICING

PRODUCT	RETAIL	GARAGE SALE	SHELLEY'S BEST
XT	N/A		
286	$100	$40	$5
386	$250	$75	$50
486	$695	$100	$60
586	$1,000+	N/A	N/A
MEMORY--1MB	$45	$25	$1.25
MONITOR	$395	$100	$10
KEYBOARD	$45	$10	$2
MOUSE	$50	$5	$1
GAMES	$35+	$10	$5
JOYSTICK	$35	$15	$5
SOUND CARD	$80	$15	$7
PRINTERS, MATRIX	$120	$20	$10
PRINTERS, LASER	$400	$100	$60

CHAPTER NINE

GARAGE, AUTO & OUTDOOR

GARAGE

AUTOMOTIVE

LAWN &
GARDEN

CAMPING
EQUIPMENT

CLEANING
SUPPLIES

RECREATION

Does anyone really decorate garages? No not really, but we do "outfit" them.

The garage is the place where we usually store lots of tools, the lawn mower and fertilizer spreader, sometimes firewood. There is usually a workbench, wet-vac, paints and stains, garden tools, wood scraps, and of course four deep freezers like I have in my garage! All of these items are easily found at garage sales.

It's nice to have a place to store all of the garage items in an organized fashion, and if you are like me, the last thing you want to do is spend hundreds of dollars on cabinets made for the garage.

I've priced special garage storage cabinets at the hardware store and came up with a solution that's just as good and quite a bit less. In fact a whole lot less!

How about spending just $10 for all the storage cabinets and Formica top! Spring and summer are usually remodeling time--

including remodeling old kitchens. What do people do with their old kitchen cabinets and Formica tops? They usually sell them in their garage sales. What wonderful storage cabinets these old kitchen cabinets make for the garage. The cabinet set that I found didn't need any repair, just a few new handles that I had been collecting in the FREE boxes at the sales.

I spray painted all the cabinets white. They were very easy to mount on the existing studs that were exposed in the garage walls. Lay the Formica back in place and you have a wonderful work area.

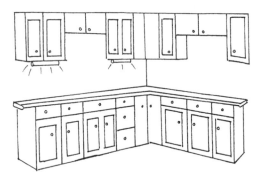

In between the base cabinets and the wall cabinets you will want a piece of Peg-Board to hold all of your tools. You can find a lot of pieces of Peg-Board in the FREE boxes at the sales. Pick these up and nail the pieces on the wall making one even sheet. Sometimes you will find an entire 4' x 8' sheet for just $1.00. You can leave the Peg-Board the original dark color or spray paint it white or any color. I use the colors that I've picked up at sales and go from there. Start digging through those hardware boxes at the sales and you will find the Peg-Board hangers to hang all of your tools. I found a whole box of assorted pieces, much more than I could ever use and it was all FREE! If you were going to purchase these little hangers they would add up in price really quickly.

Place a fluorescent light underneath the wall-mounted cabinets. You can find the fluores-

cent light sticks brand new for just $1.00 at the sales. Use the kind of fluorescent light that's either encased in plastic or a plain light stick for under the wall cabinets. Use the double fluorescent lights that are encased in metal and hang from a chain over your entire work area. Expect to pay around $2.00, including the bulbs, for the large hanging fluorescent light fixture.

Mount your 25¢ power strips at each end of the cabinets and place one in the middle so you can plug in your garage sale power tools.

Now you have a place to store all of those garage sale tools, hardware, paints and stains. I also have a heavy duty wooden work bench that I use in the garage to do painting and staining, clamping and messy work. The $8.00 Black & Decker bench grinder that was brand new is mounted on this workbench. I found the workbench at a sale for $2.00. There is at least $25 worth of wood and bolts in the $2.00 workbench!

Shelving is another popular item for the garage area and shelving is easy to find at garage sales. It's very inexpensive--sometimes even free. Shelving brackets are also easy to find at sales. I like to put large covered storage tubs on these shelves. One tub stores all of my electrical parts, another chain, another odds and ends hardware. Label them to suit your needs and you'll never be looking for that odd screw or hinge again! These tubs usually run around 50¢ to $1.00 at sales and they hold a lot!

I like to keep potting soil in one of the large tubs. It's easy to mix soils together and when I'm ready to pot I remove the lid and use it as a potting tray. The soil that spills over is easy to scrape back into the large tub. Seal the lid back on and store away. I always save the plastic laundry scoops that come in the boxes of laundry powder. They are handy for all kinds of things, especially a potting soil scoop.

Any tool or hardware item that you find in the stores you can find at local garage sales. A lot of the power tools I've found were brand new and in the box. I've purchased all kinds of saws, drills, drill bits, cordless drills, bench grinders, electric sanders, hammers, levels, screwdrivers--just about every kind of tool you can think of.

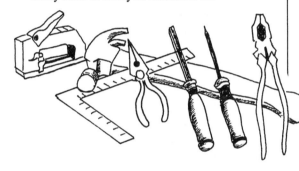

Buy all of your paints, stains, varnishes, turpentine, spray paints, and glues at sales for 10-25¢ . . . sometimes even FREE.

MOVING SALES are a great place to stock up on items for the garage. Long distance movers will not haul paints and varnishes or combustibles. You will find a lot of these items at moving sales.

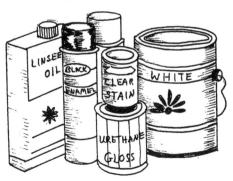

Moving sales are also a good place to buy BBQ pits, lawn mowers, snow blowers, fertilizers, garden hoses, plant food, charcoal, firewood, etc. For some reason, people usually do not, or prefer not to move these items. They would rather buy them new at their final destination.

One of my favorite buys at moving sales is firewood. Sometimes I've had to ask if they have any firewood for sale. It's an item that's often overlooked when planning a moving sale. People never even think about selling it. They were just going to leave it for the new occupants so they usually are happy to take a few dollars for the firewood. Some people give it away FREE. The most I've ever had to pay for a full cord of mixed hardwood is $25. Of course I had to load it myself, but when you consider a full cord of mixed hardwood in our area sells for $239, I didn't mind loading it!

The automatic garage door opener that we bought was only $5.00. It was the exact same brand that we were going to buy at the store and the seller even had all the paperwork and installation instructions. Without these instructions we wouldn't have considered buying it but after having installed a garage door opener before, we thought we'd give it a try. The seller said it worked and showed us the new one that she had installed with the outdoor keypad. Her old garage door opener didn't have the outdoor keypad and the children were always locking themselves out of the house. There wasn't any problem with the old opener. She did say, however, that the light didn't work. We thought we could fix it.

As it turned out, the garage door opener did work fine and has worked fine for over four years. To fix the light was very expensive, so we found a great "work around," which I highly recommend whether your garage door opener light works or not!

We bought a motion detector light at another garage sale for $2.00 and installed that on the garage wall. This is even better than having a light in the garage door opener. As soon as the garage door starts to move, the motion detector light comes on. If I go out in the garage from the kitchen--the motion detector light comes on. If I need to find something in the freezer in the garage, the light automatically comes on. This eliminates having to turn the electric lights on and off. We hardly ever turn the electric lights on any more. How many times have you left your lights on in the garage burning overnight, and wasting valuable electricity?

I highly recommend getting a motion detector spotlight and mounting it in your garage. You can set them to go out after a couple of minutes so if you are working in the garage they are not constantly lit. There is no need to turn your electric lights on and off constantly.

Since I spend so much time in the garage making all the treasures described in this book, I like to have a piece of carpet down around the work area and walking areas. I buy carpet scraps for $2.00 at sales. They are nice big pieces of carpet scraps. Sometimes they're 6' x 9' or 8' x 10'. When they get oil stained or just too dirty to clean up I pitch them and get more.

No garage is complete without a remote control, cable color television. Yes . . . there is a color television in the garage mounted up on the wall out of the way. The guys love having a TV in the garage so they can watch their weekend sports while they are out there puttering on the car or working on their latest project or helping me with my latest project!

Your normal, everyday auto stuff is found at garage sales too.

AUTOMOTIVE

My husband buys his oil and air filters at sales. They usually sell for 50¢ apiece. Quarts of oil that sell anywhere from $1.00 to $2.00 retail are found for 25¢ a quart. Anti-freeze, which sells for several dollars, can be found for 50¢ a gallon, sometimes even FREE. Transmission fluid that you would expect to pay $3.00 to $4.00 retail will cost 25-50¢ at sales.

Gas cans are another good buy. These cans are usually pretty expensive to buy because they are very well made due to government regulations. A new gas can will run anywhere from $6.00 to $10 in the store. You can pick them up at the sales for 50¢. Make sure the outside looks dry. If it's not dry then it probably leaks--find another one.

So many automotive needs will be found at moving sales. People just don't want to move a lot of these types of materials and long distance movers will not move them, so families need to get rid of this stuff.

We found brand new in-the-box side runners for our 4-wheel drive vehicle. Our car had a very high step on it and I had been pricing the runners in car catalogues. They were running around $139. We found the exact same brand that I was pricing for $10 brand new, complete with all the parts.

You can also find a lot of specialty automotive items like trailer hitches, specialty headlights, fog lamps, CB radios and radar detectors selling for just a few dollars.

Our tire chains were purchased at sales for $2.00. You can find tire chains at just about every sale. Our friend and neighbor, Scott, who is a seasoned garage sale~er says that no sale is complete without a set of tire chains and a fertilizer spreader!

Car bras and car covers are popular items. If you have ever stored an automobile, you know how expensive car covers can be. Start shopping at garage sales and you can find them, sometimes brand new for $10.

All of our cars and the children's cars are equipped with an emergency kit. These kits usually consist of jumper cables; a light that can be plugged into the cigarette lighter and sometimes pliers, screwdriver, crescent wrench, flares and signs. Kits usually come in a plastic carrying case. If the carrying case is torn, buy it anyway and pick up a piece of zippered soft-sided luggage for $1.00. The smaller size is just the right size for all of your automotive emergency supplies.

My very best automotive story involves not supplies, but automobiles. Yes, I've seen everything imaginable at garage sales. I am a firm believer that if you look long enough you will find exactly what you are looking for. I've seen lots of automobiles, from a 450 SL Mercedes Benz to the old perfectly restored Model "T"s!

My husband and I were shopping at a community sale one Saturday morning and there was a Volkswagen Rabbit with a price tag of $100. I looked at the price several times because I was sure it couldn't be right. The car was in very good condition on the inside and outside--no rust, no dents, the inside was spotless, no rips or tears and extremely clean--even the tires looked decent. I mentioned it to my husband. "Do you see the price on this car?--It's $100." As he started to walk away I asked him why he wasn't even going to inquire about the car knowing our son would love to have one at college.

"Well," he said, "there's got to be something drastically wrong with it for that price."

"Well," said I, "why don't we at least find out?" You know men--it's just like asking for directions! I decided to ask! The seller told me, "It runs, it has 189,000 miles on it, it's good for short trips but the engine needs some work." I asked him, "What kind of work?" like I'm some kind of automotive mechanic, at which point, my husband finally perked up and started kicking the tires! The owner said it for sure needed a new clutch and probably some rings but that it ran and his wife drove it daily! Sure enough, it started. I looked over the inside and it was virtually spotless. The radio and cassette player were probably worth $100. My husband thanked him for his time, stating that it was too much trouble to mess with. Throughout the rest of that community sale I knew that car was still on his mind. We stopped at another sale and I was surprised to see my friend, Barb, minding this sale. It was her sister's sale and she and her husband were helping out. We told them about the car and unbeknown to me, her husband was in the automotive business. He immediately went to the sale down the street and purchased the car!

LAWN & GARDEN

Besides outdoor tools such as lawn mowers, fertilizer spreaders, shovels, hoes, rakes, trimmers, riding lawn mowers, leaf blowers, snow blowers, weed cutters and other necessary lawn tools, you can find beautiful patio sets and umbrellas, chaise lounges, BBQ pits, BBQ tools, charcoal, flower pots, flower bulbs, trees, bushes, plants, flowers, rock, and flagstone at garage sales. Anything you can buy for outdoor living at the stores you can find at garage sales.

We had a new home so you can imagine how sparse our outdoor living area was and the yard was badly in need of landscaping, which is so very expensive. Lucky for us we shop at garage sales. Most of our landscaping materials and patio furnishings were purchased at the sales. Edging--25¢, cherry bushes--50¢, flagstone-- take it away! Even fencing is available, from wooden privacy fences to split rail, for only a few dollars! We found outdoor Toro lighting that was brand new in the box. It was a 10-light set with 100 feet of cable for just $10. I've found extra pagoda lights and spot lights to attach to the set for 25¢ apiece and several more sets of spotlights with automatic timers for just $2.00.

When we need lots of outdoor light, we just flip the switch and see beautiful new brass and glass coach lanterns all around the house. The brass lanterns were only $1.00 to $5.00!

You'll find plenty of outdoor candles in decorative tins and clay pots for 25¢ apiece. The iris and tulip garden is courtesy of garage sales. I found freshly dug iris rhizomes at a sale that were just 10¢ apiece. At that price they were worth a try and are they ever beautiful! I purchased a 5-gallon bucket filled with tulip bulbs for just 50¢. I could hardly wait until spring to see what colors they were!

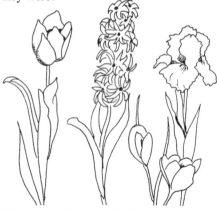

There are all kinds of bulbs to be found and the special boxed packages of seeds such as a big round container of wildflower seeds for 10¢ or a packet of catnip for 10¢--Fluffy loves it! I've found great window sill herb gardens that are still in their original wrapper, for only 50¢. They sell for $12.95 in the stores. All of our plant food and fertilizers were purchased at sales, especially moving sales. I found a brand new, never opened 8 lb. box of plant food, the most

popular brand for 50¢. All of our rose food, vegetable fertilizers, peat moss, bark and top soils are found at sales to.

We have plenty of pots--clay, ceramic, and plastic. Some were found in the FREE pile. My favorites are the very large clay pots that I like to paint and decorate myself. I so admired the large hand painted pots and vases when I was in Florence, Italy last summer, but I didn't admire the $300 price tags. I was hoping to find the right size and shape at a garage sale so I could paint it myself and sure enough, I found one that was just the right shape and in perfect condition, no chips or nicks and it was only $6.00. If you would like to try hand painting a large pot in the Florentine style, I think I can make it easy for you. Remember, you can paint just about anything with just about any kind of finish.

242

"How To"

PAINT FLORENTINE STYLE POTS AND VASES

Materials needed:
Very large ceramic or clay pot
White primer (BIN*)
Assorted bottles of acrylic paint (colors listed below)
Black paint pen
Assorted paint brushes
Spray polyurethane finish
Color picture book of Florence (at your library)
Tracing paper

*See glossary

NOTE: Look for pictures of Florentine pots or plates or something with a flower design. Make a photocopy of the picture or pictures. Blow the picture up larger if you can. Use the same colors in the picture or use Florentine colors:

Beige, cream, light gray, bright yellow, yellow green, lime green, bright royal blue, turquoise blue, muted orange, pale burgundy, shades of brown.

1 Clean the pot or vase with a soft cloth making sure there is no grit or debris anywhere.

2 Prime the entire pot or vase with primer going partially inside the top portion of the pot or vase. Let dry.

3 Apply background color or colors. Use light muted colors such as light golden brown or light gray. You may paint a solid color or use a ripped sponge and dip in several shades of the same color and let dry.

See Stipple section in the Finishes chapter.

4 On the upper third section of the pot or vase draw a rectangle approximately the same size as a recipe card, maybe a little wider if your pot is large enough. A recipe card measures 3" x 5" or try 3" x 8".

Continued . . .

Stencil the letters: A Q U A E or V I N O

inside the rectangle or free hand draw. Fill in the stenciled letters or paint the letters with black paint. Paint the rectangle outline with a line of black paint.

$$\boxed{\mathcal{AQUAE}} \qquad \boxed{\mathcal{VINO}}$$

5 Tape the photocopy design onto largest round portion of the pot or vase at four corners. Insert fabric tracing paper between pot and photocopy with colored side next to the pot. With a tracing wheel, trace around the design on the photocopy. When the design is traced, remove the photocopy and with a pencil, label the colors of the design on the pot.

E.g.,   Yellow pears label: R; Green leaves label: G

Repeat steps 4 and 5 on another section of the pot. It's up to you to decide if the pot is large enough to repeat these steps 2 or 3 more times. Allow for plenty of white space between the traced design.

6 After all the design has been traced on the pot or vase, start filling in the design with the same colors on the photocopy or use the colors listed above. Let dry.

Paint border lines at the top and bottom using different thicknesses and colors. Paint a row of "Xs" around the top. See drawing.

7 Outline the design with a thin black paint marker. THIS IS AN OPTIONAL STEP. You may not want a black outline.

8 Spray several coats of clear polyurethane allowing to dry completely between coats.

We've chosen wrought iron furniture to put out on the deck and there is always plenty to choose from at garage sales. If the price is right, I don't care what color it is because I'm going to spray paint it black anyway. We have several wonderful heavy duty wrought iron tables--round, square, rectangular, and each one was only $1.00. I found a small baker's rack, the exact same one I was admiring in a catalogue for $69 for only $5.00 at a garage sale. It was white and I simply painted it black to match the other deck furnishings. My favorite outdoor find is a black cast iron five-piece dining set. It's the old fashioned Victorian round table with four elaborate chairs. This five-piece set sells new for $500 or $600. I purchased the entire set for only $25! It will never go out of style and it will last forever!

My friend, Michaela, found a six-piece wicker set that consisted of love seat, two large chairs, a rocking chair, an end table and a coffee table for just $30. The small wicker end table would cost more than $30 at the store. Her wicker set was in excellent condition and didn't need any touch up, but it's very easy to paint wicker if you find a piece that needs it. Try painting your wicker in the new two tone style and use masking tape to tape different areas in geometric patterns. Paint the patterns a different color. It's very easy to have designer wicker at garage sale prices!

If you are going to put your wicker furnishings out doors, don't forget to give them a couple of coats of clear polyurethane to protect them from the weather.

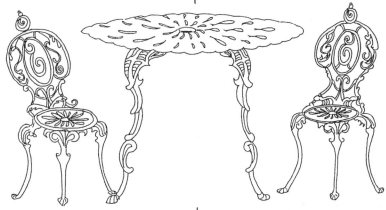

We have a black wrought iron chaise lounge, butterfly wrought iron chairs, cushioned swivel rockers and a glass-topped table with a tilt umbrella. I've seen several large glass-topped outdoor tables selling for $10 to $20 and it's easy to spray paint the metal frame any color you choose. We found a large wooden glider for $10, which sells in the stores for $100. Umbrellas are a real bargain at $5 to $10 each. You can find the very large tilt style umbrellas, the new style market umbrellas, beach umbrellas and chair umbrellas. There are folding picnic chairs, chaise lounges, beach chairs, hammocks, rattan swings, hammock swings, wooden porch swings, wood and iron park benches and lots of wonderful wicker--old and new.

Do you like to camp? Me too!

CAMPING EQUIPMENT

Our three-person domed tent with zippered and screened front was only $2.00. The kids get to sleep in it and we get the van! The Coleman two-burner cook stove and double mantle outdoor light were each $5.00, and we have enough pots and pans and plastic ware to outfit everyone in the campground. There are plenty of sleeping bags, sleeping pads and warm wool blankets to bundle up in. The very expensive sub-zero sleeping bags were only $5.00 each and I pick up

100% wool blankets whenever I can find them. They're great for picnics or camping and you can find them for 25¢ each. They may have small holes here and there, but that's OK for camping, especially when they're only 25¢!

One lucky day while out sale~ing I went to a building contractor's sale, He had all kinds of wood for sale--beautiful cedar and red-wood that were leftovers from building a deck. He had metal deck hangers, which were only 50¢ for the whole box. I checked the price at the hardware store for the metal hangers and just one was 29¢. There had to be 30 in the box. He had big sheets of lat-tice--the heavy duty kind that he was asking only $5.00 per sheet. The same lattice at the store cost over $25 a sheet. I bought so much stuff that I had to make three trips to get it all home. Luckily, he didn't live too far away. Now there was no excuse for my husband not to get started on building our deck!

CLEANING SUPPLIES

I don't remember the last time I purchased any type of cleaning items at the store. You can find everything you need at your local garage sale. Moving sales are especially good places to find cleaning supplies. I've bought big boxes of detergent, spray cans of carpet and upholstery cleaner, big bottles of carpet cleaner, furniture polish, floor wax, bathroom deodorizers, toilet bowl cleaners, stain and spot removers, scouring pads, big bags of sponges (these are also good for doing painting and crafts), bug killer, de-greasers, automotive cleaners, ammonia, silver polish, copper and brass cleaners, tile cleaner and window cleaner. A lot of these items are found in the FREE box!

All of our cleaning tools came from sales. Instead of one very old vacuum cleaner that I had to carry upstairs and downstairs, we now have three vacuum cleaners. All three are much newer and better than our original vacuum that we bought retail for $179. Now I have a vacuum on every floor for a total cost of $25. Two I found for $10 each, complete with attachments, and the other one was only $5.00. What a back saver to have one on every floor!

Our wet-dry vac was only $5.00 and the brand new carpet shampooer was $25. We couldn't get along without either of these items. We also have a handy dandy car vac that I got for $1.00 and a rechargeable dust vac for only $2.00.

RECREATION

It's so much fun to party outdoors in the summer and play with the badminton and volleyball sets that were brand new and never used for only $2.00. The wooden cro-quet set is always a big hit and was only $5.00. There are basketball boards and balls, baseballs, bats, rollerblades and bicy-cles in every size, shape and style. You can find 18-speed mountain bikes, racing bikes and bicycles built for two! I've bought sev-eral bicycles for family and friends along with a bicycle helmet. Ping pong tables are a garage sale staple along with bumper pool tables, full-size pool tables and poker tables. I've even seen dune buggies, motor scooters, motorcycles and all terrain vehicles. There are lots of rafts in every size, small sail boats, canoes, paddles, fishing boats, boat motors, and life jackets.

All kinds of exercise equipment is easily found at sales. I bought a computerized electronic treadmill for only $40. It sells at stores for $400! There are weight sets, weight benches, hand weights, ankle weights, waistband weights, sit-up bars, ex-ercise bikes, cross country and rowing ma-chines. You will also find the latest workout videos!

CHAPTER TEN

CHRISTMAS & SEASONAL

DECORATIONS

GIFT WRAP

SHRINK WRAP

HOLIDAY LIGHTS

CHRISTMAS TREES

COLLECTIBLES

LINENS

STORAGE

How fun it is to find all of your Christmas and holiday needs during the summer. No hustle and bustle, no jammed malls, no more driving around trying to find a parking space, just happy shopping at garage sales. You can virtually have your pick of all kinds of different ornaments, lights, beautiful wreaths and centerpieces--anything you can imagine to decorate your home for the holidays. You might want to add to your Christmas village collection or find the perfect Christmas tree. Maybe this is the year to buy an artificial tree or better yet, buy several of them for different areas in your home. Decorate each one in a different theme. Let the children have their very own tree and watch them have fun decorating it any way they want. How about an antique tree filled with antique ornaments and cherished family heirlooms. Trim the tree in yards and yards of old garage sale lace and beads? It's so much fun to have several trees and you can, since they are so inexpensive.

You will also find all of your Christmas linens--even your special holiday dinner service at garage sales. Find all of the much needed gift wrap, ribbon and bows at sales too. A lot of gift wrap is yours for the taking in the FREE box! You can find everything you could possibly want or need to dress up your home for the holiday season.

DECORATIONS

When I find my Christmas and holiday treasures at garage sales, I pack them away in a great big box just as soon as I get them home. When it's holiday time, I open up the great big box to see all of my "brand new" treasures. It's just as if I went out and bought everything new at department stores. It's all new to me and my family and friends. You will have forgotten how many beautiful "NEW" Christmas items you now have to decorate your home when you buy everything at garage sales in the summertime.

One of the best things about buying Christmas items at garage sales is that you are not rushed or frenzied. Remember how busy you were last Christmas and most likely every Christmas? Remember how expensive everything is? Remember how you didn't have the money to buy all of the decorating items that you wanted? Remember admiring that beautiful candle centerpiece that was $79? Remember wanting to start your Christmas village collection, only deciding to pass this year because just one little collectible house was $49? The larger village pieces cost even more, and then you need to buy all of the accessories that make your village really authentic. It all adds up so fast!

If you start buying holiday treasures now at garage sales you'll save tons of money, hours of time and have everything you could possibly want! I've found beautiful candle sets and candle wreath centerpieces that had never been used. Some were complete with a glass hurricane and candle. A few of the used centerpieces just needed a new bow or

candle. A real buy for 25¢ when you consider what you would pay for just the wreath form in a store. When shopping for holiday decorations at garage sales consider changing the bows or a few of the decorations to match your own decor. The bow may not be your color or maybe you wish that the greenery was tipped in silver or flocked. Go ahead and purchase the wreaths and center pieces just for the basics and add your own decorator touches. You are still way ahead when you can buy a wreath or centerpiece for 25¢ to 50¢ and change a few of the accessories. You can find all of the decorating accessories you need at garage sales too! Ornaments, wooden apples, decorative picks, lace, ribbon, glass hurricanes, scented candles, and battery operated lights to lace through your center piece or wreath.

All of my artificial poinsettia bushes were purchased at the sales too, for just 25¢ a bush instead of $5.99. Some were in clay pots ready to display, others were just the plain bushes. I found poinsettia garlands and large individual stem poinsettias. When strolling through the designer showrooms last Christmas they had beautiful white and gold-tipped, crystallized poinsettias in their displays. I went home and spray painted some of the large 10¢ long stemmed poinsettias white, and tipped the ends with gold paint. While the paint was still wet I sprinkled coarse Kosher salt on top, and applied a coat of high gloss polyurethane. I had the exact same designer white and gold poinsettia stems with sparkling crystals that were $15.99 in the store.

Silk and dried flowers are easy to find at garage sales. I found a big box filled with eucalyptus, silk and dried flower bouquets, wheat stems, bunches of dried roses, bags of crystal marbles, and Baby's Breath for only 50¢.

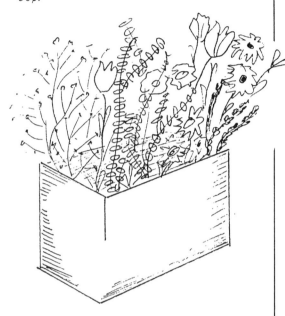

Last year, one of my favorite purchases was Christmas striking bells--the kind that play over 50 different songs. They were brand new and had never been opened. I bought them for only $2.00. I saw the exact same set in a store last year at Christmas time for over $50! I also love the large, lighted, $29.95 animated angel that I found for $1.00.! The large velvet robed Father Time Santa that sold for $79 in the department store was only $5.00 at a garage sale, brand new and in its original sealed box!

GIFT WRAP

Gift wrap and bags of bows are plentiful at sales. Moving sales are a really good place to find great big rolls of gift wrap. The bigger rolls are hard to box and pack. Most people decide just to get rid of it at their garage sale instead of packing it in a box and moving it.

You can find all different kinds of wrapping paper. Christmas wrap, birthday wrap, baby shower, wedding paper, tissue paper, and plain brown craft paper to wrap packages for mailing. Bows are plentiful, either in bags or separate beautiful brand new bows. Do you know how much just one great big bow costs in the gift shop? They are over $1.00 apiece and that's for the small ones! I've seen boxes and boxes of brand new beautiful bows in every color for just 10¢ apiece. I went to one sale where a new bride was selling all of the great big white bows that were placed on each aisle of the church. She wanted only 25¢ apiece. I bought them all!

You can find lots of wallpaper rolls at sales and they make wonderful gift wrap, in fact, wallpaper is my favorite type of gift wrap! It's easy to find leftover wallpaper rolls in the FREE box too!

A popular way to give gifts nowadays is to use one of the beautiful gift bags that you find in card and specialty shops. I like to make these gift bags myself with all the free wallpaper that I find at the sales. Wallpaper comes in so many different designs and colors, and the paper is a lot heavier than regular wrapping paper. It's easy to make gift bags out of leftover wallpaper rolls, or just use it to wrap up your packages. You'll never worry about having plenty of paper for every kind of special occasion. There are so many beautiful wallpapers around. I've picked up lots of stripes in fresh pastels which make wonderful gift wrap for children. There are lots of baby wallpaper leftovers to wrap shower and baby gifts. You can find rich foils and silk papers that are wonderful for wedding and shower gifts. The darker patterns and stripes are good to use for a man's present and all the beautiful florals make perfect wrapping paper for just about everyone. Who wants to spend $2.99 for a roll of specialty gift wrap when there is a wonderful array to choose from at garage sales?

"How To"

MAKE GIFT BAGS

SMALL, MEDIUM & LARGE

Materials needed:
Wrapping paper or wallpaper
Tacky glue
Single hole punch
Yarn or braided cord (whatever you have on hand)
Assorted boxes for sizing

1 Tape 2, 3 or 4 gift boxes together. These boxes should be the exact same size. The number of boxes to tape together depends on the size of gift bag you want to make. The boxes
make up the size and form of the gift bags.

Examples:
Small bags   3 cassette tapes
                          4 paperback books
                          Square tissue box

Medium bags   2 or 3 hard bound books
                          Several boxes taped together

Large bags   Large gift boxes
                          Packing boxes

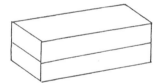

2 Lay out a large sheet of gift wrap or wallpaper. The size should be just enough to wrap up the stack of boxes just like you would wrap a present.

3 Determine the top edge of the gift bag. Do you want it taller or wider? Fold the top edge under 3/4" to 2 inches--your call. Fold this fold over again, the same size as the first fold.
If you are making a very large gift bag, use the 2 inch fold.
A smaller bag requires only a 3/4" fold.

Continued . . .

4 Position the boxes on the paper and pretend to wrap. Make sure the paper meets on the side of the boxes. Apply a line of tacky glue on the folded edge so it will adhere to the other edge of paper.

5 Lay the glued edge on top of the raw edge and glue the seam together from top to bottom. Be careful not to get any glue on the boxes inside. You want to remove the boxes when you're finished.

6 Wrap the bottom portion of the gift bag just as you would a package using tacky glue to seal down the edges. Remember to glue paper to paper and not glue to the boxes inside.

7 Remove the boxes.

8 Cut two strips of cardboard the width of the gift bag and the same depth as the top folded edge. Insert the cardboard strip under each side of the folded under edge. Measure the bottom portion of the bag and cut a piece of cardboard to match the bottom dimensions. Apply tacky glue to one side of the cardboard and lay in the bottom of the gift bag.

9 Measure 2 equal distant marks on the top two larger edges of the gift bag and use a one hole punch to punch 4 different holes. Punch through the paper and cardboard liner.

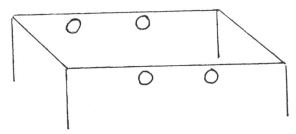

10 Cut two pieces of yarn or cording the desired length and insert a piece into the two holes on one side. Tie into a knot to secure it to the bag. Do the other side.

Make several of the gift bags at one time. It's very easy to do and it will save you lots of money. The smaller gift bags cost around $1.79 at the store and the larger bags can run $7.00 or $8.00! They're very easy to make and will cost you next to nothing when you use garage sale materials.

Among my favorite things to make for the holidays are personalized gift baskets. I can usually find all the big beautiful baskets I need at garage sales for $1.00 or less and it's so much fun to paint them, add ribbon or garage sale dried flowers and make a really beautiful basket. I love to fill the decorated baskets with beautiful soaps and bath gels or sometimes I make a theme basket with specialty foods or hobby & craft supplies.

Your favorite gardener would love to receive a gift basket filled with flower bulbs, seeds, hand tools and knee pads, or, what about a gift basket filled with special oils and vinegars that you made yourself? Pour the oils and vinegars into the lovely glass bottles and decanters that you've been buying at the sales.

If the bottle is a decanter type with a glass top, seal the bottle with a cork and include the top for later use.

I found a bottle corker at a garage sale for $1.00 and I use it all the time to seal the special vinegars and oils that I enjoy making for my friends. Buy the corks at wine making shops or at a garage sale. That's where I find mine!

Pick up some gold foil bottle toppers at a wine shop to top your bottle or seal the bottle tops with paraffin wax. You can find the paraffin wax blocks at garage sales too. I usually pay 5¢ to 25¢ for a one-pound block.

Melt the wax in an old pan and keep dipping the top of the corked bottle in the melted paraffin. Let it dry a little and then dip some more. Keep dipping until you have the desired effect.

I found a gold seal embossing kit at a garage sale for only $1.00. I set the embosser with a large S and K and press the initials with the embosser into a decorative gold seal. I cut a small piece of silk ribbon and wrap it around the bottles and stick the gold

embossed seal on top. It makes a lovely, well received personalized gift.

PLEASE BE VERY CAREFUL WHEN MELTING WAX.

Try melting colored sealing wax over the cork and bottle top. You can find sealing wax at garage sales too!

When finished assembling the gift baskets, you'll want to wrap them up in a huge sheet of cellophane and tie a beautiful fabric bow around them.

You already know to buy bows and ribbon at garage sales but do you know where to look for that huge sheet of clear cellophane? You'll probably need a very large piece-- much larger than what you can buy at craft and gift stores. The cellophane also needs to be heavy duty so it will stand up nicely when you tie a large bow around it. Where will you find this kind of cellophane? Where else . . . at a garage sale!

Look for boxes of clear sheets of window insulation--the kind that requires a hair dryer to smooth out. These boxes contain several sheets of very large heavy duty clear cellophane. The cellophane is made large enough to cover several different sizes of windows and patio doors. I find these boxes at sales all the time. Some boxes will have only a couple of sheets left in them--some are brand new and unopened. Either way, they are a terrific buy and a wonderful way to wrap up those great big baskets! You'll pay 10¢ to 25¢ a box for the window insulation.

SHRINK WRAP

Another fun thing you can do with window insulation is shrink wrap. Shrink wrap kits are available at craft and hobby shops and they sell for at least $2.00 or $3.00 a package just to shrink wrap one very small item!

Use the window insulation kits and a hair dryer and shrink wrap to your heart's content.

Even the biggest package can be shrink wrapped with these large pieces of heavy duty cellophane.

"How To"

SHRINK WRAP

Materials needed:
Window insulation sheet
Tacky glue
Hair dryer

---

1 Cut a piece of insulation sheet large enough to cover the object and tuck underneath. It's not necessary that the four end corners touch but if the sheet is large enough it is desirable.

---

2 Glue the four corners of the plastic sheet to the center bottom of the object, such as a basket, using tacky glue. Use just enough glue to hold the plastic--you don't need a lot of glue.

---

3 Turn on the hair dryer and follow the directions on the window insulation package such as how close to hold the hair dryer to the plastic. Watch it shrink up tight before your very eyes!

HOLIDAY LIGHTS

Two years ago we didn't have a single outdoor light for our house. We really couldn't afford them. Now, our house looks like the scene from the Christmas vacation movie! Remember when Chevy Chase plugs in the cord and the whole house lights up? Well . . . now that's our house at Christmas time!

Every strand of lights came from garage sales along with boxes and boxes of brand new replacement bulbs. We have so many of these that even our grandchildren will never have to buy a replacement bulb! The large outdoor style lights are attached to the house and garage. The smaller style clear lights and the lights in motion are draped all around the trees and bushes. I keep a few strands of the small clear lights draped around the large ficus tree in the dining room all year long. It's wonderful to plug in the lights when we have dinner guests.

All the lights on our many Christmas trees were purchased at garage sales too--even bubble lights! I also found a strand of lights that looked just like small candles. These I string on the antique tree for an old-fashioned authentic look. Before there was electricity, real candles were lit and placed on Christmas trees for light.

If you plan to buy lights at sales, make sure you plug in the lights and test them. Since they are so plentiful at the sales I look for the kind of lights that stay lit if one bulb burns out. I don't have the time or the patience to find that one little bad bulb. If the lights are packaged in the original carton it will say that they will stay lit. If you find bags or boxes full of used lights and they are not in their original wrapping, remove one of the lights when you plug them in to test, and see if the remainder stay lit. Either way, since you are paying only 25¢ a strand it might not matter to you. They are still such a bargain!

You can also find chile pepper lights, pumpkin Halloween lights and Easter egg lights. If there is a special holiday light made, you can find it at garage sales.

CHRISTMAS TREES

For years our family Christmas tree was a 7.5' flocked artificial tree that I purchased for $6.00, complete with stand, at a garage sale. I have since added many more trees throughout the house--all beautiful garage sale Christmas trees. There is a Christmas tree in almost every room of the house, each with its own special theme. Can you imagine trying to do this by shopping the stores at holiday time? I bet you would run out of energy before you run out of money! Take a moment now to imagine what a Christmas village, accessories for the village, Christmas tree or trees, ornaments, tree lights, outdoor lights, outdoor decorations, wreaths, table centerpieces, holiday linens and gift wrap would cost. There would be nothing left over for gifts!

Last year I splurged and bought a 9' Christmas tree to put in the entrance way. I'm sorry I did.

I did not buy this tree at a garage sale. No, I paid retail. It was on sale for half price however. Such a bargain at $250! It took me over six weeks to find just the perfect tree so I spent a lot of time and gas on top of the $250. It definitely was a mistake. I wasted $250. During the summer sale~ing months I looked and looked for a 9' tree. I did find a couple, but they were priced at $300. They were the very expensive 9' hinged trees that set up in only a few minutes. I do realize that they cost $700 to $800 in the store, but I still didn't want to pay $300! If you want a large 9', 10' or 12' tree, I think I can keep you from making the mistake I made and save you hundreds of dollars.

I think I know how to make a 9', 10' or 12' artificial tree for around $20 or less! If you are thinking of purchasing a very tall tree you might want to give this a try first. It's much better than going out and paying several hundred dollars. The worst thing that could happen is you will end up with two artificial Christmas trees. You can certainly use them both, use one, or resell them at your own garage sale. There's nothing to lose by giving it a try. Now that I've examined how the manufactured 9' tree is made, I believe it's possible to do the exact same thing with two smaller trees that you can find at garage sales for $10 or less! Two artificial trees will make one very tall Christmas tree.

Here's what I plan to do to make a large tree.

"How To"

MAKE A 9', 10' or 12' CHRISTMAS TREE

Materials needed:
2 artificial Christmas trees of the same size
(5', 6', 7', or 7.5' trees with branches that look the same)
Drill
Large Wood Dowel Screw

1 The artificial trees will either have one long pole or two shorter poles with a branched top piece. You want to attach an extra pole to the existing poles to provide the height you want.

E.g., If your trees are 5 feet tall, you will probably be working with two poles and a topper.

If your trees are 6 feet tall or taller you may be working with three poles--two poles from one complete tree and one pole from the extra tree.

These instructions are for two 7 or 7.5 foot trees. This is the most common size artificial Christmas tree and the size that I see most often at garage sales.

2 Separate the two trees and lay out their branches with them. The branches are usually color coded at the metal ends. Lay out the branches in their separate color-coded sections. You should have a total of 4 poles, 2 toppers and 2 separate sets of color-coded branches.

Continued . . .

3 Attach the two poles from one of the trees as you would normally. You now need to attach one of the poles from the other tree to the bottom of the two attached poles.

Check the ends of the poles. If there is a routed out section on the end of one of the poles to allow for placement of another pole, GREAT! If not, you will need to drill a hole in the bottom of the bottom pole and the top of the third pole.

NOTE: The extra pole will need to be cut so your tree is the height you want. Don't forget to add the measurements for the tree topper when deciding how much of the extra pole to cut off.

Make sure when attaching the third pole that the pre-drilled branch holes are at the correct angle to accept the metal end branches.

4 If you have to drill a hole to attach two poles together, insert and tightly twist a large wood dowel screw (threaded on both ends) into both of the newly drilled holes to attach the two poles together.

YOU SHOULD END UP WITH THREE POLES SNUGLY ATTACHED. THE POLE ON TOP SHOULD HAVE THE HOLE FOR THE TOPPER PIECE.

NOTE: Included with the 9 foot tree that I purchased was an extra large tree stand. This is necessary to accommodate the extra height of the tree. Make a wooden frame to attach to your regular Christmas tree stand.

A square of wooden 2 x 4s would work well.

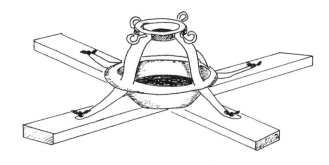

Continued . . .

5 Once the tree is sturdy and the center poles are securely attached, start attaching the branches. Count how many extra rows of holes are on the extra top pole. This is how many extra rows of branches you will need to add.

Add an extra row of the largest branches from the second tree at the bottom.

Add an extra row of the next largest branches.

You may not want to add an extra row to the next size. It's hard to say.

This is one you will have to work out yourself.

Just keep adding branches until you get a nice pyramid shape.

DECORATING THE TREE

Getting the tree out of storage, assembling it and decorating is usually a full day's task, albeit a very enjoyable task! Usually it's Mom and Dad doing the tree assembly and stringing the lights while the children eagerly await their turn to hang the ornaments, bows, garland and tinsel. I'd like to share with you some designers' tree trimming secrets and make your life a little easier at holiday time.

KNOW THAT YOU WILL HAVE TO ASSEMBLE YOUR TREE ONLY ONCE AND STRING THE LIGHTS ONLY ONCE AND YOUR TASK IS FINISHED. THAT'S RIGHT--ASSEMBLE THE TREE ONCE AND STRING THE LIGHTS ONCE . . . ONLY ONCE . . . NOT EVERY YEAR!

"How To"

DECORATE YOUR CHRISTMAS TREE

Materials needed:
Artificial Christmas tree
Miniature lights
Ornaments
Optional trim (garlands, bows, tinsel)

---

1 Assemble the tree trunk and secure in the stand.

---

2 Insert the large bottom row of branches.

---

3 Take your first strand of miniature lights and tape the receptacle end to the bottom of the tree trunk, right under the first row of branches. Wrap the string of lights around each branch and branch portions several times going out the length of the branch and wrapping and return back to tree trunk.

Continued . . .

When the strand is back to the tree trunk wrap the lights around the base of the next branch and repeat wrapping the lights around the next branch going out to the end of the branch and wrapping back to the tree trunk.

When the string of lights is used up, plug another string into the end of the first one and so on.

Repeat this process for each branch on the bottom first row.

4 Attach the next row of branches around the tree and continue wrapping the lights out from the trunk to the branch tips and back to the trunk.

Repeat this process for each branch layer until you've reached the top. You never want to see the wire for the lights, just the illumination.

A good rule of thumb is 100 lights per one foot of tree. For a six foot tree, that's 600 lights. For a nine foot tree, 900 lights! Obviously there will be more lights per foot on the larger bottom branches and less lights per foot at the tree top.

This seems like a lot of work, but remember, you will have to do this only once, never again.

How can this be?

See the next "HOW TO" STORE YOUR CHRISTMAS TREE."

5 Finish decorating the tree with ornaments, garlands, bows or tinsel.

"How To"

STORE YOUR CHRISTMAS TREE

Materials needed:
Large blanket or afghan or rope hammock
6 or 8 large hooks

After you've gone to all that work of stringing every single branch with lights there is no reason to do it again next year. This is what the professionals do to save time.

Select a storage area in an out-of-the-way place such as the ceiling of the basement, garage or tall attic.

1 Attach to the ceiling rafters long strong cup hooks approximately every two feet. Skip over a few rafters and attach more cup hooks to the rafters to match the others.

2 Make three or four small holes an equal distance apart on the opposite sides of the blanket approximately 5 or 6 six inches from the edge.

3 Remove everything from the Christmas tree except the lights.

4 Find a helper to hold up a very large blanket or afghan almost to the top of the tree. Gently push the tree over into the blanket and lay the tree down on the floor inside the blanket.

If you have a very tall tree with the extra large stand you will want to remove the stand from the tree trunk. If it is a regular size stand, you can leave it on the tree trunk.

5 Carry the blanket containing the tree into the storage area and slip the holes of the blanket over the cup hooks. It's like making a hammock for the tree.

If you have a good strong rope hammock you can use this instead of a blanket and tie up each end of the hammock to a large hook on the ceiling rafters in your garage or blanket.

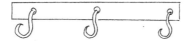

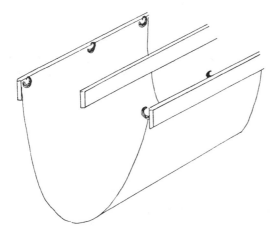

Your tree is up out of the way and next year when it's time to trim the tree, all you have to do is remove the blanket or hammock, carry the blanket containing the tree to its display area, reattach the stand and stand upright. Plug it in and it's ready for the ornaments!

COLLECTIBLES

If you are looking for collectibles and keepsakes, there are lots of commemorative ornaments, plates, and figurines sales to round out your collection.

For years I have been wanting to start collecting Christmas village houses. I always told myself that "next year" I would start. Well, next year always seemed to come and go without having a Christmas village until I started shopping at garage sales. At just one sale I found five pieces of the very expensive Dickens Village collection. The buildings were only $5.00 apiece and they were in perfect condition. They were each carefully packaged in their original boxes complete with lighting cord. Finally I had an entire village for a total of $25 instead of paying $49 for just one piece!

I found all of the little accessories at garage sales too. Just 25¢ a package for the battery operated lamp posts, fencing, trees, carriages and plenty of people to put in the village. It looks wonderful on the dining room buffet table that I made.

LINENS

Holiday table cloths are plentiful at garage sales. Some are brand new and in the original wrapping. You'll find every size and shape--round, oblong, rectangle, and square. There are so many different styles to choose from. Solid holiday colors, plaids, lace and beautiful hand crocheted tablecloths can all be found.

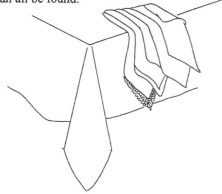

Holiday embossed fingertip towels for the bathroom and lots of kitchen towels and decorative potholders are plentiful too! Christmas will truly become a festive and fun time of year when all your decorations and accessories have been bought ahead of time and so inexpensively.

Think of the wonderful time you'll have opening that big box of garage sale Christmas decorations. I guarantee, you will have forgotten all of the lovely things you bought over the summer sale~ing months and it will be Christmas time for you when you start going through that great big box and find all of the new beautiful decorations and lovely holiday accessories. It's always a surprise and a treat to open this big box and put out all the new things I've found over the summer. You'll have much more time to truly make the house festive and put up all the outdoor lights and decorations that you bought over the summer months. No more frazzled holiday time for you, and no more empty pocketbooks or credit card payments. Everything is bought and paid for!

Put out the fine garage sale china and crystal and put that garage sale bottle of champagne in your garage sale silver wine bucket and toast to a wonderful holiday and New Year. Look around at all the wonderful new treasures you have and the smiling happy faces on your family members.

All the presents will be exquisitely wrapped with free gift wrap and wall paper and you'll have a lot more time to spend with the family and truly enjoy this special time of year. No last minute shopping for picked over ornaments and lights. No more checking the price tags to see if you can afford it. No more overloading the charge card and no more standing in line. Everything you could possibly want is in the storage room waiting to be unpacked and enjoyed! Have fun!

STORAGE

Since metal file cabinets are so inexpensive at garage sales, buy them for storage. No longer will you have stacks and stacks of boxes piled up. Label the front of each drawer and when you need an item, you will know right where to go and get it. Label one drawer Christmas lights, another could be labeled Christmas village, another drawer for ornaments, a drawer for Easter, and a drawer for Halloween.

Put all of your gift wrap, wallpaper rolls, ribbon and bows in another drawer. Put in a roll of tape and a pair of scissors and you will always be prepared to wrap a beautiful present. Store silk flowers and wreaths, raffia, ribbon floral foam and all the things you would use to make decorative arrangements. Once you start garage sale~ing and have so many things, it's very important to be organized. This is a very easy and space saving way to store your decorating treasures.

GLOSSARY

Bullion fringe: Twisted cord fringe.

Boxing: Fabric strip separating top and bottom pieces.

Claw tool: Staple and tack remover.

Coax adapter: A coax connector that attaches on the older twin lead antenna.

Coaxial cable: A cable that has a center conductor shielded with black plastic--used to connect televisions to cable outlets or a cable used in some computer networking systems.

Crackle: Painting technique--aged, cracked appearance.

Crimping: Small regular folds or ridges.

Dart: Sewing a tapered tuck.

Decoupage: Decorating a surface with paper cutouts.

Deglosser: Product that removes sheen from wood furniture.

Double welt: Two parallel cords wrapped in fabric.

Dowel: A round wood stick or rod.

Duvet: The outer fabric covering for a comforter.

Eggshell: Refers to the type & hardness of paint. Use when distressing or antiqueing.

E6000: An industrial strength sealant and adhesive used for non-porous materials.

Filigree: Intricate, delicate fabric trim.

Finial: A top ornament of wood or metal.

Flyspecks: The brown dots of paint or stain used in distressing furniture.

Fray Check: A solution that locks fabric threads to prevent fraying.

Fresh Start: An acrylic based primer that can be used for glass, metal and plastic.

Gel stain: A very thick gel like stain that does not run.

Gimp: Ornamental braid.

Glazing points: Metal pins to hold glass or mirror.

Gold leaf: Paper thin sheets of gold.

Gro-lite: Electric bulbs used for plants.

Inlay: Tiny pieces of decorative wood set into a surface.

Jig saw: A power saw with a narrow, vertical reciprocating blade.

Kerf: A groove made by a saw.

Linseed Oil: A product used for wood surfaces.

Masonite: A pressed fiber type fabric available in 4' x 8' sheets. The same material used for Pegboard.

Miter: A beveled cut made at a 45 degree angle.

Mod-Podge: A water based sealer, glue or finish for all surfaces.

Oil pigment: Tubes of thick oil-based artists color.

Ottoman: An upholstered low seat or footstool.

Peg-Board: Masonite board that is full of small holes.

Primer: An undercoat of paint used to prepare a surface.

Router: A tool used to make decorative edges or to gouge shapes in wood.

Saber saw: See jigsaw.

Sconce: A decorative wall bracket for candles or lights.

Spindle: A notched and shaped piece of wood.

Staple puller: See claw tool.

Stiffener: A water-based product used to stiffen fabric products.

Stipple: A reverse painting technique achieved by sponging paint off a surface.

Swag: To hang in an arc or curve.

Tacking strip: Cardboard strip with metal tacks.

Tie wire: A 16-gauge bendable wire.

Tuffet: A stool or low seat.

Upholster needle: A large, long curved sewing needle with large eye.

Verdigris: Antiqued copper.

Welt: Cord that is encased and stitched in fabric.

BIN: A quick drying primer-sealer-bonder for glass, glossy surfaces, metals, new wood, plaster

MOLDING

Screen Molding

Quarter Round

Cove Molding

Crown Molding

Outside Corner

Outside Crown Corner

Inside Crown Corner

Casing

Rosette

APPENDIX

NOTE:

The items marked in the retail column were mostly priced at a discount store or at the lowest available sale price.

The items marked in the garage sale column were the typical or lowest price I've ever seen this item at a sale.

The items in Shelley's Best column were the very best price I've ever purchased this particular item. All items in Shelley's Best column were either new or in excellent condition.

N/A   Not applicable, meaning I did not try to bargain or I did not purchase this particular item   or in some cases, prices were not available.

ITEM	RETAIL PRICE	GARAGE SALE	SHELLEY'S BEST
286 MOTHER BOARD	N/A	$ 5.00	$ 2.86
386 MOTHER BOARD	N/A	$ 5.00	$ 1.00
4 MB RAM	$ 140.00	$ 20.00	$ 10.00
45 RECORDS	N/A	$ 0.50	$ 0.20
486 MOTHER BOARD	N/A	$ 30.00	$ 5.00
8 TRACK, AMPLIFIER, SPEAKERS	N/A	$ 25.00	$ 3.00
ACRYLIC NAIL SET	$ 10.00	$ 2.00	$ 0.50
ACRYLIC NAIL SUPPLIES	N/A	N/A	$ 0.25
ADIRONDACK CHAIRS, WOOD	$ 50.00	$ 20.00	$ 10.00
AIR PURIFIER	$ 12.99	$ 1.00	$ 0.50
AMERICAN FLAG & POLE KIT	$ 9.99	$ 2.00	$ 1.00
AMERICAN FLAG, LARGE	$ 9.99	$ 2.00	$ 1.00
AMERICAN FLAG, SMALL	$ 1.99	$ 0.25	$ 0.25
AMPLIFIER	$ 100.00	$ 25.00	$ 3.00
AMPLIFIER, SURROUND SOUND	$ 100.00	$ 15.00	$ 15.00
ANDIRONS, BRASS	N/A	$ 20.00	$ 5.00
ANTIQUE 2 TIER SILENT BUTLER	$ 350.00	N/A	$ 10.00
ANTIQUE MAPLE CHEST	$ 300.00	$ 200.00	$ 30.00
ANTIQUE OAK WASHSTAND	$ 300.00	$ 150.00	$ 20.00
ANTIQUE VICTORIAN CHAIR	$ 100.00	$ 40.00	$ 5.00
ANTIQUE, INLAID WOOD SILENT BUTLER	$ 350.00	$ 150.00	$ 10.00
ANTIQUE, MAHOGANY TABLE CIRCA 1900	$ 150.00	$ 15.00	$ 8.00
ANTIQUE, MAPLE DRESSER W/ MIRROR	$ 400.00	$ 300.00	$ 30.00
AREA RUGS 6 X 9	$ 50.00	$ 20.00	$ 10.00
AREA RUGS, DHURRIE, LARGE	$ 79.00	$ 10.00	$ 5.00

ITEM	RETAIL PRICE	GARAGE SALE	SHELLEY'S BEST
AREA RUGS, DHURRIE, SMALL	$ 12.99	$ 3.00	$ 0.25
AREA RUGS, OVAL BRAIDED, LARGE	$ 129.00	$ 35.00	$ 10.00
AREA RUGS, OVAL BRAIDED, SMALL	$ 9.99	$ 8.00	$ 3.00
ARMOIRE, LARGE, BEVELED MIRROR	$ 1,499.00	$ 500.00	$ 500.00
ARMOIRE, LARGE, PINE	$ 699.00	$ 150.00	$ 100.00
ARTIFICIAL FLOWER ARRANGEMENTS	$ 10.00	$ 2.00	$ 0.50
AUTOMOBILE ANTI-FREEZE - 1 Gal	$ 5.39	$ 1.00	$ 0.50
AUTOMOBILE BRAS	$ 69.00	$ 15.00	$ 5.00
AUTOMOBILE CAR TOP CARRIERS	$ 69.00	$ 20.00	$ 5.00
AUTOMOBILE COVERS	$ 59.00	$ 25.00	$ 8.00
AUTOMOBILE TROUBLE LIGHTS	$ 15.00	$ 5.00	$ 2.00
AUTOMOTIVE FILTERS	$ 3.49	$ 1.00	$ 0.25
AUTOMOTIVE OIL 10W40	$ 1.00	$ 0.50	$ 0.25
AX & MAUL	$ 19.95	$ 5.00	$ 2.00
BABY OIL	$ 1.99	$ 0.50	$ 0.25
BABY'S BREATH, BUNCH	$ 1.99	$ 0.50	$ 0.10
BACKPACKING COOKING UTENSILS	N/A	$ 2.00	$ 1.00
BACKPACKS	$ 19.95	$ 5.00	$ 1.00
BACKPACKS, MOUNTAIN STYLE, METAL	$ 49.00	$ 10.00	$ 8.00
BACON COOKER, MICROWAVE	$ 9.99	$ 0.25	$ 0.25
BADMINTON/VOLLEYBALL SET	$ 19.95	$ 3.00	$ 3.00
BAKER'S RACK, MEDIUM SIZE	$ 189.00	$ 40.00	$ 30.00
BAKER'S RACK, LARGE	$ 1,000.00	$ 150.00	$ 150.00
BAKER'S RACK, SMALL	$ 69.96	$ 15.00	$ 5.00
BAKEWARE, ASSORTED	$ 3.00	$ 1.00	$ 0.25
BAR STOOLS, OAK & CANE	$ 20.00	$ 5.00	$ 1.00
BAR STOOLS, SWIVEL BACK, OAK	$ 100.00	$ 20.00	$ 10.00
BASKETS, LARGE	$ 15.00	$ 5.00	$ 1.00
BASKETS, SMALL	$ 1.00	$ 0.25	FREE
BASKETS, VERY LARGE	$ 25.00	$ 5.00	$ 2.00
BATHROOM CLEANER	$ 3.00	$ 0.50	$ 0.25
BATHROOM CLEANER, SPRAY	$ 3.00	$ 0.50	$ 0.25
BATHTUB DOORS, GLASS W/TRACK	N/A	$ 10.00	N/A
BATTERIES	$ 2.00	$ 0.50	$ 0.10
BATTING, 15 YDS	$ 45.00	$ 5.00	$ 2.00
BBQ GRILL, GAS WITH SIDE BURNER	$ 169.00	$ 40.00	$ 35.00
BBQ GRILLS, GAS	$ 100.00	$ 20.00	$ 10.00
BBQ PIT COVERS	$ 7.99	$ 2.00	$ 0.50
BBQ PIT, KETTLE, LARGE	$ 59.95	$ 7.00	$ 5.00
BBQ PIT, KETTLE, SMALL	$ 12.95	$ 2.00	$ 2.00
BBQ PIT, PICNIC STYLE, GAS	$ 19.95	$ 8.00	N/A
BBQ PIT, PORTABLE, CHARCOAL	$ 7.99	$ 0.50	$ 0.50
BED PILLOWS, KING, DOWN	$ 39.00	$ 5.00	$ 1.00

ITEM	RETAIL PRICE	GARAGE SALE	SHELLEY'S BEST
BED PILLOWS, STANDARD	$ 10.00	$ 2.00	$ 1.00
BED TRAY, BEECH	$ 9.99	$ 5.00	$ 2.00
BED TRAY, WICKER	$ 19.95	$ 5.00	$ 5.00
BED, CANOPY, DOUBLE	$ 89.00	$ 10.00	$ 10.00
BED, QUEEN AIRBED	$ 29.95	$ 5.00	$ 3.00
BED, RICE, QUEEN SIZE, CHERRY	$ 1,000.00	$ 250.00	$ 250.00
BEDFRAME KING	$ 59.00	$ 10.00	$ 3.00
BEDFRAME, DOUBLE	$ 39.00	$ 10.00	$ 2.00
BEDROOM END TABLE, 1 DRAWER	$ 89.00	$ 20.00	$ 3.00
BEDROOM END TABLE, 2 DRAWER	$ 119.00	$ 20.00	$ 5.00
BEDS, BUNK, METAL	$ 149.00	$ 40.00	$ 25.00
BEDS, BUNK, WOOD	$ 50.00	$ 25.00	$ 25.00
BEDS, TRUNDLE	$ 169.00	$ 35.00	$ 25.00
BENCHGRINDER, 1/4 HORSEPOWER	$ 35.00	$ 10.00	$ 5.00
BINDERS, 3 RING	$ 2.00	$ 0.50	$ 0.25
BINOCULARS	$ 39.00	$ 5.00	$ 5.00
BIRD BATH, STONE	$ 49.00	$ 10.00	$ 5.00
BIRD FEEDERS	$ 5.00	$ 2.00	$ 0.25
BIRDSEED 20#	$ 3.00	$ 0.50	$ 0.50
BLANKET, STADIUM STYLE IN POUCH	$ 19.99	$ 5.00	$ 1.00
BLANKET, WOOL	$ 25.00	$ 5.00	$ 1.00
BLANKET, WOOL, MOVING TYPE	N/A	$ 1.00	$ 0.25
BLANKETS, HUDSON BAY WOOL	$ 99.00	$ 15.00	$ 1.00
BLANKETS, KING SIZE	$ 20.00	$ 5.00	$ 1.00
BLANKETS, QUEEN VELOUR	$ 19.99	$ 5.00	$ 1.00
BLANKETS, SATIN EDGE, KING	$ 35.00	$ 5.00	$ 1.00
BLANKETS, VELOUR, QUEEN	$ 20.00	$ 5.00	$ 1.00
BLANKETS, WOOL, KING SIZE	$ 89.00	$ 5.00	$ 2.00
BLENDER	$ 29.99	$ 5.00	$ 3.00
BLENDER, HAND	$ 29.00	$ 8.00	$ 3.00
BLOOD PRESSURE MONITOR, DIGITAL	$ 59.00	$ 10.00	$ 8.00
BLOODY MARY MIX	$ 2.99	$ 0.50	$ 0.25
BLOW DRYER, LARGE	$ 19.00	$ 5.00	$ 1.00
BLOW DRYER, PORTABLE	$ 19.00	$ 5.00	$ 0.50
BOLTS	N/A	N/A	FREE
BOMBAY CHEST, FRENCH	$ 1,200.00	$ 300.00	$ 150.00
BOOKS, COFFEE TABLE STYLE	N/A	$ 5.00	$ 1.00
BOOKS, HARDBOUND, BESTSELLERS	$ 20.00	$ 5.00	$ 0.50
BOOKS, PAPERBACK	$ 5.00	$ 0.50	$ 0.10
BOOKSHELVES, WALL UNIT	$ 100.00	$ 30.00	$ 15.00
BOOKSHELVES, WOOD	$ 59.00	$ 15.00	$ 5.00
BOOKSHELVES, WOOD, 5 SHELF	$ 80.00	$ 20.00	$ 15.00
BOOM BOX, DUAL CASSETTE	$ 49.00	$ 10.00	$ 5.00

ITEM	RETAIL PRICE	GARAGE SALE	SHELLEY'S BEST
BOWLS, ONION SOUP	$ 1.99	$ 0.50	$ 0.25
BRACKETS, CURTAIN & DRAPERY	$ 2.00	$ 0.25	FREE
BRASS & CRYSTAL LAMPS, LARGE	$ 59.00	$ 10.00	$ 5.00
BRASS & GLASS TABLE, SET OF 3	$ 89.00	$ 25.00	$ 10.00
BRASS BOWLS, DECORATIVE	$ 15.00	$ 3.00	$ 0.25
BRASS CANDLESTICKS	$ 5.00	$ 1.00	$ 0.25
BRASS CANDLESTICKS, LARGE	$ 20.00	$ 5.00	$ 2.00
BRASS HOUR GLASS, LARGE	$ 15.00	$ 3.00	$ 0.50
BRASS LAMPS, LARGE	$ 150.00	$ 10.00	$ 3.00
BRASS LAMPS, SMALL	$ 25.00	$ 4.00	$ 0.50
BREAD BASKET, SILVER	$ 12.99	$ 5.00	$ 0.50
BREAD MAKER	$ 119.00	$ 50.00	$ 15.00
BREAD MAKERS	$ 129.00	$ 50.00	$ 15.00
BRICK	N/A	N/A	FREE
BRIDAL GOWNS	N/A	$ 75.00	$ 10.00
BRIDESMAID GOWNS	N/A	$ 10.00	$ 1.00
BRIEFCASE, LEATHER	$ 89.00	$ 10.00	$ 2.00
BRIEFCASE, LEATHER	$ 300.00	$ 25.00	$ 15.00
BROOM	$ 7.99	$ 1.00	$ 0.10
BUBBLE BATH	$ 8.00	$ 1.00	$ 0.25
BUD VASES	$ 5.00	$ 0.50	FREE
BUG REPELLENT	$ 7.00	$ 0.50	FREE
BUG SPRAY	$ 3.00	$ 0.50	FREE
BUG ZAPPER, ELECTRIC	$ 13.99	$ 5.00	$ 1.00
BULB PLANTER	$ 3.00	$ 1.00	$ 0.25
BULBS, AMARYLLIS	$ 6.99	$ 2.00	$ 0.50
BULBS, IRIS	$ 12.99	$ 3.00	$ 0.25
BUTTER DISH, SILVER	$ 19.99	$ 5.00	$ 1.00
BUTTER DISH, CRYSTAL	$ 15.00	$ 3.00	$ 1.00
CALCULATORS, BATTERY	$ 10.00	$ 1.00	$ 0.50
CALCULATORS, SOLAR	$ 6.00	$ 1.00	$ 1.00
CAMCORDER 8MM	$ 600.00	$ 100.00	$ 100.00
CAMCORDER CASE	$ 49.00	$ 15.00	$ 5.00
CAMCORDER, FULL SIZE	$ 500.00	$ 75.00	$ 40.00
CAMERAS, ASSORTED	N/A	$ 10.00	$ 5.00
CAMP LANTERN, PROPANE	$ 19.95	$ 5.00	$ 5.00
CAMP STOVE, PROPANE	$ 29.95	$ 5.00	$ 5.00
CAN OPENER, ELECTRIC	$ 24.95	$ 5.00	$ 2.00
CAN OPENER, UNDER COUNTER	$ 25.00	$ 5.00	$ 3.00
CANDELABRA LAMP SHADES	$ 2.99	$ 0.50	$ 0.25
CANDLE SNUFFER, BRASS	$ 9.99	$ 2.00	$ 0.25
CANDLE SNUFFER, SILVERPLATE	$ 12.99	$ 3.00	$ 1.00
CANDLEHOLDER, 3 ARM, BRASS	$ 19.99	$ 5.00	$ 2.00

ITEM	RETAIL PRICE	GARAGE SALE	SHELLEY'S BEST
CANDLEHOLDER, 5 ARM SILVER	$ 49.00	$ 10.00	$ 5.00
CANDLES, CITRONELLA	$ 2.99	$ 1.00	$ 0.10
CANING CONTAINER, LARGE	$ 12.00	$ 5.00	$ 2.00
CANING JARS	N/A	N/A	FREE
CANISTER SETS, CERAMIC	$ 29.99	$ 5.00	$ 5.00
CANISTER SETS, COPPER	$ 39.95	$ 10.00	$ 8.00
CANNED FOODS, LARGE CANS	$ 9.99	$ 2.00	$ 2.00
CANVAS PICNIC CANOPY	$ 79.99	$ 10.00	N/A
CAR MATS, 4 PIECE	$ 29.95	$ 5.00	$ 3.00
CAR WAX	$ 2.99	$ 0.50	FREE
CARPENTER'S SQUARE, LARGE	$ 6.00	$ 5.00	$ 1.00
CARPET CLEANER	$ 129.00	$ 40.00	$ 25.00
CARPET CLEANING SOLUTION	$ 8.00	$ 3.00	$ 0.50
CARPET REMNANTS, NEW	N/A	$ 1.00	$ 0.50
CASSETTE PLAYER, SINGLE	$ 59.00	$ 25.00	$ 10.00
CASSETTE PLAYER, RECORDER DUAL	$ 89.00	$ 25.00	$ 10.00
CASSETTE TAPES	$ 5.99	$ 1.00	$ 0.50
CASSETTE TAPES, BLANK	$ 1.99	$ 0.50	$ 0.25
CAULK	$ 3.99	$ 0.50	$ 0.25
CAULKING GUN	$ 4.99	$ 1.00	$ 0.25
CD CASES	$ 1.00	$ 0.25	$ 0.10
CD HOLDER, WOOD TOWER	$ 30.00	$ 10.00	$ 5.00
CD HOLDER, LEATHER CASE	$ 6.00	$ 2.00	$ 0.50
CD PLAYERS	$ 100.00	$ 25.00	$ 10.00
CD PLAYERS, PORTABLE	$ 100.00	$ 35.00	$ 25.00
CDs	$ 10.00	$ 5.00	$ 1.00
CD, CHANGER	$ 149.00	$ 50.00	$ 30.00
CD, PLAYER	$ 89.00	$ 10.00	$ 10.00
CD-ROM, DOUBLE SPIN	$ 69.00	$ 30.00	$ 10.00
CEDAR CHEST, LARGE	$ 300.00	$ 50.00	$ 30.00
CEILING FANS	$ 69.00	$ 15.00	$ 5.00
CERAMIC MOUSSE PAN	$ 9.99	$ 1.00	$ 1.00
CERAMIC QUICHE PAN	$ 9.99	$ 2.00	$ 1.00
CERAMIC TILE TRIVETS	$ 2.99	$ 1.00	$ 0.25
CHAIN SAW, GAS 12"	$ 129.00	$ 25.00	$ 10.00
CHAIN SAW, GAS 16"	$ 159.99	$ 50.00	$ 25.00
CHAIN, DECORATIVE	0.89/ ft.	N/A	FREE
CHAIR, ADIRONDACK	$ 59.00	$ 15.00	$ 8.00
CHAIR, CANE & CHROME KITCHEN	$ 14.99	$ 5.00	$ 2.00
CHAIR, CLUB, UPHOLSTERED	$ 250.00	$ 60.00	$ 15.00
CHAIR, CLUB, UPHOLSTERED, SOILED	N/A	$ 10.00	$ 1.00
CHAIR, LADDER BACK	$ 59.00	$ 10.00	$ 5.00
CHAIR, LEATHER OVERSTUFFED	$ 499.00	$ 75.00	$ 75.00

ITEM	RETAIL PRICE	GARAGE SALE	SHELLEY'S BEST
CHAIR, LOUIS XV, CANE	$ 250.00	$ 75.00	$ 15.00
CHAIR, OAK WINDSOR	$ 19.00	$ 7.50	$ 5.00
CHAIR, RECLINER, NEW STYLE	$ 300.00	$ 75.00	$ 50.00
CHAIR, SECRETARIAL	$ 49.00	$ 10.00	$ 5.00
CHAIR, WINGBACK, UPHOLSTERED	$ 199.00	$ 25.00	$ 15.00
CHAIR, WOODEN, CANE & CHROME	$ 25.00	$ 5.00	$ 2.00
CHAISE LOUNGE, PLASTIC WEBBING	$ 14.99	$ 5.00	$ 2.00
CHAISE LOUNGE, RESIN	$ 39.99	$ 10.00	$ 7.00
CHANDELIER, BRASS & GLASS	$ 100.00	$ 25.00	$ 7.00
CHANDELIER, BRONZE & CRYSTAL 5 LT	$ 100.00	$ 10.00	$ 5.00
CHANDELIER, CRYSTAL, 6 LIGHT	$ 199.00	$ 10.00	$ 5.00
CHANDELIER, CRYSTAL, LARGE	$ 200.00	$ 50.00	$ 5.00
CHANDELIER, CRYSTAL, SMALL	$ 100.00	$ 20.00	$ 2.00
CHANDELIER, GOLD LEAF, 5 LT	$ 100.00	$ 5.00	$ 1.50
CHANDELIER, MILK GLASS	$ 29.00	$ 5.00	$ 0.50
CHANDELIER, WROUGHT IRON	$ 79.00	$ 10.00	$ 2.00
CHEST, 2 DRAWER, FLORENTINE GOLD	$ 169.00	$ 75.00	$ 25.00
CHINA SERVICE FOR 8	N/A	$ 10.00	$ 5.00
CHIP & DIP, CRYSTAL	$ 20.00	$ 5.00	$ 1.00
CHIP & DIP, PLASTIC	$ 10.00	$ 4.00	$ 2.00
CHIP & DIP, POTTERY	$ 25.00	$ 5.00	$ 3.00
CHIP & DIP, SILVER	$ 20.00	$ 5.00	$ 3.00
CHOPPER, MINI ELECTRIC	$ 19.95	$ 3.00	$ 1.00
CHOPPING BLOCK, LARGE FLOOR TYPE	$ 250.00	$ 100.00	$ 50.00
CHRISTMAS ANGEL, ANIMATED	$ 19.00	$ 5.00	$ 2.00
CHRISTMAS BOWS	$ 0.99	$ 0.25	FREE
CHRISTMAS CARDS	$ 8.00	$ 1.00	$ 0.25
CHRISTMAS CENTERPIECES	$ 15.99	$ 5.00	$ 0.25
CHRISTMAS CHINA, SERVICE FOR 4	$ 19.99	$ 5.00	$ 5.00
CHRISTMAS CRECHE, LARGE	$ 29.00	$ 5.00	$ 0.25
CHRISTMAS LAWN FIGURES	$ 24.99	$ 5.00	$ 1.00
CHRISTMAS LIGHTS 100 CT	$ 10.00	$ 2.00	$ 0.50
CHRISTMAS LIGHTS 50 CT	$ 5.00	$ 1.00	$ 0.25
CHRISTMAS LIGHTS, OUTDOOR LARGE	$ 10.00	$ 100.00	$ 0.25
CHRISTMAS MUSICAL BELLS	$ 69.00	$ 5.00	$ 2.00
CHRISTMAS ORNAMENTS	N/A	N/A	FREE
CHRISTMAS ORNAMENTS, BOXED NEW	$ 7.00	$ 1.00	$ 0.25
CHRISTMAS TABLECLOTHS	$ 10.00	$ 2.00	$ 2.00
CHRISTMAS TOPPER	$ 10.00	$ 1.00	FREE
CHRISTMAS TREE SKIRT	$ 10.00	$ 2.00	$ 0.50
CHRISTMAS TREE STANDS	$ 10.00	$ 1.00	FREE
CHRISTMAS TREES, 7.5 FT	$ 100.00	$ 100.00	$ 5.00
CHRISTMAS TREES, SMALL	$ 60.00	$ 10.00	$ 2.00

ITEM	RETAIL PRICE	GARAGE SALE	SHELLEY'S BEST
CHRISTMAS TREES, TABLETOP	$ 20.00	$ 5.00	$ 0.50
CHRISTMAS WRAP	$ 2.99	$ 1.00	FREE
CHRISTMAS WREATH, CERAMIC DICKENS	$ 25.00	$ 14.99	$ 2.00
CHRISTMAS WREATHS, LARGE	$ 35.00	$ 10.00	$ 1.00
CLOCK RADIO	$ 15.00	$ 5.00	$ 1.00
CLOCK, ALARM DIGITAL	$ 10.00	$ 1.00	$ 0.25
CLOCK, ANNIVERSARY	$ 39.00	$ 12.00	$ 5.00
CLOCK, ANTIQUE MANTLE CHIME	$ 195.00	$ 75.00	$ 25.00
CLOCK, ANTIQUE STRIKER WALL	$ 195.00	$ 20.00	$ 17.00
CLOCK, QUARTZ	$ 12.99	$ 5.00	$ 2.00
CLOCK, QUARTZ WORLD TIME	$ 50.00	$ 10.00	$ 8.00
CLOCK, SCHOOLHOUSE, CHIME	$ 149.00	$ 10.00	$ 8.00
CLOCK, WALL	$ 10.00	$ 5.00	$ 2.00
CLOCKS, MANTLE, CRYSTAL	$ 19.99	$ 5.00	$ 2.00
CLOCKS, MANTLE, WOOD, CHIMES	$ 49.99	$ 10.00	$ 8.00
CLOSET DOOR, MIRRORED 6'	$ 150.00	$ 30.00	$ 30.00
COCKTAIL DRESSES	N/A	$ 10.00	$ 1.00
COFFEE FILTERS	$ 1.00	$ 0.50	$ 0.10
COFFEE POT FILTER, BASKET	$ 0.75	$ 0.25	$ 0.25
COFFEE POT FILTER, CONE	$ 1.19	$ 0.25	$ 0.25
COFFEE POT, ELECTRIC, LARGE	$ 69.96	$ 10.00	$ 5.00
COFFEE POT, ELECTRIC, SMALL	$ 19.95	$ 5.00	$ 1.50
COFFEE POT, REPLACEMENT GLASS	$ 3.00	$ 0.50	$ 0.25
COFFEE POT, UNDER COUNTER	$ 35.00	$ 15.00	$ 5.00
COFFEE TABLE, BRASS	$ 49.00	$ 10.00	$ 5.00
COFFEE TABLE, GLASS AND BAMBOO	$ 100.00	$ 20.00	$ 5.00
COFFEE TABLE, OAK	$ 129.00	$ 25.00	$ 8.00
COFFEE TABLE, PINE	$ 129.00	$ 30.00	$ 15.00
COFFEE TABLE, WOOD	N/A	$ 10.00	$ 3.00
COLOR TV, CASIO PORTABLE	$ 149.00	$ 30.00	$ 15.00
COMFORTER SET, EYELET	$ 59.00	$ 15.00	$ 5.00
COMFORTER, DOWN FILLED QUEEN	$ 69.00	$ 10.00	$ 5.00
COMPUTER 286	N/A	$ 40.00	$ 25.00
COMPUTER 386	N/A	$ 50.00	$ 25.00
COMPUTER 486	$ 300.00	$ 150.00	$ 100.00
COMPUTER CARRYING CASE	$ 79.00	$ 10.00	$ 7.00
COMPUTER DESK UNIT, PRTCLE BOARD	$ 69.00	$ 15.00	$ 5.00
COMPUTER DESK UNIT, WOOD	$ 129.00	$ 25.00	$ 10.00
COMPUTER ETHERNET CARD	N/A	N/A	$ 0.25
COMPUTER GAMES	N/A	$ 5.00	$ 2.00
COMPUTER KEYBOARD	$ 49.00	$ 25.00	$ 5.00
COMPUTER MAXI TOWER W/POWER	$ 119.95	$ 10.00	$ 5.00
COMPUTER MOUSE	$ 49.00	$ 5.00	$ 0.50

ITEM	RETAIL PRICE	GARAGE SALE	SHELLEY'S BEST
COMPUTER PAPER	N/A	N/A	FREE
COMPUTER POWER SUPPLY	$ 49.99	$ 5.00	$ 5.00
COMPUTER SOFTWARE, ASSORTED	N/A	N/A	$ 5.00
COMPUTER WORKSTATION	$ 100.00	$ 30.00	$ 15.00
CONCRETE MIX, BAG	$ 1.99	$ 0.25	$ 0.25
CONCRETE STEPPING STONES	$ 2.97	$ 0.25	FREE
CONSOLE COOLER	$ 15.99	$ 5.99	$ 1.00
COOLER, LARGE	$ 25.00	$ 8.00	$ 5.00
COOLER, SMALL	$ 17.00	$ 5.00	$ 3.00
COOLER, SOFT SIDED	$ 4.99	$ 1.00	$ 0.25
COOLER, PARTY STYLE 85 QT.	$ 99.00	$ 25.00	$ 10.00
COPPER & BRASS CLEANER	$ 5.00	$ 1.00	FREE
COPPER BUCKETS, LARGE	$ 69.00	$ 30.00	$ 20.00
COPPER BUCKETS, SMALL	$ 10.00	$ 5.00	$ 2.00
COPPER BUCKETS, VERY LARGE	$ 150.00	$ 35.00	$ 20.00
CORNING WARE LIDS	N/A	$ 1.00	$ 0.25
CORNING WARE, 2 QT CASSEROLE	$ 10.00	$ 3.00	$ 1.00
CORNING WARE, 3 PIECE SET	$ 15.00	$ 3.00	$ 1.00
CRAFT PAINT	$ 0.89	$ 0.25	$ 0.10
CREDENZA, OFFICE WOOD	$ 269.99	$ 100.00	$ 50.00
CRIMPING IRONS	$ 7.99	$ 1.00	$ 0.50
CROCK POT, LARGE	$ 29.95	$ 10.00	$ 2.00
CROCK POT, POTPOURRI	$ 9.99	$ 5.00	$ 0.50
CROCK POT, SMALL	$ 8.99	$ 3.00	$ 1.00
CROCKERY SERVICE, PFALTZGRAF	N/A	$ 75.00	$ 10.00
CROQUET SETS	$ 19.95	$ 7.00	$ 5.00
CRYSTAL BOWLS, LARGE	$ 40.00	$ 10.00	$ 2.00
CRYSTAL BOWLS, SMALL	$ 14.99	$ 8.00	$ 0.25
CRYSTAL CANDY DISHES	$ 9.99	$ 10.00	$ 1.00
CRYSTAL DECANTER SET	$ 39.00	$ 8.00	$ 3.00
CRYSTAL DECANTERS, LEAD	$ 99.00	$ 25.00	$ 1.00
CRYSTAL DECANTERS, PRESSED	$ 29.95	$ 5.00	$ 1.00
CRYSTAL PUNCH BOWL	$ 14.99	$ 5.00	$ 2.00
CRYSTAL PUNCH BOWL WITH CUPS	$ 19.99	$ 5.00	$ 3.00
CRYSTAL VASES	$ 29.99	$ 5.00	$ 0.50
CRYSTAL WINE BUCKET WITH GLASSES	$ 49.99	$ 10.00	$ 5.00
CRYSTAL WINE GOBLETS, LEAD	$ 40.00	$ 5.00	$ 3.00
CRYSTAL, ASSORTED GLASSWARE	$ 3.99	$ 1.00	$ 0.10
CRYSTAL, CANDLEHOLDERS	$ 9.95	$ 1.00	$ 0.50
CRYSTAL, HURRICANES	$ 9.95	$ 2.00	$ 0.25
CRYSTAL, IRISH COFFEE MUGS	$ 4.99	$ 1.00	$ 0.25
CRYSTAL, PRESSED MUGS	$ 2.99	$ 0.10	$ 0.10
CRYSTAL, WINE GRAN VIN	$ 10.00	$ 0.50	$ 0.20

ITEM	RETAIL PRICE	GARAGE SALE	SHELLEY'S BEST
CURIO CABINET, CHERRY	$ 249.00	$ 75.00	$ 5.00
CURIO CABINET, WOOD	$ 24.95	$ 5.00	$ 3.00
CURLING IRON	$ 9.99	$ 2.00	$ 1.00
CURTAINS, AUSTRIAN PANELS	$ 19.99	$ 2.00	$ 0.50
CURTAINS, PRISCILLA	$ 19.99	$ 5.00	$ 1.00
DE-GLOSSER	$ 8.99	$ 1.00	FREE
DEHYDRATOR, 4 SHELF	$ 49.99	$ 10.00	$ 5.00
DESK CHAIR, EXECUTIVE	$ 200.00	$ 25.00	$ 2.00
DESK LAMPS, HALOGEN	$ 19.99	$ 5.00	$ 2.00
DESK PAD	$ 6.99	$ 2.00	$ 1.00
DESK SET, PEN & PENCIL, MARBLE	$ 24.99	$ 5.00	$ 0.50
DESK, OFFICE, LARGE	$ 250.00	$ 125.00	$ 100.00
DESK, OFFICE, SMALL	$ 150.00	$ 80.00	$ 25.00
DESK, STUDENT	$ 100.00	$ 25.00	$ 5.00
DIFFUSERS	$ 8.99	$ 1.00	$ 0.25
DINING ROOM CHAIRS, QUEEN ANN	$ 129.00	$ 35.00	$ 20.00
DINING ROOM CHAIRS, UPHOLSTERED	$ 100.00	$ 40.00	$ 12.50
DINNER LINENS, DAMASK	$ 2.49	$ 1.00	$ 0.25
DINNERWARE, PLASTIC, SERVICE FOR 4	$ 24.95	$ 5.00	$ 4.00
DINNERWARE, SERVICE 4, GLASS	$ 19.99	$ 5.00	$ 3.00
DISHWASHER, BUILT IN	$ 300.00	$ 50.00	$ 25.00
DISK DRIVES	$ 250.00	$ 20.00	$ 5.00
DOG BOWLS	$ 1.95	$ 0.25	$ 0.25
DOG HOUSE, IGLOO, LARGE	$ 89.00	$ 20.00	$ 8.00
DOG HOUSE, IGLOO, SMALL	$ 59.00	$ 15.00	$ 3.00
DOG RUNS, CHAIN LINK	$ 150.00	$ 50.00	$ 20.00
DOOR HANDLE, DEAD BOLT, NEW	$ 39.95	$ 10.00	$ 3.00
DOOR HANDLES, NEW	$ 12.99	$ 5.00	$ 1.00
DOOR KNOCKER, BRASS	$ 20.00	$ 5.00	$ 1.00
DOOR STOPS, DECORATIVE	$ 25.00	$ 5.00	$ 3.00
DOOR STOPS, RUBBER	$ 1.00	$ 0.25	$ 0.25
DOORS, FRENCH, WOOD 6'	$ 299.00	$ 50.00	$ 10.00
DOORS, INTERIOR SIX PANEL	$ 79.00	$ 25.00	$ 5.00
DOORS, INTERIOR, HOLLOW	$ 20.00	$ 5.00	$ 2.00
DOORS, IRON PROTECTION	$ 249.99	$ 50.00	$ 5.00
DOORS, LOUVERED, 2 PANEL	$ 40.00	$ 10.00	$ 2.00
DOORS, SLIDING PATIO	$ 149.00	$ 10.00	$ 10.00
DOORS, SLIDING SHOWER	$ 89.00	$ 10.00	$ 5.00
DOORS, STORM	$ 99.00	$ 10.00	$ 5.00
DOUBLE MATTRESS & BOX SPRING	$ 499.00	$ 50.00	$ 15.00
DOUBLE MATTRESS, NEW	$ 149.00	$ 30.00	$ 5.00
DRAPERY TIEBACKS	$ 10.00	$ 1.00	$ 0.25
DRAPES, LINED, LARGE	$ 50.00	$ 25.00	$ 2.00

ITEM	RETAIL PRICE	GARAGE SALE	SHELLEY'S BEST
DRAPES, SHEER GATHERED TOP	N/A	$ 5.00	$ 1.00
DRAPES, SHEER, ROD POCKET	N/A	$ 5.00	$ 0.25
DRAWER LINERS, QUILTED	$ 8.99	$ 2.00	$ 0.25
DRESSER, DOUBLE, FRENCH	$ 189.00	$ 25.00	$ 10.00
DREXEL TWO DRAWER CHEST	$ 999.00	$ 175.00	$ 120.00
DRIED FLOWER TOPIARIES	$ 14.99	$ 5.00	$ 1.00
DRILL BIT SET	$ 19.99	$ 2.00	$ 2.00
DRILL, CORDLESS	$ 69.95	$ 15.00	$ 7.00
DRILL, ELECTRIC	$ 35.00	$ 10.00	$ 5.00
DRILLS, CORDLESS	$ 50.00	$ 10.00	$ 5.00
DRIVEWAY SALT	N/A	$ 0.25	$ 0.10
DRYER VENT	N/A	N/A	$ 0.25
DRYER, LARGE CAPACITY	$ 359.00	$ 100.00	$ 50.00
DUST MOP	$ 5.99	$ 1.00	$ 0.10
DUST RUFFLE, BATTENBURG	$ 19.95	$ 5.00	$ 2.00
DUST RUFFLES	$ 10.00	$ 2.00	$ 0.50
DUSTBUSTER	$ 19.99	$ 5.00	$ 2.00
DUSTER, LAMBSWOOL	$ 9.99	$ 2.00	$ 0.50
DUSTER, LAMBSWOOL	$ 9.99	$ 1.00	$ 1.00
ELECTRIC MIXER - HAND HELD	$ 19.95	$ 3.00	$ 1.00
ELECTRIC OUTLET BOX	$ 2.00	$ 0.25	FREE
ELECTRIC ROLLERS	$ 19.99	$ 5.00	$ 2.00
ELECTRIC ROLLERS, TRAVEL SIZE	$ 16.99	$ 5.00	$ 1.00
ELECTRIC SKILLET	$ 29.95	$ 3.00	$ 1.00
ELECTRIC SWITCH PLATES	$ 2.00	$ 0.35	FREE
ELECTRIC SWITCHES	$ 0.50	$ 0.25	FREE
ELECTRICAL WIRING, ROMEX	N/A	N/A	$ 0.50
ENCYCLOPEDIAS, FULL SET	N/A	$ 25.00	$ 5.00
END TABLE, INLAID WOOD, ITALIAN	$ 269.00	$ 15.00	$ 8.00
END TABLE, PINE	$ 119.00	$ 10.00	$ 5.00
END TABLES, BRASS & GLASS	$ 29.00	$ 10.00	$ 5.00
END TABLES, CHERRY	$ 159.00	$ 15.00	$ 5.00
END TABLES, OAK	$ 159.00	$ 15.00	$ 5.00
END TABLES, WOODEN	N/A	$ 5.00	$ 5.00
ENTERTAINMENT CENTER, OAK	$ 250.00	$ 75.00	$ 35.00
ENTERTAINMENT CENTER, VENEER	$ 100.00	$ 25.00	$ 15.00
EUCALYPTUS	$ 1.99	$ 1.00	$ 0.25
EUROPEAN ELECTRIC CONVERSION KIT	$ 19.99	$ 5.00	$ 1.00
EXERCISE BIKES, DELUXE	$ 100.00	$ 35.00	$ 25.00
EXERCISE BIKES, OLD STYLE	$ 49.00	$ 10.00	$ 5.00
EXPRESSO MAKER	$ 50.00	$ 20.00	$ 5.00
EXTENSION CORD 100' OUTDOOR	$ 14.99	$ 5.00	$ 2.00
EXTENSION CORD INSIDE	$ 1.29	$ 0.50	$ 0.10

ITEM	RETAIL PRICE	GARAGE SALE	SHELLEY'S BEST
EXTENSION CORD, HEAVY DUTY 25'	$ 15.00	$ 2.00	$ 1.00
FABRIC, YARD	N/A	N/A	$ 0.25
FAN LIGHT KIT	$ 19.99	$ 10.00	$ 3.00
FAN, ATTIC	$ 199.00	$ 50.00	$ 25.00
FAN, BOX	$ 14.99	$ 5.00	$ 3.00
FAN, CEILING	$ 59.00	$ 5.00	$ 5.00
FAN, DECORATIVE	$ 14.99	$ 5.00	$ 2.00
FAN, OSCILLATING	$ 18.99	$ 5.00	$ 2.00
FAN, STAND UP, OSCILLATING	$ 29.99	$ 10.00	$ 5.00
FAN, WINDOW	$ 24.99	$ 8.00	$ 3.00
FAT WOOD, BAG	$ 15.00	$ 1.00	$ 1.00
FAUCET BRASS	$ 49.99	$ 10.00	$ 5.00
FAUCET CHROME	$ 29.99	$ 5.99	$ 3.00
FAUCETS, BAR TYPE	$ 39.00	$ 10.00	$ 5.00
FAUCETS, KITCHEN	$ 40.00	$ 5.00	$ 3.00
FAX MACHINE	$ 299.00	$ 50.00	$ 35.00
FEATHERBED, QUEEN	$ 39.95	$ 10.00	$ 5.00
FENCING, SPLIT RAIL, 50'	N/A	N/A	$ 15.00
FERTILIZER SPREADER, HAND HELD	$ 10.00	$ 1.00	$ 0.50
FERTILIZER SPREADER, PUSH	N/A	$ 10.00	$ 3.00
FERTILIZER, LARGE BAG	$ 8.00	$ 2.00	$ 1.00
FILE CABINET 2 DRAWER, WOOD	$ 50.00	$ 20.00	$ 10.00
FILE CABINET, 2 DRAWER	$ 15.00	$ 5.00	$ 2.00
FILE CABINET, 4 DRAWER	$ 99.00	$ 15.00	$ 10.00
FILE FOLDERS & METAL HOLDER	N/A	$ 1.00	FREE
FIRE ESCAPE CHAIN LADDERS	$ 29.99	$ 8.00	$ 5.00
FIRE EXTINGUISHERS	N/A	N/A	$ 2.00
FIREPLACE FAN, BRASS	$ 129.00	$ 25.00	$ 5.00
FIREPLACE LOGS, PRESSED WOOD	$ 0.99	$ 0.25	FREE
FIREPLACE MATCHES	$ 1.99	$ 0.50	$ 0.10
FIREPLACE SCREEN, BRASS	$ 49.95	$ 5.00	$ 3.00
FIREPLACE TOOLS, HEAVY BRASS	$ 39.95	$ 20.00	$ 2.00
FIREPLACE UTENSILS	$ 59.00	$ 12.00	$ 2.00
FIREPLACE, OUTDOOR CLAY	$ 89.00	$ 20.00	$ 10.00
FIREWOOD, CORD, OAK	$ 239.00	$ 50.00	$ 25.00
FIREWOOD, STACK	$ 59.00	$ 10.00	FREE
FLAGSTONE	N/A	N/A	FREE
FLASHLIGHT, ELECTRIC CHARGER	$ 15.00	$ 5.00	$ 1.00
FLASHLIGHTS, LARGE	$ 4.99	$ 1.00	$ 0.25
FLASHLIGHTS, SMALL	$ 1.99	$ 0.50	$ 0.25
FLATWARE, GOLD	$ 39.00	$ 10.00	$ 2.00
FLATWARE, SILVERPLATED	$ 149.00	$ 25.00	$ 10.00
FLATWARE, SILVERPLATED, ANTIQUE	N/A	N/A	$ 5.00

ITEM	RETAIL PRICE	GARAGE SALE	SHELLEY'S BEST
FLOOR MAT, PLASTIC	$ 17.99	$ 5.00	$ 1.00
FLOOR PILLOWS, LARGE	$ 19.99	$ 3.00	$ 0.25
FLORAL FOAM, LARGE BAG	N/A	$ 1.00	$ 0.25
FLOWER BOXES, REDWOOD	$ 19.99	$ 5.00	$ 1.00
FLOWER BUSHES, SILK	$ 3.99	$ 0.50	$ 0.10
FLOWER POT, GRECIAN URN, PLASTER	$ 10.99	$ 5.00	$ 2.00
FLOWER POT, GRECIAN URN, PLASTIC	$ 4.99	$ 2.00	$ 1.00
FLOWER POT, URN, CONCRETE	$ 49.00	$ 5.00	$ 3.00
FLOWER POTS, DECORATIVE	$ 14.99	$ 2.00	$ 0.50
FLOWER POTS, LARGE CLAY	$ 9.95	$ 2.00	$ 1.00
FLOWER POTS, LARGE PLASTIC	$ 19.95	$ 5.00	FREE
FLOWER POTS, SMALL	$ 0.79	$ 0.25	FREE
FLOWER POTS, SMALL CLAY	$ 0.99	$ 0.50	FREE
FLOWER POTS, STRAWBERRY	$ 12.99	$ 5.00	$ 1.00
FLOWER POTS, VERY LARGE	$ 25.00	$ 8.00	$ 2.00
FLOWER SEED PACKETS	$ 0.89	$ 0.25	$ 0.05
FLOWERS, DRIED BUNCH	$ 5.00	$ 1.00	$ 0.25
FLOWERS, SILK, STEM	$ 1.00	$ 0.25	$ 0.10
FLUORESCENT LITE STICK	$ 15.99	$ 3.00	$ 1.00
FLUORESCENT SHOP LIGHTS	$ 12.00	$ 2.00	$ 1.00
FONDUE FORKS, SET OF 8	N/A	$ 2.00	$ 0.25
FOOD PROCESSOR, LARGE	$ 139.00	$ 25.00	$ 5.00
FOOD PROCESSOR, SMALL	$ 29.95	$ 8.00	$ 3.00
FOOD SLICER, ELECTRIC	$ 79.00	$ 25.00	$ 10.00
FOOT MASSAGER BATH, ELECTRIC	$ 24.99	$ 5.00	$ 1.00
FOOT MASSAGER, ELECTRIC	$ 24.99	$ 5.00	$ 1.00
FRAME, BRASS 5 X 7	$ 9.99	$ 2.00	$ 1.00
FRAME, BRASS 8 X 10	$ 19.99	$ 4.00	$ 1.00
FRAME, DIPLOMA STYLE 8 X 10	$ 1.99	$ 0.50	$ 0.10
FRAMES, MINIATURE BRASS	$ 3.99	$ 1.00	$ 0.25
FRAMES, MINIATURE SILVER	$ 3.99	$ 1.00	$ 0.25
FRAME, SILVER 5 X 7	$ 19.99	$ 3.00	$ 1.00
FRAME, SILVER 8 X 10	$ 24.99	$ 5.00	$ 1.00
FRAME, ORNATE WOOD, SMALL	$ 19.99	$ 5.00	$ 0.50
FRAME, ORNATE WOOD, LARGE	$ 100.00	$ 25.00	$ 10.00
FRAME, PLAIN WOOD	$ 8.99	$ 2.00	$ 1.00
FUTON, QUEEN	$ 119.00	$ 20.00	$ 2.00
GARAGE DOOR OPENER W/REMOTE	$ 129.00	$ 25.00	$ 5.00
GARDEN EDGING, 20 FT.	$ 3.00	$ 1.00	$ 0.50
GARDEN FABRIC SHEETING, ROLL	$ 8.00	$ 2.00	$ 0.50
GARDEN HOSE REEL	$ 19.99	$ 5.00	$ 4.00
GARDEN HOSE, 50'	$ 6.00	$ 1.00	$ 0.50
GARDEN PISTOL NOZZLE	$ 4.00	$ 0.50	$ 0.25

ITEM	RETAIL PRICE	GARAGE SALE	SHELLEY'S BEST
GARDEN SOAKER HOSE 50'	$ 5.00	$ 1.00	$ 0.50
GARDEN STATUARY, LARGE	$ 49.00	$ 5.00	$ 5.00
GARDEN, STATUARY, SMALL	$ 12.99	$ 5.00	$ 2.00
GARDENING TOOLS - SET OF 3	$ 2.95	$ 1.00	$ 0.30
GARMENT BAGS	$ 8.99	$ 1.00	$ 1.00
GAS CAN, 2.5 GAL	$ 2.99	$ 0.50	$ 0.50
GLADIOLUS BULBS	$ 0.30	$ 0.10	$ 0.10
GLASS ROUND, 36"	$ 79.00	$ 10.00	$ 5.00
GLASS TABLE ROUND, 24"	$ 9.99	$ 3.00	$ 0.50
GLASS, SALAD BOWLS	$ 1.00	$ 0.50	$ 0.25
GLASS, SALAD PLATES	$ 1.00	$ 0.50	$ 0.25
GLASS, WATER PITCHERS	$ 9.99	$ 5.00	$ 1.00
GLASSES, ASSORTED	$ 1.00	$ 0.25	FREE
GLASSES, CHAMPAGNE FLUTES	$ 1.99	$ 0.50	$ 0.10
GLASSES, CORDIAL	$ 1.00	$ 0.25	$ 0.25
GLASSES, JUICE	$ 1.00	$ 0.25	$ 0.10
GLASSWARE, COCKTAIL & WINE	$ 5.00	$ 0.50	$ 0.05
GLASSWARE, COFFEE MUGS	$ 1.99	$ 0.50	$ 0.25
GLASSWARE, MASON JAR MUGS	$ 0.79	$ 0.25	$ 0.10
GLIDER, WOOD	$ 99.00	$ 20.00	$ 10.00
GLOBE WITH CHERRY STAND, LIGHTED	$ 69.00	$ 10.00	$ 5.00
GLUE, EPOXY	$ 4.99	$ 1.00	FREE
GLUE, SUPER	$ 1.29	$ 0.25	FREE
GLUE, WOOD 8 OZ	$ 2.00	$ 0.50	$ 0.25
GOLF TRAVEL BAG, NEW	$ 49.00	$ 10.00	$ 5.00
GOURMET FOOD GIFT ITEMS	N/A	$ 5.00	$ 0.25
GRASS & WEED KILLER	$ 14.00	$ 1.00	$ 0.50
GRATER, CHEESE	$ 10.99	$ 0.25	$ 0.25
GREETING CARDS	$ 1.50	$ 0.20	$ 0.05
GRILL, SMOKER	$ 35.00	$ 10.00	$ 5.00
GUN CABINET, OAK	$ 99.00	$ 25.00	$ 10.00
GUN RACK, WALL WOOD, 3	$ 19.00	$ 3.00	$ 1.00
HALL TREE, MIRRORED OAK	$ 259.00	$ 75.00	$ 50.00
HAMMER	$ 19.95	$ 1.00	$ 0.25
HAMMOCK W/STAND	$ 34.99	$ 10.00	$ 6.00
HAMMOCK, HANGING	$ 29.99	$ 5.00	$ 3.00
HAMMOCKS, METAL FRAME	$ 39.00	$ 10.00	$ 5.00
HANDTRUCK	$ 30.00	$ 8.00	$ 5.00
HEADPHONE RADIO	$ 12.99	$ 1.00	$ 0.50
HEADPHONES	$ 10.00	$ 1.00	$ 0.25
HEATING PAD	$ 12.99	$ 2.00	$ 1.00
HEATING PAD WITH VIBRATOR	$ 29.99	$ 5.00	$ 3.00
HEATING PAD, MICROWAVE	$ 9.99	$ 3.00	$ 1.00

ITEM	RETAIL PRICE	GARAGE SALE	SHELLEY'S BEST
HINGES	N/A	N/A	FREE
HOME GYM	$ 350.00	$ 75.00	$ 35.00
HOT DOG COOKER, ELECTRIC	$ 20.00	$ 5.00	$ 2.00
HOT PLATE, ELECTRIC	$ 12.00	$ 3.00	$ 1.00
HOT ROLLERS, FULL SET	$ 19.99	$ 5.00	$ 2.00
HOT ROLLERS, TRAVEL SIZE	$ 15.00	$ 5.00	$ 2.00
HOT TUB SUPPLIES - BOX	N/A	N/A	$ 2.00
HUMIDIFIERS, DESK TYPE	$ 25.00	$ 5.00	$ 3.00
HUMIDIFIERS, ROOM	$ 45.00	$ 5.00	$ 5.00
HURRICANE GLASS GLOBES	$ 6.99	$ 1.00	FREE
ICE CREAM MAKER, ELECTRIC	$ 29.99	$ 10.00	$ 5.00
ICE CREAM MAKERS, ELECTRIC	$ 20.00	$ 8.00	$ 3.00
ICE CRUSHER, ELECTRIC	$ 29.95	$ 5.00	$ 3.00
ICE CRUSHER, HAND	$ 19.95	$ 5.00	$ 2.00
IRIS RHIZOMES	$ 3.99	$ 0.20	$ 0.20
IRON TRIVETS	$ 1.99	$ 0.50	$ 0.25
IRONING BOARDS	$ 12.00	$ 2.00	$ 1.00
IRONING BOARDS, HIDEAWAY	$ 100.00	$ 20.00	$ 10.00
IRONING BOARDS, PORTABLE	N/A	N/A	$ 1.00
IRONS, ELECTRIC	$ 25.00	$ 2.00	$ 1.00
IRONS, TRAVEL	$ 19.99	$ 3.00	$ 1.00
JOIST HANGERS	$ 0.30	$ 0.05	$ 0.05
JOYSTICKS	$ 30.00	$ 5.00	$ 3.00
KENNELS, LARGE	$ 100.00	$ 40.00	$ 25.00
KENNELS, SMALL	$ 30.00	$ 5.00	$ 3.00
KEYBOARDS, CASIO, LARGE	$ 179.00	$ 50.00	$ 25.00
KEYBOARDS, CASIO, SMALL	$ 79.00	$ 20.00	$ 5.00
KITCHEN GADGETS	$ 1.99	$ 0.25	$ 0.05
KITCHEN HUTCH, OAK	$ 249.00	$ 50.00	$ 40.00
KITCHEN SET, GLASS TOP, 4 CHAIRS	$ 99.00	$ 25.00	$ 15.00
KITCHEN TABLE & 4 CHAIRS, OAK	$ 400.00	$ 100.00	$ 75.00
KITCHEN TABLE, BUTCHER BLOCK TOP	$ 129.00	$ 20.00	$ 10.00
KITCHEN TABLE, OAK FARMHOUSE	$ 169.00	$ 60.00	$ 40.00
KITTY LITTER BOXES	$ 2.49	$ 0.50	$ 0.10
KITTY LITTER, CLUMP 8# BOX	$ 5.99	$ 1.50	$ 0.50
KNIFE, PUTTY	$ 1.99	$ 0.50	$ 0.05
KNIFE, UTILITY	$ 3.95	$ 0.50	$ 0.25
LADDER, EXTENSION 16' METAL	$ 40.00	$ 20.00	$ 10.00
LADDER, STEP 6' METAL	$ 29.99	$ 5.00	$ 1.00
LAMP OIL	$ 2.99	$ 0.50	FREE
LAMP, TORCHIERE	$ 30.00	$ 5.00	$ 2.00
LAMP, CAMPING, DOUBLE MANTLE	$ 1.00	$ 0.50	$ 0.50
LAMP, CHRISTMAS, SMALL	$ 1.00	$ 0.50	$ 0.10

ITEM	RETAIL PRICE	GARAGE SALE	SHELLEY'S BEST
LAMP, ELECTRIC LARGE	$ 30.00	$ 3.00	$ 1.00
LAMP, ELECTRIC SMALL	$ 0.50	$ 0.25	$ 0.25
LAMP, MINI-READING, BATTERY	$ 1.00	$ 0.50	$ 0.50
LAMP, TENSOR	$ 1.00	$ 0.50	$ 0.25
LAMP, HANGING, SWAG	$ 29.99	$ 1.00	$ 1.00
LAMPS, CRYSTAL, LARGE	$ 69.95	$ 20.00	$ 5.00
LAMPS, CRYSTAL, MEDIUM	$ 39.00	$ 10.00	$ 3.00
LAMPS, CRYSTAL, SMALL	$ 19.95	$ 5.00	$ 1.00
LAMPS, METAL TOLE, DESK	$ 59.00	$ 25.00	$ 2.00
LAMPS, METAL TOLE, FLOOR	$ 59.00	$ 10.00	$ 1.00
LAMPS, MILK GLASS	$ 29.00	$ 5.00	$ 0.25
LAMPS, OUTDOOR COACH, BRASS	$ 39.00	$ 5.00	$ 3.00
LAMPS, PIANO, BRASS	$ 19.95	$ 5.00	$ 2.00
LAMPSHADES, LARGE	$ 18.99	$ 3.00	$ 0.50
LAMPSHADES, METAL TOLE	$ 24.99	$ 5.00	$ 0.25
LAMPSHADES, SMALL	$ 6.99	$ 1.00	$ 0.25
LATTICE, 4 X 8	$ 14.99	$ 5.00	$ 2.00
LATTICE, PIECES	N/A	N/A	FREE
LAUNDRY BASKETS, PLASTIC	$ 2.00	$ 0.50	$ 0.25
LAUNDRY HAMPER, OAK	$ 569.00	$ 25.00	$ 10.00
LAUNDRY HAMPER, WICKER	$ 24.95	$ 5.00	$ 5.00
LAWN EDGER	$ 3.99	$ 2.00	$ 1.00
LAWN FOOD, 20#	$ 15.00	$ 2.00	$ 1.00
LAWN MOWER, 4HP, 20"	$ 199.00	$ 50.00	$ 25.00
LAWN TRIMMERS	$ 40.00	$ 10.00	$ 5.00
LEVEL SMALL	$ 3.99	$ 1.00	$ 0.25
LEVEL, 2 '	$ 12.00	$ 4.00	$ 2.00
LIGHT FIXTURE, BATHROOM 3 LIGHT	$ 12.00	$ 5.00	$ 1.00
LIGHT FIXTURE, BATHROOM 6 LIGHT	$ 25.00	$ 5.00	$ 3.00
LIGHT, CORDLESS CLOSET	$ 4.99	$ 1.00	$ 0.10
LIGHTBULBS, APPLIANCE	$ 2.99	$ 0.50	$ 0.10
LIGHTBULBS, CHANDELIER	$ 1.99	$ 0.50	$ 0.10
LIGHTBULBS, FLOOD	$ 5.99	$ 1.00	$ 0.25
LIGHTBULBS, GROLITE 150 WATT	$ 7.99	$ 2.00	$ 0.50
LIGHTBULBS, GROLITE 75 WATT	$ 4.99	$ 1.00	$ 0.50
LIGHTBULBS, NIGHT, PACKAGE	$ 1.99	$ 0.50	$ 0.10
LIGHTBULBS, SPOT	$ 4.99	$ 1.00	$ 0.25
LIGHTING, OUTDOOR TIKI TORCHES	$ 10.99	$ 3.00	$ 0.50
LIGHTING, OUTDOOR, FESTIVE	$ 4.99	$ 1.00	$ 1.00
LIGHTING, OUTDOOR, SOLAR	$ 25.00	$ 5.00	$ 3.00
LIGHTS, CLAMP	$ 7.00	$ 1.00	$ 0.25
LIGHTS, FLUORESCENT STICK	$ 17.00	$ 3.00	$ 1.00
LIGHTS, MOTION DETECTOR	$ 15.00	$ 5.00	$ 3.00

ITEM	RETAIL PRICE	GARAGE SALE	SHELLEY'S BEST
LIGHTS, RECESSED	$ 15.00	$ 1.00	$ 0.50
LIGHTS, TRACK, 4'	$ 30.00	$ 5.00	$ 2.00
LINSEED OIL	$ 6.99	$ 1.00	FREE
LIQUOR, KAHLUA\QT.	$ 24.95	$ 4.00	$ 2.00
LLADRO FIGURINES	$ 130.00	$ 20.00	$ 20.00
LLADRO FIGURINES, SMALL	$ 100.00	$ 15.00	$ 15.00
LOVE SEAT, QUEEN ANNE	$ 300.00	$ 50.00	$ 25.00
LOVESEAT, 2 CUSHION - EXCELLENT	$ 289.00	$ 75.00	$ 30.00
LOVESEAT, TUFTED	$ 239.00	$ 75.00	$ 25.00
LUGGAGE CART	$ 8.99	$ 1.00	$ 0.50
LUGGAGE SOFTSIDE	N/A	$ 5.00	$ 1.00
LUGGAGE VALET, CHERRY	$ 29.95	$ 10.00	$ 1.00
LUGGAGE, GARMENT BAG	N/A	$ 5.00	$ 2.00
LUGGAGE, LARGE	N/A	$ 20.00	$ 5.00
LUGGAGE, LARGE, WITH WHEELS	N/A	$ 20.00	$ 5.00
LUGGAGE, SMALL	N/A	$ 5.00	$ 3.00
MAGNIFYING GLASS	$ 2.99	$ 1.00	$ 0.25
MAILBOX, RURAL	$ 7.00	$ 3.00	$ 2.00
MAKEUP, SEALED	N/A	$ 0.50	$ 0.25
MAKEUP MIRRORS, LIGHTED	$ 19.95	$ 5.00	$ 1.00
MARBLE TABLE TOP 24"	$ 50.00	$ 10.00	$ 5.00
MARGARITA MIX	$ 2.99	$ 0.25	$ 0.25
MASKING TAPE	$ 1.29	$ 0.25	$ 0.25
MASONITE PEG-BOARD PANELS	$ 9.99	$ 1.00	FREE
MATS, ASTROTURF	$ 8.99	$ 1.00	$ 0.25
MATS, OUTDOOR	$ 8.99	$ 1.00	$ 0.25
MATS, SISAL	$ 4.99	$ 1.00	$ 0.25
MATTRESS & BOX SPRING, NEW	$ 500.00	$ 100.00	$ 50.00
MATTRESS PAD, KING	$ 19.99	$ 5.00	$ 1.00
MATTRESS PAD, QUEEN OR FULL	$ 14.99	$ 3.00	$ 0.25
MEDICINE CABINET, WITH MIRROR	$ 39.00	$ 5.00	$ 3.00
METAL SHELVING, 5 SHELF	$ 15.00	$ 5.00	$ 2.00
MICROWAVE BACON COOKER	$ 2.99	$ 0.50	$ 0.25
MICROWAVE BAKEWARE	$ 8.99	$ 1.00	$ 0.25
MICROWAVE OVEN, LARGE	$ 189.00	$ 60.00	$ 30.00
MICROWAVE OVEN, SMALL	$ 89.00	$ 20.00	$ 12.00
MICROWAVE, BUILT IN	$ 199.00	$ 25.00	$ 25.00
MICROWAVE, OVER THE RANGE	$ 279.00	$ 50.00	$ 35.00
MINI-BLINDS, ASSORTED SIZES	N/A	$ 1.00	$ 1.00
MINI-BLINDS, LARGE	N/A	$ 5.00	$ 1.00
MINI-BLINDS, SMALL	N/A	$ 1.00	$ 0.50
MIRROR, CHEVAL CHERRY	$ 99.00	$ 25.00	$ 15.00
MIRROR 30 X 72, CHIPPED EDGE	N/A	$ 5.00	$ 5.00

ITEM	RETAIL PRICE	GARAGE SALE	SHELLEY'S BEST
MIRROR, ASSORTED PIECES	N/A	N/A	$ 4.00
MIRROR, LIGHTED MAKEUP	$ 24.99	$ 5.00	$ 2.00
MIRROR, UNFRAMED 30 X 40	$ 49.99	$ 20.00	$ 4.00
MIRROR, UNFRAMED 50 X 60	$ 189.00	$ 20.00	$ 10.00
MIRRORED CLOSET DOORS, 6'	$ 129.00	$ 30.00	$ 25.00
MITER BOX WITH SAW	$ 8.99	$ 5.00	$ 2.00
MIX-MASTER	$ 100.00	$ 15.00	$ 0.50
MODEMS	$ 49.95	$ 5.00	N/A
MOLECULAR ROLLERS, FULL SET	$ 29.95	$ 8.00	$ 3.00
MONITOR, COLOR	$ 250.00	$ 100.00	$ 10.00
MOP	$ 5.99	$ 1.00	$ 0.10
MOUSE PAD	N/A	N/A	FREE
MUGS, CERAMIC	$ 0.99	$ 0.50	$ 0.05
MUSIC BOX	N/A	$ 19.99	$ 1.00
NAIL POLISH	$ 2.99	$ 0.25	$ 0.10
NAILS, ALL SIZES	N/A	N/A	FREE
NAPKIN RINGS, SILVER	$ 10.00	$ 5.00	$ 1.00
NORDIC TRACK	$ 350.00	$ 125.00	$ 75.00
OIL LAMPS, CRYSTAL	$ 39.95	$ 5.00	$ 0.50
OPERA GLASSES	$ 14.99	$ 2.00	$ 1.00
OTTOMAN, RECTANGLE	$ 129.00	$ 10.00	$ 3.00
OTTOMAN, ROUND	$ 99.00	$ 5.00	$ 1.00
OUTDOOR BEACH CHAIRS, CANVAS	$ 12.99	$ 2.00	$ 0.50
OUTDOOR BUSHES, CHERRY	N/A	N/A	$ 0.50
OUTDOOR CHAIRS, PLASTIC WEBBING	$ 5.99	$ 1.00	$ 0.50
OUTDOOR RESIN CHAISE LOUNGE	$ 40.00	$ 20.00	$ 8.00
OUTDOOR RESIN TABLE 48"	$ 59.00	$ 10.00	$ 8.00
OUTDOOR RESIN CHAIR	$ 10.99	$ 3.00	$ 3.00
OUTDOOR SUNDIAL, STONE	N/A	$ 10.00	$ 5.00
PACKING TAPE	$ 3.99	$ 0.50	$ 0.50
PAINT	N/A	N/A	FREE
PAINT BRUSHES, ASSORTED	N/A	$ 0.50	$ 0.10
PAINT ROLLERS, NEW	$ 3.00	$ 0.50	$ 0.50
PAINT STRIPPER	$ 10.00	$ 1.00	$ 0.50
PAINT, GALLON	$ 10.00	$ 3.00	FREE
PAINT, QUART	N/A	$ 1.00	FREE
PANELS, LACE	$ 9.99	$ 1.00	$ 0.50
PANELS, SHEER	$ 8.99	$ 1.00	$ 0.20
PAPER CLIP HOLDER	$ 1.99	$ 0.25	$ 0.25
PAPER CLIPS, STAPLES	$ 1.49	$ 0.50	$ 0.10
PAPER CUPCAKE HOLDERS, BOX OF 500	N/A	N/A	$ 0.25
PAPER STACKER, 3 TIER	$ 4.99	$ 2.00	$ 0.50
PAPER TOWEL HOLDER, PLASTIC	$ 1.99	$ 0.25	FREE

ITEM	RETAIL PRICE	GARAGE SALE	SHELLEY'S BEST
PAPER TOWEL HOLDER, WOOD	$ 6.99	$ 1.00	$ 0.50
PARK BENCH, WOOD & IRON	$ 69.00	$ 10.00	$ 5.00
PATIO BISTRO SET	$ 149.00	$ 20.00	$ 15.00
PATIO CANVAS AWNING	N/A	N/A	$ 10.00
PATIO CHAIRS, IRON	$ 49.95	$ 15.00	$ 2.00
PATIO CHAIRS, PADDED SWIVEL ROCKER	$ 199.00	$ 25.00	$ 15.00
PATIO CHAIRS, WROUGHT IRON ROCKER	$ 179.00	$ 25.00	$ 10.00
PATIO CHAIRS, WROUGHT IRON SWIVEL	$ 49.00	$ 5.00	$ 1.50
PATIO SET, 5 PIECE CAST IRON	$ 699.00	$ 50.00	$ 25.00
PATIO SET, WROUGHT IRON, 5 PIECE	$ 400.00	$ 50.00	$ 30.00
PATIO TABLE, ROUND 48"	$ 99.00	$ 20.00	$ 10.00
PATIO TABLES, IRON	$ 19.95	$ 5.00	$ 1.00
PATIO UMBRELLA STANDS, PLASTIC	$ 10.99	$ 1.00	$ 1.00
PATIO UMBRELLA, MARKET STYLE	$ 69.00	$ 25.00	$ 10.00
PATIO UMBRELLAS	$ 59.00	$ 10.00	$ 5.00
PECAN HALVES, 2# BAG	$ 4.99	N/A	$ 1.00
PEEP HOLE	$ 8.99	$ 1.00	FREE
PENCIL SHARPER, ELECTRIC	$ 19.95	$ 5.00	$ 1.00
PENCIL SHARPER, WALL	$ 4.99	$ 1.00	$ 0.25
PEPPER MILL, WOOD	$ 19.99	$ 5.00	$ 2.00
PERFUME, FULL BOTTLES	N/A	$ 3.00	$ 0.50
PERFUMED POWDERS	N/A	$ 1.00	$ 0.25
PET BEDS	$ 19.99	$ 1.00	$ 0.50
PHOTO ALBUMS	$ 4.99	$ 1.00	$ 0.25
PICKUP TRUCK BOXES	$ 99.00	$ 25.00	$ 10.00
PICNIC BASKET, WICKER	$ 20.00	$ 5.00	$ 2.00
PICTURE FRAME STANDS, BRASS	$ 19.99	$ 2.00	$ 0.50
PICTURE FRAMES, CERAMIC	$ 9.99	$ 1.00	$ 0.25
PICTURE MATS	N/A	N/A	$ 0.10
PILLOW SHAMS	$ 10.00	$ 1.00	$ 0.25
PILLOWCASE, KING SIZE	$ 9.99	$ 1.00	$ 0.25
PILLOWCASE, REGULAR	$ 7.99	$ 0.50	$ 0.05
PILLOWS, ASSORTED TOSS	$ 14.99	$ 2.00	$ 0.25
PILLOWS, NECKROLL	$ 14.99	$ 2.00	$ 0.25
PING PONG TABLE	$ 199.00	$ 25.00	$ 15.00
PLACEMATS, BATTENBURG LACE	N/A	$ 1.00	$ 0.25
PLACEMATS, SET OF 4	$ 10.00	$ 3.00	$ 1.00
PLANT FOOD, 4 LB BOX	$ 12.99	$ 1.00	$ 0.25
PLANT FOOD, LIQUID	$ 3.00	$ 1.00	$ 0.25
PLANT SPIKES	$ 6.99	$ 1.00	$ 0.10
PLANT STAND, VICTORIAN OAK	$ 39.00	$ 10.00	$ 3.00
PLANT STANDS, CHERRY & MARBLE	$ 39.00	$ 10.00	$ 1.00
PLANT STANDS, WROUGHT IRON	$ 12.00	$ 1.00	$ 0.25

ITEM	RETAIL PRICE	GARAGE SALE	SHELLEY'S BEST
PLANTER BOX, REDWOOD 2'	$ 8.00	$ 1.00	$ 1.00
PLANTER BOX, REDWOOD 4'	$ 15.00	$ 1.00	$ 1.00
PLANTERS, BRASS, VERY LARGE	$ 40.00	$ 10.00	$ 3.00
PLANTERS, RESIN	$ 10.00	$ 2.00	FREE
PLANTS & BUSHES, ARTIFICIAL	$ 2.99	$ 0.50	$ 0.25
PLANTS, ARTIFICIAL MUMS	$ 2.99	$ 0.50	$ 0.25
PLANTS, LARGE FLOOR	$ 79.00	$ 10.00	$ 3.00
PLANTS, SMALL	$ 3.99	$ 1.00	$ 0.25
PLASTIC FOOD STORAGE CONTAINERS	$ 0.50	$ 0.10	FREE
PLASTIC PAIL, 5 QT	$ 2.99	$ 0.50	$ 0.10
PLASTIC SEWING BOX, LARGE	$ 14.99	$ 2.00	$ 0.50
PLASTIC STORAGE BOXES, LARGE	$ 6.99	$ 1.00	$ 1.00
PLASTIC STORAGE BOXES, MEDIUM	$ 4.99	$ 1.00	$ 0.50
PLASTIC STORAGE BOXES, SMALL	$ 2.99	$ 0.50	$ 0.25
PLASTIC WARE, GLASSES, SET OF 8	$ 20.00	$ 5.00	$ 2.00
PLASTIC WIRE STORAGE PIECES	$ 2.99	$ 0.25	$ 0.25
PLATE STAND, 3 TIER	$ 14.99	$ 5.00	$ 0.25
PLIERS	N/A	$ 0.25	$ 0.25
PLYWOOD PANELS	$ 10.00	$ 1.00	FREE
POLYURETHANE	N/A	N/A	FREE
PORCELAIN, DELFT, LARGE	$ 29.00	$ 8.00	$ 3.00
PORCELAIN, DELFT, SMALL	$ 15.00	$ 1.00	$ 0.50
PORCH SWING, WOOD	$ 50.00	$ 8.00	$ 5.00
PORTABLE CAMPING TOILET	$ 79.97	$ 10.00	$ 5.00
POTHOLDERS	$ 1.99	$ 0.50	$ 0.10
POTHOLDERS, CHRISTMAS	$ 1.99	$ 0.50	$ 0.10
POTPOURRI	$ 8.99	$ 1.00	$ 0.25
POTTING SOIL	$ 1.00	$ 0.25	$ 0.25
POWER PAINTER, WAGER HEAVY DUTY	$ 69.00	$ 15.00	$ 8.00
POWER STRIP	$ 7.99	$ 2.00	$ 0.50
POWER STRIP, INDUSTRIAL 5'	$ 30.00	$ 5.00	$ 3.00
POWER WASH, AUTOMOBILE	$ 15.00	$ 5.00	$ 3.00
PREHUNG DOOR, NEW	$ 89.00	$ 40.00	$ 25.00
PRINTERS, DOT MATRIX	$ 89.00	$ 50.00	$ 10.00
PRINTERS, LASER	$ 250.00	$ 100.00	$ 50.00
PROPANE FUEL, 16 OZ.	$ 1.49	$ 0.50	$ 0.25
PRUNING SHEARS	$ 10.00	$ 1.00	$ 0.25
RADIO SCANNER	$ 139.00	$ 40.00	$ 5.00
RADIO, CAR WITH CASSETTE	$ 99.00	$ 10.00	$ 5.00
RAKE, BOW	$ 12.00	$ 3.00	$ 1.00
RAKE, FAN	$ 9.00	$ 2.00	$ 1.00
RAMEKINS, CERAMIC	$ 1.99	$ 0.50	$ 0.20
RANGE HOOD W/LIGHT & FAN	N/A	$ 15.00	$ 5.00

ITEM	RETAIL PRICE	GARAGE SALE	SHELLEY'S BEST
RANGE HOOD, PAINTED	$ 60.00	$ 10.00	$ 5.00
RANGE HOOD, STAINLESS	$ 79.99	$ 10.00	$ 5.00
RAZORS, ELECTRIC	$ 25.00	$ 5.00	$ 2.00
RAZORS, ELECTRIC	$ 24.99	$ 5.00	$ 2.00
RECORD ALBUMS	N/A	$ 0.50	$ 0.25
REDWOOD LUMBER	N/A	$ 2.00	FREE
REED BLINDS, ASSORTED SIZES	$ 19.99	$ 5.00	$ 1.00
REFRIGERATOR, DESK SIZE	$ 129.00	$ 50.00	$ 18.00
REFRIGERATOR, FREEZER, ICE MAKER	$ 450.00	$ 200.00	$ 125.00
REFRIGERATOR, SIDE-BY-SIDE	$ 899.00	$ 300.00	$ 150.00
REMOTE CONTROL, UNIVERSAL	$ 12.00	$ 4.00	$ 2.00
ROCKING CHAIR, ANTIQUE CANE	$ 100.00	N/A	$ 2.00
RODS, CURTAIN	N/A	N/A	FREE
RODS, DRAPERY	N/A	N/A	FREE
ROLLING CARTS, PLASTIC	$ 19.99	$ 5.00	$ 1.00
ROOT FEEDERS WITH SPIKES	N/A	$ 3.00	$ 1.00
ROTISSERIE	$ 50.00	$ 10.00	$ 3.00
ROUTER TABLE	$ 49.99	$ 10.00	$ 5.00
ROUTER, 1.5 HORSEPOWER	$ 60.00	$ 5.00	$ 2.00
ROWING MACHINES	$ 159.00	$ 25.00	$ 25.00
RUBBERMAID CONTAINERS, LARGE	$ 2.99	$ 0.50	$ 0.10
RUG, FLOKATI WOOL, LARGE	N/A	$ 15.00	$ 8.00
RUG, KARISTAN WOOL RUNNER	$ 99.00	$ 10.00	$ 2.00
RUG, LAMB'S WOOL	$ 59.00	$ 10.00	$ 5.00
RUG, PERSIAN BALUCHI	$ 300.00	$ 15.00	$ 15.00
RUGS, BATHROOM	$ 10.00	$ 1.00	$ 0.50
SACHET PILLOWS	$ 6.99	$ 1.00	$ 0.25
SALAD SPINNER	$ 15.00	$ 1.00	$ 0.50
SALT & PEPPER SHAKERS, SILVER	$ 10.00	$ 5.00	$ 1.00
SALT & PEPPER SHAKERS, WOOD	$ 12.00	$ 3.00	$ 2.00
SALT/PEPPER SHAKERS, GLASS	$ 1.00	$ 1.00	$ 0.25
SANDER, ELECTRIC	$ 39.95	$ 5.00	$ 3.00
SANDPAPER	$ 1.99	N/A	FREE
SANDWICH MAKERS, ELECTRIC	$ 20.00	$ 5.00	$ 3.00
SAW, HAND	$ 9.95	$ 1.00	$ 1.00
SAW, MITER	$ 200.00	$ 50.00	$ 50.00
SAW, POWER	$ 29.95	$ 8.00	$ 5.00
SAW, RECIPROCATING	$ 125.00	$ 25.00	$ 15.00
SAW, SABER	$ 19.95	$ 5.00	$ 2.00
SAW, TABLE	$ 329.00	$ 40.00	$ 40.00
SCALE, BATHROOM	$ 34.99	$ 5.00	$ 5.00
SCALE, FOOD	$ 6.99	$ 0.50	$ 0.50
SCONCE, SILVER 3 CANDLE	$ 14.99	$ 2.00	$ 0.50

ITEM	RETAIL PRICE	GARAGE SALE	SHELLEY'S BEST
SCONCES, CANDLE	$ 20.00	$ 5.00	$ 0.50
SCONCES, WALL, ELECTRIC	$ 25.00	$ 5.00	$ 0.50
SCREW DRIVERS	$ 0.99	$ 0.25	$ 0.10
SECURITY SYSTEM PANELS	$ 150.00	$ 3.00	$ 1.00
SEWING MACHINE CABINETS	$ 129.00	$ 5.00	$ 2.00
SEWING MACHINES WITH CABINET	$ 259.00	$ 25.00	$ 25.00
SEWING MACHINES, PORTABLE	$ 179.00	$ 25.00	$ 25.00
SHADES, FABRIC, LARGE	N/A	N/A	$ 3.00
SHADES, FABRIC, SMALL	N/A	N/A	$ 1.00
SHEET SET, SATIN, KING SIZE	$ 49.95	$ 5.00	$ 3.00
SHEETS, DOUBLE	$ 9.99	$ 0.25	$ 0.25
SHEETS, KING SIZE, FITTED	$ 15.95	$ 0.25	$ 0.25
SHEETS, KING SIZE, FLAT	$ 15.95	$ 0.25	$ 0.25
SHEETS, TWIN	$ 9.99	$ 0.25	$ 0.25
SHELF BRACKETS	$ 0.60	$ 0.25	$ 0.10
SHELF BRACKETS, IRON DECORATIVE	$ 3.99	$ 1.00	$ 0.50
SHELF RAILING, DECORATOR	$ 10.00	$ 3.00	$ 1.00
SHELVES WOOD, SMALL	$ 40.00	$ 15.00	$ 5.00
SHELVES, METAL, LARGE	$ 10.99	$ 5.00	$ 5.00
SHELVES, METAL, SMALL	$ 7.99	$ 5.00	$ 1.00
SHELVES, PLASTIC, 4 SHELF	$ 24.99	$ 5.00	$ 2.00
SHELVES, WICKER, 5 SHELF	$ 79.99	$ 10.00	$ 2.00
SHELVES, WOOD, LARGE	$ 119.00	$ 40.00	$ 15.00
SHELVING, WIRE, PLASTIC COATING	$ 1.99	$ 1.00	$ 0.50
SHOE BUFFER, ELECTRIC	$ 29.95	$ 5.00	$ 1.00
SHOE SHINE KIT, WOOD W/POLISH	$ 19.95	$ 5.00	$ 3.00
SHOERACK, OVER THE DOOR	$ 20.00	$ 8.00	$ 1.00
SHOVEL	$ 19.95	$ 3.00	$ 2.00
SHOWER CADDY	$ 2.99	$ 0.25	$ 0.25
SHOWER DOORS, GLASS	$ 100.00	$ 20.00	$ 10.00
SHOWER HEAD MASSAGER	$ 19.99	$ 2.00	$ 2.00
SHUTTERS, 4	N/A	N/A	$ 1.00
SHUTTERS, PLANTATION, LARGE	N/A	N/A	$ 10.00
SILVER 4 PIECE COFFEE & TEA SERVICE	N/A	N/A	$ 3.00
SILVER 5 PIECE COFFEE & TEA SERVICE	$ 499.00	$ 50.00	$ 25.00
SILVER BRUSH, COMB, MIRROR SET	$ 19.99	$ 10.00	$ 0.50
SILVER CLEANER	$ 3.00	$ 0.50	FREE
SILVER EXPANDABLE TRIVET	$ 12.99	$ 1.00	$ 0.25
SILVER LADLE	$ 14.99	$ 3.00	$ 1.00
SILVERPLATED BRANDY WARMER	$ 19.99	$ 5.00	$ 1.00
SILVERPLATED BUTTER DISH	$ 9.99	$ 3.00	$ 1.00
SILVERPLATED CHAMPAGNE BUCKET	$ 39.99	$ 10.00	$ 2.00
SILVERPLATED ICE BUCKET W/LID	$ 49.99	$ 10.00	$ 2.00

ITEM	RETAIL PRICE	GARAGE SALE	SHELLEY'S BEST
SINK WITH COUNTER & BASE	$ 119.00	$ 25.00	$ 10.00
SINK, BAR STYLE, SMALL, BRASS	$ 79.00	$ 25.00	$ 15.00
SINK, BAR STYLE, SMALL, STAINLESS	$ 59.00	$ 10.00	$ 3.00
SINK, KITCHEN, STAINLESS, DUAL	$ 100.00	$ 20.00	$ 5.00
SINK, LAUNDRY STYLE	$ 89.00	$ 10.00	$ 2.00
SINK, PEDESTAL	$ 69.00	$ 25.00	$ 15.00
SINK, ROUND, OVAL	N/A	N/A	$ 2.00
SINK, MARBLE WITH VANITY	N/A	$ 25.00	$ 8.00
SIT-UP BAR	$ 10.99	$ 1.00	$ 0.50
SIT-UP BENCH	$ 29.95	$ 5.99	$ 2.00
SKYLIGHTS	$ 139.00	$ 10.00	$ 10.00
SNOW BLOWER, 3 HP	$ 200.00	$ 50.00	$ 10.00
SNOW SHOVEL, HEAVY DUTY	$ 10.00	$ 2.00	$ 1.00
SNOW SHOVEL	$ 5.00	$ 1.00	FREE
SNUG SACKS, QUILTED	$ 19.99	$ 5.00	$ 1.00
SOAP DISH, CRYSTAL	$ 3.99	$ 1.00	$ 0.25
SOAP DISH, SILVER	$ 4.99	$ 1.00	$ 0.50
SOAP GIFT PACKAGE	N/A	N/A	$ 0.50
SOFA BED, QUEEN SIZE	N/A	$ 125.00	$ 50.00
SOFA TABLE, CHERRY WITH DRAWERS	$ 149.00	$ 40.00	$ 15.00
SOFA TABLE, OAK	$ 189.00	$ 50.00	$ 30.00
SOFA, 3 CUSHION, EXCELLENT	$ 400.00	$ 150.00	$ 75.00
SOFA, CAMEL BACK, WOOD LEGS	$ 389.00	$ 75.00	$ 40.00
SOFA, DOWN CUSHION	$ 1,000.00	$ 200.00	$ 60.00
SOFA, LEATHER	$ 999.00	$ 250.00	$ 200.00
SOFA, SECTIONAL	$ 699.00	$ 100.00	$ 50.00
SOUP TUREENS, LARGE	$ 29.99	$ 15.00	$ 5.00
SPA, 9 JETS, SEAT 6	$ 2,495.00	$ 1,000.00	$ 600.00
SPACE HEATERS, ELECTRIC	$ 19.95	$ 5.00	$ 2.00
SPACE HEATERS, KEROSENE	$ 80.00	$ 20.00	$ 5.00
SPANISH MOSS, LARGE BAG	$ 1.39	$ 0.50	$ 0.10
SPEAKERS, LARGE	N/A	$ 20.00	$ 10.00
SPEAKERS, MEDIUM	N/A	$ 10.00	$ 5.00
SPEAKERS, SMALL	N/A	$ 5.00	$ 0.25
SPICE RACK W/ SPICES	$ 19.95	$ 5.00	$ 2.00
SPICES	$ 2.99	$ 0.50	$ 0.10
SPRAY PAINT	$ 2.99	$ 0.50	FREE
SPRINKLER, CIRCULAR	$ 5.00	$ 1.00	$ 0.25
SPRINKLER, IMPULSE	$ 9.00	$ 1.00	$ 0.25
SPRINKLER, OSCILLATING	$ 12.99	$ 1.00	$ 0.25
SQUARE LACE TOPPER	$ 7.99	$ 1.00	$ 0.50
STAIN	N/A	N/A	FREE
STAINLESS STEEL, 12 PC COOKWARE	$ 119.00	$ 15.00	$ 8.00

ITEM	RETAIL PRICE	GARAGE SALE	SHELLEY'S BEST
STAPLE GUN	$ 12.95	$ 1.00	$ 1.00
STAPLE GUN, ELECTRIC	$ 29.95	$ 8.00	$ 5.00
STAPLERS	$ 8.99	$ 1.00	$ 0.25
STAPLES, OFFICE	$ 0.99	$ 0.25	$ 0.10
STAPLES, STAPLE GUN	$ 1.29	$ 0.25	$ 0.10
STATIONARY	$ 8.99	$ 1.00	$ 0.25
STEAK KNIVES, SET OF 6	$ 19.99	$ 1.00	$ 0.50
STEAMER, ELECTRIC	$ 29.95	$ 10.00	$ 1.00
STEEL 2 DOOR CABINET	$ 129.00	$ 25.00	$ 15.00
STEP LADDER, METAL, 3 STEP	$ 20.00	$ 3.00	$ 0.50
STEP LADDER, WOOD, 2 STEP	$ 10.00	$ 3.00	$ 1.00
STEP STOOL	$ 6.95	$ 1.00	$ 0.50
STEP STOOL, PLASTIC	$ 12.99	$ 1.00	$ 0.50
STEPSTOOL, METAL	$ 9.99	$ 1.00	$ 0.50
STEPSTOOL, WOOD	$ 6.95	$ 1.00	$ 1.00
STEREO RACK SYSTEM, CD PLAYER	N/A	N/A	$ 40.00
STERNO	$ 1.49	$ 0.25	$ 0.10
STEREO SYSTEM	$ 100.00	$ 10.00	$ 5.00
STOOLS, BAMBOO	$ 15.99	$ 5.00	$ 2.00
STOOLS, CHERRY VANITY	$ 149.00	$ 20.00	$ 15.00
STOVE, ELECTRIC, SELF CLEANING	$ 399.00	$ 100.00	$ 30.00
STUD FINDER	$ 4.99	$ 1.00	$ 0.25
SWAG HOOKS	$ 1.99	$ 0.25	FREE
SWAG LIGHT KIT	$ 15.00	$ 3.00	$ 0.25
TABLE TOPS, GLASS, BEVELED EDGE	$ 89.00	$ 15.00	$ 5.00
TABLE, COFFEE, LARGE	$ 299.00	$ 25.00	$ 10.00
TABLE, COFFEE, MEDIUM	$ 149.00	$ 25.00	$ 2.00
TABLE, DRAFTING	$ 119.00	$ 25.00	$ 5.00
TABLE, FOLDING CARD	N/A	$ 20.00	$ 5.00
TABLE, FOLDING PICNIC, METAL, LARGE	$ 39.00	$ 10.00	$ 5.00
TABLE, LEATHER TOP MAHOGANY	$ 189.00	$ 25.00	$ 1.00
TABLE, ROUND 24"	$ 9.99	$ 2.00	$ 0.25
TABLECLOTH, CHRISTMAS	$ 9.99	$ 2.00	$ 2.00
TABLECLOTH, LACE, LARGE	$ 14.99	$ 5.00	$ 2.00
TABLECLOTH, ROUND LACE	$ 14.99	$ 5.00	$ 1.00
TABLECLOTH, SATIN TRIM, LARGE	$ 14.99	$ 5.00	$ 2.00
TABLECLOTH, PAPER NEW	$ 2.99	$ 0.50	$ 0.25
TAPE DISPENSER	$ 3.99	$ 1.00	$ 0.50
TAPE MEASURE 25'	$ 8.00	$ 1.00	$ 0.50
TAPE, MASKING	$ 1.00	$ 0.25	$ 0.10
TAPE, PACKING	$ 3.00	$ 1.00	$ 0.50
TATO TWISTER	$ 19.95	$ 5.00	$ 3.00
TEA KETTLE, BRASS	$ 12.99	$ 2.00	$ 0.75

ITEM	RETAIL PRICE	GARAGE SALE	SHELLEY'S BEST
TEA KETTLE, COPPER	$ 14.99	$ 5.00	$ 1.00
TEA KETTLE, STAINLESS	$ 12.99	$ 2.00	$ 1.00
TEA TABLE, CHERRY	$ 79.00	$ 10.00	$ 5.00
TEACART, WROUGHT IRON	$ 100.00	$ 25.00	$ 20.00
TELEPHONE CABLE	N/A	N/A	$ 0.50
TELEPHONE CORD	$ 1.99	$ 0.25	$ 0.10
TELEPHONE JACK	$ 2.99	$ 0.25	FREE
TELEPHONE, CORDLESS	$ 79.00	$ 25.00	$ 5.00
TELEPHONE, SPEAKERS	$ 12.99	$ 5.00	$ 1.00
TELEPHONES	$ 29.00	$ 10.00	$ 0.50
TELEPHONES, PORTABLE	$ 69.00	$ 20.00	$ 10.00
TELEPHONES, SPEAKER	$ 59.00	$ 30.00	$ 10.00
TELESCOPE	$ 119.00	$ 20.00	$ 10.00
TENT SCREEN	$ 69.00	$ 15.00	$ 10.00
TENT, LARGE	$ 119.00	$ 25.00	$ 10.00
TENT, SMALL	$ 39.00	$ 8.00	$ 2.00
THERMOMETERS, OUTDOOR	$ 12.99	$ 1.00	$ 0.25
THERMOS, LARGE	$ 8.99	$ 2.00	$ 1.00
THERMOS, SMALL	$ 2.99	$ 1.00	$ 0.50
THERMOSTATS, WHOLE HOUSE	NA	N/A	$ 3.00
THROW, FAUX LEOPARD	$ 60.00	$ 5.00	$ 2.00
THROW, PENDLETON WOOL	$ 89.00	$ 5.00	$ 1.00
TIMERS, PLUG IN	$ 10.00	$ 2.00	$ 0.50
TIRE CHAINS	N/A	N/A	$ 3.00
TIRES	N/A	N/A	$ 3.00
TOASTER OVEN	$ 29.95	$ 15.00	$ 5.00
TOASTER OVEN CABINET MOUNT	$ 19.95	$ 5.00	$ 0.50
TOASTER, 4 SLICE	$ 19.99	$ 5.00	$ 3.00
TOMATO CAGES	N/A	N/A	FREE
TOOL CHEST CABINET, 13 DRAWER	$ 250.00	$ 75.00	$ 40.00
TOOLS GARDEN	$ 9.99	$ 2.00	$ 0.50
TOP SOIL, 40#	$ 1.50	$ 1.00	$ 0.50
TOWEL BAR, BATH, BRASS	$ 14.99	$ 2.00	$ 1.00
TOWEL RACK, ROUND, CHROME	$ 4.99	$ 1.00	$ 0.25
TOWEL RACK, ROUND, GOLD	$ 6.99	$ 1.00	$ 0.25
TOWELS, BATH	$ 6.99	$ 2.00	$ 1.00
TOWELS, BEACH	$ 9.99	$ 1.00	$ 0.25
TOWELS, CHRISTMAS	$ 9.99	$ 1.00	$ 0.25
TOWELS, EMBELLISHED HAND, NEW	$ 12.00	$ 1.00	$ 0.50
TOWELS, KITCHEN	$ 2.99	$ 0.50	$ 0.10
TOWELS, KITCHEN, CHRISTMAS	$ 2.99	$ 1.00	$ 0.25
TOWELS, USED	N/A	$ 0.25	$ 0.10
TRACTOR, LAWN	$ 799.00	$ 250.00	$ 250.00

ITEM	RETAIL PRICE	GARAGE SALE	SHELLEY'S BEST
TRASH CAN, 32 GAL PLASTIC	$ 9.99	$ 0.25	$ 0.25
TRASH CAN, 32 GALLON	$ 6.99	$ 0.25	$ 0.25
TRASH COMPACTOR	N/A	N/A	$ 15.00
TREADMILL, ELECTRIC, -COMPUTER	$ 299.00	$ 75.00	$ 40.00
TRELLIS, FAN	$ 10.00	$ 2.00	$ 1.00
TROUBLE LIGHT	$ 10.00	$ 2.00	$ 2.00
TRUNK, ANTIQUE, CAMEL BACK	$ 350.00	$ 30.00	$ 30.00
TRUNKS, WICKER & BRASS	$ 59.00	$ 10.00	$ 10.00
TURNTABLE	N/A	$ 20.00	$ 5.00
TURPENTINE	$ 3.99	$ 1.00	FREE
TV CART & CABINET, SWIVEL	$ 69.00	$ 25.00	$ 20.00
TV CART, SWIVEL	$ 69.00	$ 25.00	$ 15.00
TV TRAYS, WOOD, SET OF 4	$ 19.99	$ 5.00	$ 3.00
TV, 15" GE COLOR	$ 129.00	$ 20.00	$ 5.00
TV, 15" SONY COLOR	$ 189.00	$ 25.00	$ 15.00
TV, 19" SONY COLOR W/REMOTE	$ 249.00	$ 35.00	$ 20.00
TV, POCKET SIZE, CASIO COLOR	$ 149.00	$ 30.00	$ 15.00
TYPEWRITER, ELECTRIC	$ 129.00	$ 25.00	$ 5.00
UMBRELLA HURRICANE LIGHT	$ 25.00	$ 2.00	$ 0.25
UMBRELLA STAND	$ 19.99	$ 5.00	$ 1.00
UMBRELLAS, GOLF	N/A	$ 3.00	$ 1.00
UMBRELLAS, HAND	$ 14.99	$ 1.00	$ 1.00
UMBRELLAS, PATIO 7.5'	$ 89.00	$ 10.00	$ 5.00
UNDER CABINET FLUORESCENT LIGHT	$ 9.99	$ 2.00	$ 1.00
UPHOLSTERY FOAM--2,3,4,6"	N/A	N/A	$ 2.00
VACUUM CLEANER BAGS PK	$ 3.99	$ 0.50	$ 0.10
VACUUM CLEANERS, UPRIGHT	$ 100.00	$ 10.00	$ 5.00
VACUUM KITCHEN BAG SEALER	$ 49.00	$ 5.00	$ 2.00
VACUUM, CANISTER	$ 100.00	$ 10.00	$ 3.00
VACUUM, DIRT DEVIL DELUXE UPRIGHT	$ 179.00	$ 10.00	$ 8.00
VACUUM, DIRT DEVIL HANDVAC	$ 39.00	$ 5.00	$ 5.00
VALANCE, JABOTS, TRIPLE, LINED	$ 139.00	$ 10.00	$ 5.00
VARNISH	N/A	N/A	FREE
VASE, CLOISONNE, LARGE	$ 49.00	$ 8.00	$ 1.00
VASE, CLOISONNE, SMALL	$ 9.99	$ 1.00	$ 0.50
VASES	$ 5.99	$ 0.50	FREE
VCR, 4 HEAD, ZENITH WORKING	$ 169.00	$ 10.00	$ 5.00
VCR, TAPE NOT WORKING	N/A	N/A	FREE
VELCRO ROLLERS, SET	$ 5.99	$ 1.00	$ 0.25
VERTICAL BLINDS, 6'	$ 79.00	$ 10.00	$ 5.00
VHS MOVIES	$ 12.99	$ 5.00	$ 0.50
VHS TAPES	$ 1.99	$ 1.00	$ 0.50
VOLLEYBALL, BADMINTON SET	$ 19.99	$ 5.00	$ 3.00

ITEM	RETAIL PRICE	GARAGE SALE	SHELLEY'S BEST
WAFFLE MAKER	$ 30.00	$ 10.00	$ 5.00
WAFFLE MAKER, ANTIQUE	N/A	$ 10.00	$ 2.00
WALLPAPER BORDERS	N/A	$ 4.99	$ 0.25
WALLPAPER HANGING KITS	$ 12.00	$ 3.00	$ 1.00
WALLPAPER ROLLS	N/A	N/A	FREE
WARMER, COFFEE CUP	N/A	$ 1.00	$ 0.25
WARMING TRAY, ELECTRIC	$ 14.99	$ 5.00	$ 1.00
WASHER DRYER HOSES	N/A	N/A	$ 0.50
WASHER, LARGE CAPACITY	$ 389.00	$ 100.00	$ 75.00
WASHER/DRYER APARTMENT STYLE	$ 700.00	$ 150.00	$ 100.00
WASTEBASKETS, PLASTIC	$ 2.99	$ 0.50	$ 0.25
WATER JARS, LARGE	N/A	$ 5.00	$ 2.00
WATER SEAL, WATERPROOFER, 5 GAL	$ 34.95	$ 5.00	$ 3.00
WATERING CAN, 2 GALLON	$ 2.99	$ 0.50	$ 0.10
WATERING KIT, DRIP	$ 19.95	$ 2.00	$ 1.00
WEATHER STRIPPING	N/A	$ 1.00	$ 0.25
WEIGHT LIFTING BENCH	$ 69.00	$ 10.00	$ 5.00
WEIGHT SCALE	$ 19.99	$ 5.00	$ 2.00
WEIGHT SETS, FULL SIZE	$ 49.99	$ 10.00	$ 5.00
WEIGHTS, ANKLE	$ 9.99	$ 1.00	$ 0.50
WEIGHTS, HAND	$ 9.99	$ 1.00	$ 1.00
WEIGHTS, WAISTBAND	$ 14.99	$ 1.00	$ 0.50
WET-DRY VAC, 5 GAL	$ 35.00	$ 10.00	$ 5.00
WHEELBARROW, LARGE	$ 50.00	$ 10.00	$ 5.00
WHEELBARROW, SMALL	$ 30.00	$ 5.00	$ 3.00
WHISKEY	$ 12.95	$ 5.00	$ 4.00
WICKER TABLE, VICTORIAN	$ 89.00	$ 10.00	$ 5.00
WILDFLOWER SEEDS	$ 9.95	$ 1.00	$ 0.10
WINDOW INSULATION, PLASTIC	N/A	$ 1.00	$ 0.25
WINDOW WELL COVER, PLASTIC	$ 7.99	$ 1.00	$ 1.00
WINDOW, GREENHOUSE	$ 189.00	$ 25.00	$ 25.00
WINDOWS, HOUSE	N/A	$ 5.00	N/A
WINE RACK, METAL, 32 BOTTLES	N/A	N/A	$ 2.00
WINE RACK, OAK, 24 BOTTLES	$ 39.00	$ 5.00	$ 3.00
WINE, ASSORTED	N/A	N/A	$ 1.00
WINE, CHAMPAGNE, FRENCH	$ 24.95	$ 2.00	$ 2.00
WINE, CHARDONNAY	$ 12.95	$ 2.00	$ 2.00
WINE, CHIANTI, BASKET BOTTLE	$ 9.99	$ 1.00	$ 0.50
WIRE HANGING BASKET, 3 TIER	$ 3.99	$ 1.00	$ 0.50
WIRE, WELDED SHEETS	$ 5.00	$ 1.00	$ 0.50
WOK, LARGE	$ 19.99	$ 5.00	$ 2.00
WOK, SMALL	$ 14.99	$ 3.00	$ 1.00

ITEM	RETAIL PRICE	GARAGE SALE	SHELLEY'S BEST
WOOD DECORATIVE SHELVES	$ 19.99	$ 3.00	$ 0.50
WOOD SEALER	N/A	N/A	FREE
WOOD VEGETABLE BIN	$ 49.00	$ 10.00	$ 5.00
WORD PROCESSOR	$ 249.00	$ 100.00	$ 25.00
WORK BENCH	N/A	$ 25.00	$ 3.00
WORK GLOVES	$ 1.00	$ 0.25	$ 0.10
WORKMATE, BLACK & DECKER	$ 89.00	$ 20.00	$ 10.00
WREATHS, DRIED FLOWERS	N/A	$ 5.00	$ 1.00
WREATHS, EUCALYPTUS	N/A	$ 3.00	$ 1.00
WREATHS, GRAPEVINE, LARGE	N/A	$ 3.00	$ 2.00
WREATHS, GRAPEVINE, SMALL	N/A	$ 1.00	$ 0.50
WREATHS, SILK FLOWERS, LARGE	N/A	$ 8.00	$ 5.00
WREATHS, SILK FLOWERS, SMALL	N/A	$ 5.00	$ 1.00
WREATHS, STRAW	N/A	$ 1.00	$ 0.50
WRENCHES	N/A	$ 1.00	$ 0.25
YARDSTICKS	N/A	N/A	$ 0.10
Z BRICK	$ 9.99	$ 2.50	$ 1.00